Learning Android

Learning Android

Marko Gargenta

O'REILLY®

Beijing · Cambridge · Farnham · Köln · Sebastopol · Tokyo

Learning Android
by Marko Gargenta

Published by O'Reilly Media, Inc., 1005 Gravenstein Highway North, Sebastopol, CA 95472.

O'Reilly books may be purchased for educational, business, or sales promotional use. Online editions are also available for most titles (*http://my.safaribooksonline.com*). For more information, contact our corporate/institutional sales department: (800) 998-9938 or *corporate@oreilly.com*.

Editors: Andy Oram and Brian Jepson	**Indexer:** Jay Marchand
Production Editor: Holly Bauer	**Cover Designer:** Karen Montgomery
Copyeditor: Genevieve d'Entremont	**Interior Designer:** David Futato
Proofreader: Jennifer Knight	**Illustrator:** Robert Romano

Printing History:

    March 2011:   First Edition.

ISBN: 978-1-449-39050-1

[LSI]

1299695720

Table of Contents

Preface

This book sprang from years of delivering the Marakana Android Bootcamp training class to thousands of software developers at some of the largest mobile companies located on four continents around the world. Teaching this class, over time I saw what works and what doesn't. This book is a distilled version of the Android Bootcamp training course that I developed at Marakana and fine-tuned over numerous engagements.

My background is in Java from back before it was even called that. From the beginning, I was very interested in embedded development as a way to program various devices that surround us in everyday life. Because Java primarily took off in web application development, most of my experience in the previous decade has been in building large enterprise systems. Then Android arrived, and once again I became very excited about building software for nontraditional computers. My current interests lie in using Android on devices that may not even resemble a typical phone.

This book teaches anyone who knows Java (or a similar language) how to develop a reasonably complex Android application. I hope you find this book fairly comprehensive and that you find the example-based learning reasonably motivating. The goal of *Learning Android* is to get you to *think* in Android terms.

What's Inside

Chapter 1, Android Overview
   Is an introduction to Android and its history

Chapter 2, The Stack
   Is an overview of the Android operating system and all its parts from a very high level

Chapter 3, Quick Start
   Helps you set up your environment for Android application development

Chapter 4, Main Building Blocks
   Explains the Android components application developers use to put together an app

Chapter 5, Yamba Project Overview
Explains the Yamba application that we'll build together through this book and use as an example to learn Android's various features

Chapter 6, Android User Interface
Explains how to build the user interface for your application

Chapter 7, Preferences, the Filesystem, the Options Menu, and Intents
Covers some of the operating system features that make an application developer's life easier

Chapter 8, Services
Covers building an Android service to process background tasks

Chapter 9, The Database
Explains the Android framework's support for the built-in SQLite database and how to use it to persist the data in your own application

Chapter 10, Lists and Adapters
Covers an important feature of Android that allows large data sets to be linked efficiently to relatively small screens

Chapter 11, Broadcast Receivers
Explains how to use the publish-subscribe mechanism in Android to respond to various system and user-defined messages

Chapter 12, Content Providers
Shows how to design a content provider to share data between applications, in this case using it to enable our app widget to display data on the home screen

Chapter 13, System Services
Introduces various system services that an app developer can tap into

Chapter 14, The Android Interface Definition Language
Covers building an inter-process communication mechanism to allow for remote access to a service from another application

Chapter 15, The Native Development Kit (NDK)
Introduces how to write native C code as part of your Android application

Conventions Used in This Book

The following typographical conventions are used in this book:

Italic
Indicates new terms, URLs, email addresses, filenames, and file extensions.

`Constant width`
Used for program listings, as well as within paragraphs to refer to program elements such as variable or function names, data types, and XML entities.

`Constant width bold`
Shows commands or other text that should be typed literally by the user.

Constant width italic
> Shows text that should be replaced with user-supplied values or by values determined by context.

 This icon signifies a tip, suggestion, or general note.

 This icon indicates a warning or caution.

Using Code Examples

This book is here to help you get your job done. In general, you may use the code in this book in your programs and documentation. You do not need to contact us for permission unless you're reproducing a significant portion of the code. For example, writing a program that uses several chunks of code from this book does not require permission. Selling or distributing a CD-ROM of examples from O'Reilly books does require permission. Answering a question by citing this book and quoting example code does not require permission. Incorporating a significant amount of example code from this book into your product's documentation does require permission.

We appreciate, but do not require, attribution. An attribution usually includes the title, author, publisher, and ISBN. For example: "*Learning Android* by Marko Gargenta (O'Reilly). Copyright 2011 Marko Gargenta, 978-1-449-39050-1."

If you feel your use of code examples falls outside fair use or the permission given here, feel free to contact us at *permissions@oreilly.com*.

Safari® Books Online

 Safari Books Online is an on-demand digital library that lets you easily search over 7,500 technology and creative reference books and videos to find the answers you need quickly.

With a subscription, you can read any page and watch any video from our library online. Read books on your cell phone and mobile devices. Access new titles before they are available for print, get exclusive access to manuscripts in development, and post feedback for the authors. Copy and paste code samples, organize your favorites, download chapters, bookmark key sections, create notes, print out pages, and benefit from tons of other time-saving features.

O'Reilly Media has uploaded this book to the Safari Books Online service. To have full digital access to this book and others on similar topics from O'Reilly and other publishers, sign up for free at *http://my.safaribooksonline.com*.

How to Contact Us

Please address comments and questions concerning this book to the publisher:

O'Reilly Media, Inc.
1005 Gravenstein Highway North
Sebastopol, CA 95472
800-998-9938 (in the United States or Canada)
707-829-0515 (international or local)
707 829-0104 (fax)

We have a web page for this book, where we list errata, examples, and any additional information. You can access this page at:

http://oreilly.com/catalog/9781449390501/

To comment or ask technical questions about this book, send email to:

bookquestions@oreilly.com

For more information about our books, courses, conferences, and news, see our website at *http://oreilly.com*.

Find us on Facebook: *http://facebook.com/oreilly*

Follow us on Twitter: *http://twitter.com/oreillymedia*

Watch us on YouTube: *http://www.youtube.com/oreillymedia*

Acknowledgments

This book is truly a result of outstanding teamwork. First, I'd like to thank my editors at O'Reilly, Andy Oram and Brian Jepson. Andy, your comments were spot-on and constructive. Brian, thank you for persuading me to take on writing this book in the first place.

I would like to thank all my technical editors: Dan Bornstein, Hervé Guihot, Frank Maker III, and Bill Schrickel. Thank you for diligently reading my half-baked drafts and providing valuable comments.

This book wouldn't be what it is without field testing it on our numerous clients. You were the true pioneers on the cutting edge of Android, and your projects are all very inspiring. Thank you for your trust.

I'd like to thank my team at Marakana—Aleksandar (Saša) Gargenta, Ken Jones, and Laurent Tonon—for bringing back firsthand feedback from teaching Android Boot-camp courses using the draft of this book. Saša, special thanks to you for sending me back to the drawing board more times than I'd like to admit. This book is probably months past due because of your in-depth technical comments.

And finally, a huge thanks to my wife, Lisa, and daughter, Kylie. I know what a sacrifice it was for you while I was crisscrossing the world working on this material. Thank you for supporting me along the way.

## CHAPTER 1

Android Overview

In this chapter, you will learn how Android came about. We'll take a look at its history to help us understand its future. As this mobile environment enters a make-or-break year, we look at the key players in this ecosystem, what motivates them, and what strengths and weaknesses they bring to the table.

By the end of this chapter, you will better understand the ecosystem from a business point of view, which should help clarify the technology choices and how they relate to long-term advantages for various platforms.

Android Overview

Android is a comprehensive open source platform designed for mobile devices. It is championed by Google and owned by Open Handset Alliance (*http://www.openhand setalliance.com/*). The goal of the alliance is to "accelerate innovation in mobile and offer consumers a richer, less expensive, and better mobile experience." Android is the vehicle to do so.

As such, Android is revolutionizing the mobile space. For the first time, it is a truly open platform that separates the hardware from the software that runs on it. This allows for a much larger number of devices to run the same applications and creates a much richer ecosystem for developers and consumers.

Let's break down some of these buzz words and see what's behind them.

Comprehensive

Android is a comprehensive platform, which means it is a complete software stack for a mobile device.

For developers, Android provides all the tools and frameworks for developing mobile apps quickly and easily. The Android SDK is all you need to start developing for Android; you don't even need a physical phone.

For users, Android just works right out of the box. Additionally, users can customize their phone experience substantially.

For manufacturers, it is the complete solution for running their devices. Other than some hardware-specific drivers, Android provides everything else to make their devices work.

Open Source Platform

Android is an open source platform. The entire stack, from low-level Linux modules all the way to native libraries, and from the application framework to complete applications, is totally open.

More so, Android is licensed under business-friendly licenses (Apache/MIT) so that others can freely extend it and use it for variety of purposes. Even some third-party open source libraries that were brought into the Android stack were rewritten under new license terms.

So, as a developer, you have access to the entire platform source code. This allows you to see how the guts of the Android operating system work. As manufacturer, you can easily port Android OS to your specific hardware. You can also add your own proprietary secret sauce, and you do not have to push it back to the development community if you don't want to.

There's no need to license Android. You can start using it and modifying it today, and there are no strings attached. More so, Android has many hooks at various levels of the platform, allowing anyone to extend it in unforeseen ways.

 There are couple of minor low-level pieces of code that are proprietary to each vendor, such as the software stack for the cellular, WiFi, and Bluetooth radios. Android tries hard to abstract those components with interfaces so that vendor-specific code can be managed easily.

Designed for Mobile Devices

Android is a purpose-built platform for mobile devices. When designing Android, the team looked at which mobile device constraints likely were not going to change for the foreseeable future. For one, mobile devices are battery powered, and battery performance likely is not going to get much better any time soon. Second, the small size of mobile devices means that they will always be limited in terms of memory and speed.

These constraints were taken into consideration from the get-go and were addressed throughout the platform. The result is an overall better user experience.

Android was designed to run on all sorts of physical devices. Android doesn't make any assumptions about a device's screen size, resolution, chipset, and so on. Its core is designed to be portable.

History

The history of Android is interesting and offers some perspective on what the future might hold.

These are the key events of the past few years:

- In 2005, Google buys Android, Inc. The world thinks a "gPhone" is about to come out.
- Everything goes quiet for a while.
- In 2007, the Open Handset Alliance is announced. Android is officially open sourced.
- In 2008, the Android SDK 1.0 is released. The G1 phone, manufactured by HTC and sold by the wireless carrier T-Mobile USA, follows shortly afterward.
- 2009 sees a proliferation of Android-based devices. New versions of the operating system are released: Cupcake (1.5), Donut (1.6), and Eclair (2.0 and 2.1). More than 20 devices run Android.
- In 2010, Android is second only to Blackberry as the best-selling smart phone platform. Froyo (Android 2.2) is released and so are more than 60 devices that run it.

In 2005, when Google purchased Android, Inc., the world thought Google was about to enter the smart phone market, and there were widespread speculations about a device called the gPhone.

Google's CEO, Eric Schmidt, made it clear right away that Android's ambitions were much larger than a single phone. Instead, they envisioned a platform that would enable many phones and other devices.

Google's Motivation

Google's motivation for supporting the Android project seems to be having Android everywhere and by doing that, creating a level playing field for mobile devices. Ultimately, Google is a media company, and its business model is based on selling advertising. If everyone is using Android, then Google can provide additional services on top of it and compete fairly. This is unlike the business models of other software vendors who depend on licensing fees.

Although Google does license some proprietary apps, such as Gmail and Maps, and makes some money off the Android market, its primary motivation is still the advertising revenue that those apps bring in.

Open Handset Alliance

For this to be bigger than just Google, Android is owned by the Open Handset Alliance, a nonprofit group formed by key mobile operators, manufacturers, carriers, and others. The alliance is committed to openness and innovation for the mobile user experience.

In practice, the alliance is still very young and many members are still learning to work with each other. Google happens to be putting the most muscle behind the Android project at the moment.

 The first version of the Android SDK was released without an actual phone on the market. The point of this is that you don't really need a phone for Android development. There are some exceptions (hardware sensors, telephony, etc.), but for the most part the Android SDK contains everything you'll need for developing on this platform.

Android Versions

Like any software, Android is improved over time, which is reflected in its version numbers. However, the relationship between different version numbers can be confusing. Table 1-1 helps explain that.

Table 1-1. Android versions through Android 2.3

Android version	API level	Nickname
Android 1.0	1	
Android 1.1	2	
Android 1.5	3	Cupcake
Android 1.6	4	Donut
Android 2.0	5	Eclair
Android 2.01	6	Eclair
Android 2.1	7	Eclair
Android 2.2	8	Froyo (frozen yogurt)
Android 2.3	9	Gingerbread
Android 2.3.3	10	Gingerbread
Android 3.0	11	Honeycomb

The Android version number itself partly tells the story of the software platform's major and minor releases. What is most important is the API level. Version numbers change all the time, sometimes because the APIs have changed, and other times because of minor bug fixes or performance improvements.

As application developers, you will want to make sure you know which API level your application is targeting in order to run. That API level will determine which devices can and cannot run your application.

Typically your objective is to have your application run on as many devices as possible. So, with that in mind, try to shoot for an API level that is as low as possible. Keep in mind the distribution of Android versions on real devices out there. Figure 1-1 shows a snapshot of the Android Device Dashboard (*http://developer.android.com/resources/dashboard/platform-versions.html*) from mid-2010.

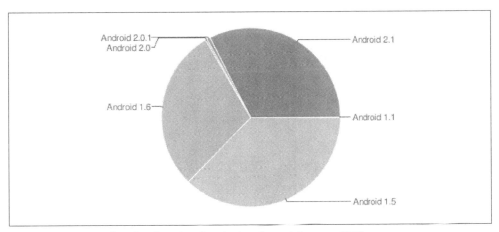

Figure 1-1. Historical Android version distribution through January 2011

You may notice that there are not a lot of users of Android 1.5 and 1.6. You may also notice that not a lot of users have the latest and greatest Android 2.3, but the number of 2.x users is growing. This is because everyone with 1.0 and 1.1 got upgraded over the air (OTA) automatically to 1.5. On the other hand, users who still have devices with Android 1.5 and 1.6 likely will never be able to upgrade to 2.x versions. Their older devices do not have the relevant firmware, and most manufacturers are not planning on releasing firmware upgrades as they are busy working on new models.

With that in mind, you will probably choose 1.6 or 2.0 as your minimum development target, unless you truly need the features of the latest version.

Summary

The Android operating system was designed from the ground up to be a comprehensive open source platform for mobile devices. It is a game-changer in the industry and has enjoyed great success.

In the next chapter, we'll take a look at the entire Android operating system at a high level to gain a technical understanding of how all the pieces fit together.

## CHAPTER 2

The Stack

This is the 9,000-foot overview of the Android platform. Although you're concerned primarily with writing Android applications, understanding the layout of the system will help shape your understanding about what you can or cannot do easily with Android.

By the end of this chapter, you'll understand how the whole system works, at least from the high level.

Stack Overview

The Android operating system is like a cake consisting of various layers. Each layer has its own characteristics and purpose. The layers are not cleanly separated but often seep into each other.

When you read through this chapter, keep in mind that I am concerned only with the big picture of the entire system and will get into the nitty-gritty details later on. Figure 2-1 shows the parts of the Android stack.

Linux

Android is built on top of Linux. Linux is a great operating system and the poster child of open source. There are many good reasons for choosing Linux as the base of the Android stack. Some of the main ones are its portability, security, and features.

Portability

Linux is a portable platform that is relatively easy to compile on various hardware architectures. What Linux brings to Android is a level of hardware abstractions. By basing Android on Linux, we don't have to worry too much about underlying hardware features. Most low-level parts of Linux have been written in fairly portable C code, which allows for third parties to port Android to a variety of devices.

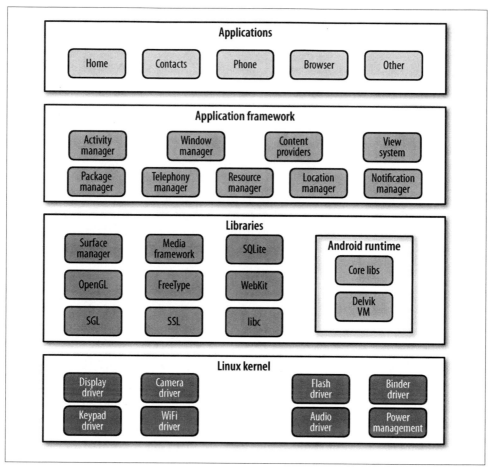

Figure 2-1. Android stack

Security

Linux is a highly secure system, having been tried and tested through some very harsh environments over the decades. Android heavily relies on Linux for security. All Android applications run as separate Linux processes with permissions set by the Linux system. As such, Android passes many security concerns to the underlying Linux system.

Features

Linux comes with a lot of very useful features. Android leverages many of them, such as support for memory management, power management, and networking.

Native Libraries

The native libraries are C/C++ libraries, often taken from the open source community in order to provide necessary services to the Android application layer. Among others, they include:

Webkit
> A fast web-rendering engine used by Safari, Chrome, and other browsers

SQLite
> A full-featured SQL database

Apache Harmony
> An open source implementation of Java

OpenGL
> 3D graphics libraries

OpenSSL
> The secure locket layer

Although many of these libraries are used as-is, one notable exception is Bionic, which is basically a rewritten version of the standard C library. Bionic is used for two reasons:

Technology
> To make it purpose-built for tiny, battery-powered devices

License
> To make it license-friendly for others who might want to adopt it and change it

> GNU libc, the default C library for Linux, is licensed under a GPL license, which requires any changes that you release publicly to be pushed back to the open source community. As such, it might not be the most business-friendly open source license when a company wants to keep their derivative work proprietary. Bionic, on the other hand, is licensed under an Apache/MIT license, which doesn't require derivative works to be open sourced.

Dalvik

Dalvik is a purpose-built virtual machine designed specifically for Android, developed by Dan Bornstein and his team at Google.

The Java virtual machine (VM) was designed to be a one-size-fits-all solution, and the Dalvik team felt they could do a better job by focusing strictly on mobile devices. They looked at which constraints specific to a mobile environment are least likely to change in the near future. One of these is battery life, and the other is processing power. Dalvik was built from the ground up to address those constraints.

Another side effect of replacing the Java VM with the Dalvik VM is the licensing. Whereas the Java language, Java tools, and Java libraries are free, the Java virtual machine is not. This was more of an issue back in 2005 when the work on Dalvik started. Nowadays, there are open source alternatives to Sun's Java VM, namely the OpenJDK (*http://openjdk.java.net/*) and Apache Harmony (*http://harmony.apache .org/*) projects.

By developing a truly open source and license-friendly virtual machine, Android yet again provides a full-featured platform that others are encouraged to adopt for a variety of devices without having to worry about the license.

Android and Java

In Java, you write your Java source file, compile it into a Java byte code using the Java compiler, and then run this byte code on the Java VM. In Android, things are different. You still write the Java source file, and you still compile it to Java byte code using the same Java compiler. But at that point, you recompile it once again using the Dalvik compiler to Dalvik byte code. It is this Dalvik byte code that is then executed on the Dalvik VM. Figure 2-2 illustrates this comparison between standard Java (on the left) in Android using Dalvik (on the right).

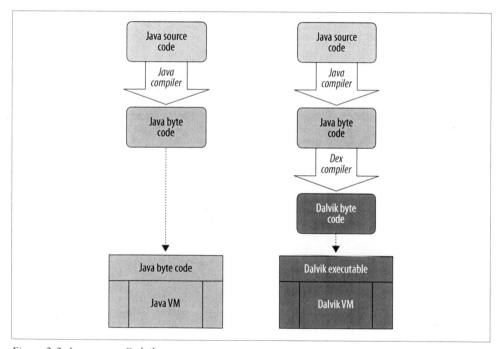

Figure 2-2. Java versus Dalvik

It might sound like you have to do a lot more work with Android when it comes to Java. However, all these compilation steps are automated by tools such as Eclipse or Ant, and you never notice the additional steps.

You may wonder, why not compile straight from Java into the Dalvik byte code? There are a couple of good reasons for the extra steps. Back in 2005, when work on Dalvik started, the Java language was going through frequent changes, but the Java byte code was more or less set in stone. So, the Android team chose to base Dalvik on Java byte code instead of Java source code.

A side effect of this is that in theory you could write Android applications in any other language that compiles down to Java byte code. For example, you could use Python or Ruby. I say "in theory" because in practice the appropriate libraries that are part of the SDK would need to be available. But it is likely that the open source community will come up with a solution to that in the future.

Another thing to keep in mind is that Android Java is a nonstandard collection of Java classes. Java typically ships in:

Java Standard Edition
    Used for development on basic desktop-type applications
Java Enterprise Edition (aka J2EE or JavaEE)
    Used for development of enterprise applications
Java Micro Edition (aka J2ME or JavaME)
    Java for mobile applications

Android's Java set of libraries is closest to Java Standard Edition. The major difference is that Java user interface libraries (AWT and Swing) have been taken out and replaced with Android-specific user interface libraries. Android also adds quite a few new features to standard Java while supporting most of Java's standard features. So, you have most of your favorite Java libraries at your disposal, plus many new ones.

Application Framework

The application framework is a rich environment that provides numerous services to help you, the app developer, get your job done. This is the best-documented and most extensively covered part of the platform because it is this layer that empowers developers to get creative and bring fantastic applications to the market.

In the application framework layer, you will find numerous Java libraries specifically built for Android. You will also find many services (or *managers*) that provide the ecosystem of capabilities your application can tap into, such as location, sensors, WiFi, telephony, and so on.

As you explore Android application development, most of your focus will be on this part of the stack, and you will get to use many of the application framework components.

Applications

And finally, there are the applications that you and other developers create. These applications are what end users find valuable about Android. They can come preinstalled on the device or can be downloaded from one of the many Android markets.

The APK

An application is a single application package (APK) file. An APK file roughly has three main components. An API consists of the following major components:

Dalvik executable
> This is all your Java source code compiled down to a Dalvik executable. This is the code that runs your application.

Resources
> Resources are everything that is not code. Your application may contain a number of images and audio/video clips, as well as numerous XML files describing layouts, language packs, and so on. Collectively, these items are the resources.

Native libraries
> Optionally, your application may include some native code, such as C/C++ libraries. These libraries could be packaged together with your APK file.

Application Signing

Android applications must be signed before they can be installed on a device. For development purposes, we'll be signing our example applications with a debug key—a key that you already have on your development platform. However, when you distribute your application commercially, you'll want to sign it with your own key. The Android developer document titled "Signing Your Application" (*http://developer.an droid.com/guide/publishing/app-signing.html*) has the details.

Application Distribution

One way in which Android is quite different from other platforms is the distribution of its apps. On most other platforms, such as iPhone, a single vendor holds a monopoly over the distribution of applications. On Android, there are many different stores, or markets. Each market has its own set of policies with respect to what is allowed, how the revenue is split, and so on. As such, Android is much more of a free market space in which vendors compete for business.

In practice, the biggest market currently is Android Market, run by Google. It is unclear whether Google means to just seed the market space while other stores develop or plans to make it a profitable venture.

Applications can also be distributed via the Web. When you download an APK file from a website through the browser, the application represented by the APK file is installed automatically on your phone.

What about viruses, malware, spyware, and other bad things?

With its decentralized application distribution system, it is certainly possible for an unsuspecting user to download a malicious app that consequently does bad things. For example, there have been reports of phishing attacks via fake banking apps (*http://www .downloadsquad.com/2010/01/12/phishing-attack-hits-android-market-be-careful -about-banking/*).

So, Android leaves it to the marketplace to sort it out. Eventually, there will be stores that are more reputable and those that are less so, at least in theory. Google relies on user reports for policing its Android Market, but other stores may choose to do more proactive testing and raise the bar on what gets into the store in the first place.

Summary

In this chapter, you got a big-picture overview of what comprises the Android operating system and how its various pieces fit together. You now understand what makes Android so complete, open, and attractive to developers.

In the next chapter, we'll look at how to set up your development environment so you can get up to speed quickly. We'll also look at a simple Hello World application and dissect it to help you understand the various pieces of an Android application.

## CHAPTER 3

Quick Start

In this chapter, you will learn how to set up your environment for Android development. I'll go beyond just listing where you can download the software, and will cover some of the best practices in getting set up. I'll look at development operating system choices as well as the Android tools available. You will see the good, the bad, and the ugly of the various tool and platform choices that you're about to make (or that someone else has already made for you).

By the end of this chapter, you will have your entire development environment set up. You'll be able to write a Hello World application, build it, and run it on the emulator (or a physical device, if you want).

 I'm going to use ~ to refer to your home directory. On Mac OS X, that's typically something like */Users/marko*. On Linux, it would be */home/ marko*, and on Windows Vista and 7, *C:\Users\marko* (in Windows XP, it would be *C:\Documents and Settings\marko*). Also, I'm going to use Unix-style forward slashes and not Windows backslashes to denote file path separators.

So, if you're on Windows, just change ~ to *C:\Users***YourUserName** and / to \. Other than that, everything should be pretty much for different operating systems, regardless of whether you use OS X, Linux, or Windows.

Installing the Android SDK

The Android Software Development Kit (SDK) is all you need to develop applications for Android. The SDK comes with a set of tools as well as a platform to run it and see it all work. You can download the Android SDK for your particular platform from the Android SDK Download page (*http://developer.android.com/sdk/index.html*).

Once you download it, unzip (or on Linux, *untar*) it into a folder that is easy to get to. Further examples in the book will assume your SDK is in the folder ~/android-sdk. If it's in a different location, use that location instead of ~/android-sdk. For example:

Windows
> C:\apps\android-sdk-windows

Linux
> /home/**YourUserName**/android-sdk-linux_86

Mac OS X
> /Users/**YourUserName**/android-sdk-mac_86

 For Windows users, I strongly recommend choosing directories without spaces in them. This is because we'll be doing work on the command line and spaces just complicate things. Because the Windows XP home directory is in *C:\Documents and Settings*, I would recommend putting *android-sdk* in a top-level directory that you create, such as *C:\apps*.

However, on Windows Vista or 7, you can simply extract *android-sdk* into *C:\Users***YourUserName**.

Setting Up a PATH to Tools

The Android SDK has a folder that contains all its major tools. Since we're going to use these tools from the command line, it is *very* helpful to add your ~/android-sdk/tools/ and your ~/android-skd/platform-tools/ directories to your system PATH variable. This will make it easier to access your tools without having to navigate to their specific location every single time.

Details for setting up the PATH variable depend on the platform; see step 2 of the document "Installing Android SDK" (*http://developer.android.com/sdk/installing.html*).

Installing Eclipse

Eclipse is an open source collection of programming tools originally created by IBM for Java. Nowadays, most developers in the Java community favor Eclipse as their Integrated Development Environment (IDE) of choice. Eclipse lives at *http://eclipse.org*.

Eclipse has a lot of time-saving features, which I'll be pointing out as we continue. Keep in mind that, although powerful, Eclipse tends to be very resource-hungry, and so you might want to restart it once a day if it starts running sluggishly.

Although you can do Android development with any favorite text editor or integrated development environment (IDE), most developers seem to be using Eclipse, and thus that's what I use in this book.

If you choose not to use Eclipse, please refer to "Developing in Other IDEs" (*http://developer.android.com/guide/developing/other-ide.html*).

Download Eclipse at *http://www.eclipse.org/downloads/*. I recommend Eclipse IDE for Java Developers (*not* the twice-as-large Eclipse for Java EE Developers). You can install it in any directory you'd like.

Eclipse Workspace

Eclipse organizes all your work by projects. Projects are placed in a workspace, which is a location you choose. So, where you put your workspace is significant. I recommend *~/workspace* as a simple place for your code. On Windows, however, I recommend storing your workspace in a directory that doesn't have spaces in it (they complicate anything you might do at the command line). *C:\workspace* is a good choice for Windows users.

Setting Up Android Development Tools

You also need to set up Android Tools for Eclipse. The instructions are:

1. Start Eclipse, then select Help→Install New Software (see Figure 3-1).
2. In the Available Software dialog, click Add.
3. In the Add Site dialog that appears, enter a name for the remote site (for example, "Android Plugin") in the "Name" field.
4. In the "Location" field, enter this URL: `https://dl-ssl.google.com/android/eclipse/`.
5. Click OK.
6. Back in the Available Software view, you should now see "Developer Tools" added to the list. Select the checkbox next to Developer Tools, which will automatically select the nested tools Android DDMS and Android Development Tools. Click Next.
7. In the resulting Install Details dialog, the Android DDMS and Android Development Tools features are listed. Click Next to read and accept the license agreement and install any dependencies, then click Finish.
8. Restart Eclipse.

 If you have trouble downloading the plug-in, you can try using "http" in the URL instead of "https" (https is preferred for security reasons).

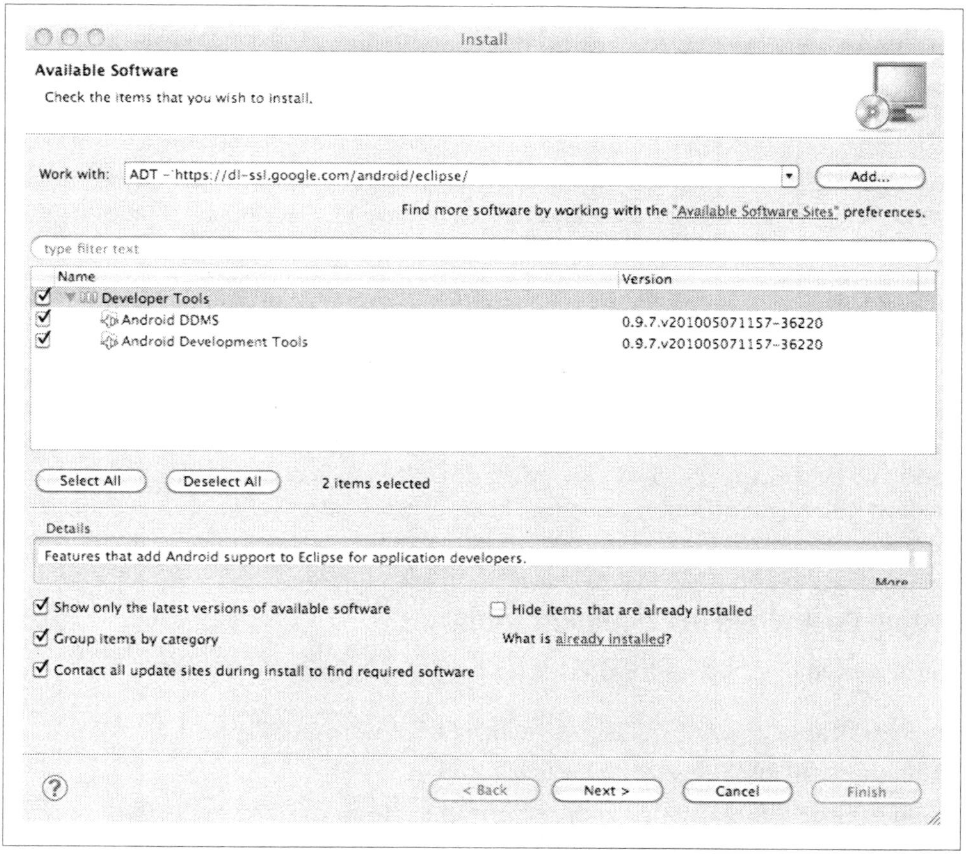

Figure 3-1. Install new software

Hello, World

To make sure everything is set up properly, we're going to write a simple Hello World program. As a matter of fact, there's not much for us to write, but a lot to understand. This is because Eclipse will create the project shell for us from some predefined templates.

Creating a New Project

In Eclipse, choose File→New→Android Project. Sometimes (especially the first time you run Eclipse) the Android tools may not be appear there right away. They should show up in the future after you've used them for the first time. If Android Project is not an option under File→New, choose Other and look for Android Project in there.

In the new project dialog window, fill out the following:

1. "Project name" is an Eclipse construct. Eclipse organizes everything into projects. A project name should be one word. I like to use the CamelCase (*http://en.wikipedia .org/wiki/Camel_case_(programming)*) naming convention here. Go ahead and type HelloWorld.

2. Next, you need to choose the *build target*. The build target tells the build tools which version of the Android platform you are building for. In here you should see a list of available platforms and add-ons you have installed as part of your SDK. Go ahead and pick one of the newer ones, such as Android 2.2 (but don't choose the targets named Google APIs—those are Google's proprietary extensions to the Android platform). For our purposes, we'll stick to Android Open Source versions of the Android platform.

3. You need to fill out your project properties next. The application name is the plain English name of your application. Go ahead and enter something like Hello, World!!!.

4. The package name is a Java construct. In Java, all source code is organized into packages. Packages are important because, among other things, they specify the visibility of objects between the various Java classes in your project. In Android, packages are also important for application signing purposes. Your package name should be the reverse of your domain name with optional subdomains. I might use com.example.calculator if I were building a calculator app and my domain name was *example.com*. I'm going to be using com.marakana for my package name here.

5. You can optionally specify an activity. I haven't covered activities yet (you'll learn about them in Chapter 6), but think of them as corresponding to the various screens in your application. An activity is going to be represented by a Java class, and therefore its name should adhere to Java class naming conventions: start with an upper-case letter and use CamelCase to separate words. So, type HelloWorld for your activity name.

6. The minimum SDK version is the minimum version of Android—as represented by API level—that is required for the device to run this application. You want this number to be as low as possible so that your app can run on as many devices as possible. I'm going to put 8 here to represent Android 2.2, which I know I have installed.

Finally, click on the Finish button, and Eclipse will create your project. Let's look at the various files that this process created in Figure 3-2.

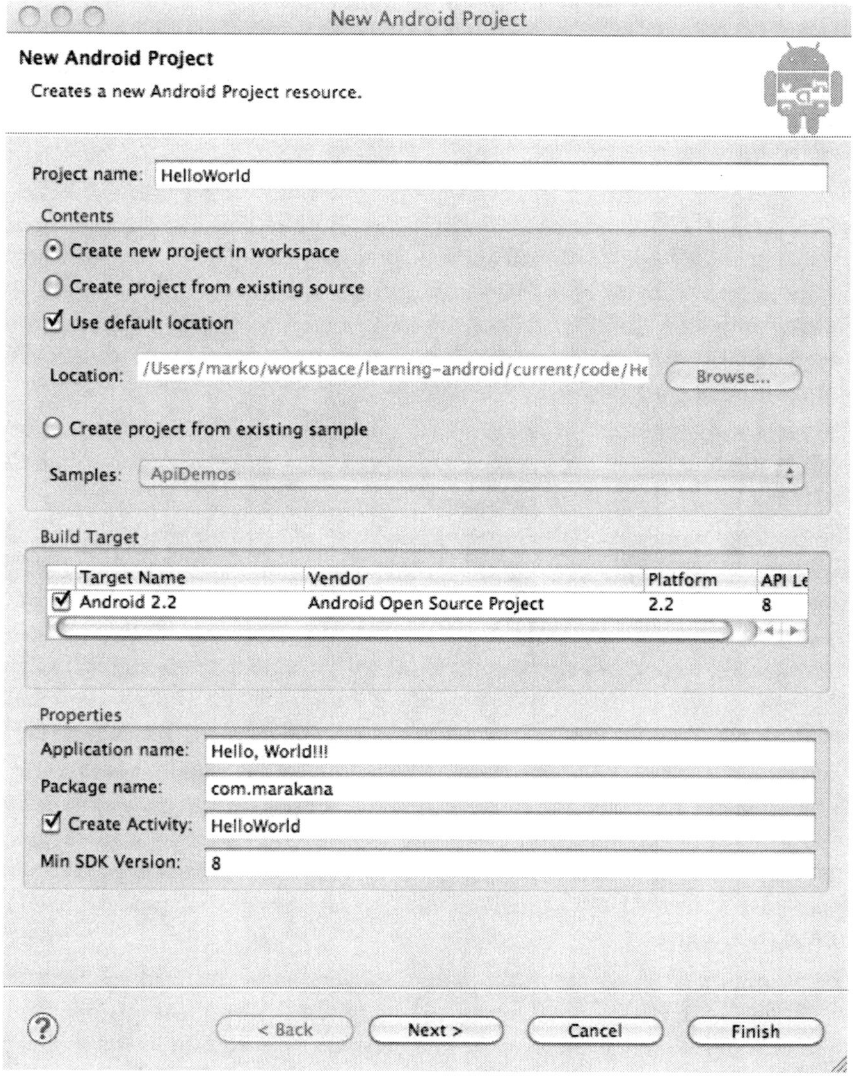

Figure 3-2. HelloWorld new project window

Manifest File

The manifest file glues everything together. It is this file that explains what the application consists of, what all its main building blocks are, what permissions it requires, and so on (see Example 3-1).

Example 3-1. AndroidManifest.xml

```xml
<?xml version="1.0" encoding="utf-8"?>
<manifest xmlns:android="http://schemas.android.com/apk/res/android"
  package="com.marakana" android:versionCode="1" android:versionName="1.0">
  <application android:icon="@drawable/icon" android:label="@string/app_name">
    <activity android:name=".HelloWorld" android:label="@string/app_name">
      <intent-filter>
        <action android:name="android.intent.action.MAIN" />
        <category android:name="android.intent.category.LAUNCHER" />
      </intent-filter>
    </activity>

  </application>
  <uses-sdk android:minSdkVersion="8" />

</manifest>
```

Layout XML Code

The layout file specifies the layout of your screen. In this case, shown in Example 3-2, we have only one screen, and it's loaded by the *HelloWorld.java* code seen in Example 3-5.

Example 3-2. res/layout/main.xml

```xml
<?xml version="1.0" encoding="utf-8"?>
<LinearLayout xmlns:android="http://schemas.android.com/apk/res/android"
        android:orientation="vertical" android:layout_width="fill_parent"
        android:layout_height="fill_parent">
        <TextView android:layout_width="fill_parent"
                android:layout_height="wrap_content" android:text="@string/hello" />
</LinearLayout>
```

Strings

This is another XML file that contains all the text that your application uses. For example, the names of buttons, labels, default text, and similar types of strings go into this file. This is the best practice for separating the concerns of various files, even if they are XML files. In other words, layout XML is responsible for the layout of widgets, but strings XML is responsible for their textual content (see Example 3-3).

Example 3-3. res/values/strings.xml

```xml
<?xml version="1.0" encoding="utf-8"?>
<resources>
    <string name="hello">Hello World, HelloWorld!</string>
    <string name="app_name">Hello, World!!!</string>
</resources>
```

The R File

The R file is the glue between the world of Java and the world of resources (see Example 3-4). It is an automatically generated file, and as such, you never modify it. It is recreated every time you change anything in the *res* directory, for example, when you add an image or XML file.

You don't need to look at this file much. We will use the data in it quite a bit, but we'll use Eclipse to help us refer to values stored in this file.

Example 3-4. gen/com/marakana/R.java

```
/* AUTO-GENERATED FILE.  DO NOT MODIFY.
 *
 * This class was automatically generated by the
 * aapt tool from the resource data it found.  It
 * should not be modified by hand.
 */

package com.marakana;

public final class R {
    public static final class attr {
    }
    public static final class drawable {
        public static final int icon=0x7f020000;
    }
    public static final class layout {
        public static final int main=0x7f030000;
    }
    public static final class string {
        public static final int app_name=0x7f040001;
        public static final int hello=0x7f040000;
    }
}
```

Java Source Code

The Java code is what drives everything. This is the code that ultimately gets converted to a Dalvik executable and runs your application (see Example 3-5).

Example 3-5. HelloWorld.java

```
package com.marakana;

import android.app.Activity;
import android.os.Bundle;

public class HelloWorld extends Activity {
  /** Called when the activity is first created. */
  @Override
  public void onCreate(Bundle savedInstanceState) {
    super.onCreate(savedInstanceState);
```

```
        setContentView(R.layout.main);
    }
}
```

The Emulator

Running your application on a physical device versus an emulated device is pretty much the same thing. That is because the emulator is an actual code emulator, meaning it runs the same code base as the actual device, all the way down to the machine layer.

 A simulator and an emulator sound very similar, but are fundamentally different. To emulate means to imitate the machine executing the binary code. So, an emulator is sort of like a virtual machine. A simulator merely simulates the behavior of the code at a higher level. Android SDK ships with a true emulator, based on QEMU (*http://wiki.qemu.org/Main _Page*).

To use the emulator, we'll have to create an Android Virtual Device (AVD). The easiest way to do that is to start the android tool via Eclipse.

To create a new AVD, start the tool called Android SDK and AVD Manager (see Figure 3-3). You can start this tool from Eclipse by clicking on the icon or via the command line by starting the tool called android, which is located in your *SDK/tools* directory.

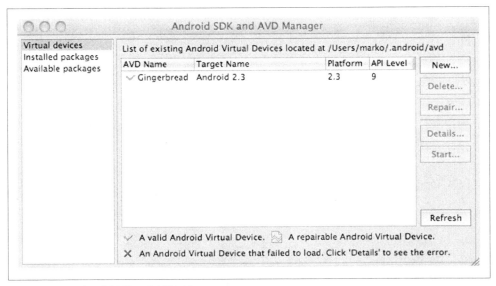

Figure 3-3. Android SDK and AVD Manager

From within the Android SDK and AVD Manager window, choosing "New..." pops up a Create New AVD dialog window (see Figure 3-4). In this dialog, you specify the parameters for your new AVD. The name can be any name you choose. The target designates which version of Android you want installed on this particular AVD. The list of possible targets is based on platforms and add-ons that you have installed into your SDK. If you don't have any targets, go back to the Android SDK and AVD Manager window and choose the "Available packages" tab to install at least one platform, for example, Android 2.3 - API level 9.

Each AVD can have an SD card. You can just specify a number here for your built-in card, in megabytes. The skin is the look and feel of your device as well as its form factor. The Hardware option lets you fine-tune what this AVD does and doesn't support.

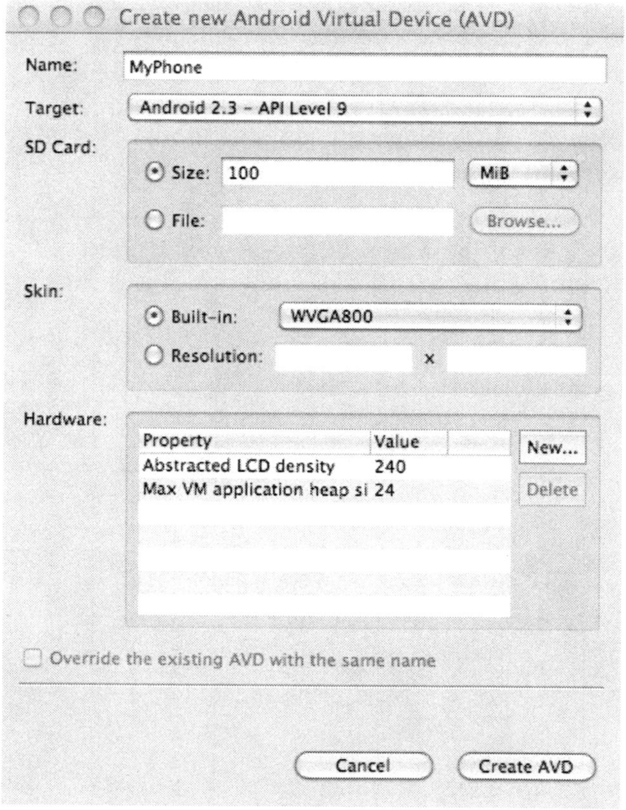

Figure 3-4. New AVD dialog

Once you are done with this dialog, you will have an AVD in your list. Go ahead and start it, and an emulator will pop up (see Figure 3-5).

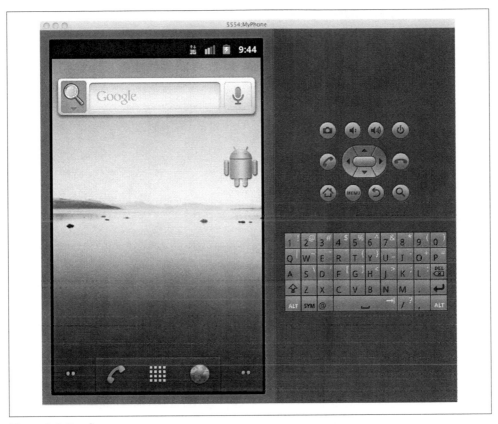

Figure 3-5. Emulator

An Emulator Versus a Physical Phone

For the most part, running your application on the emulator is identical to running it on a physical phone. There are some notable exceptions, mostly things that are just hard to virtualize, such as sensors. Other hardware-related features such as telephony and location services, can be simulated in the emulator.

Summary

Setting up the Android development environment basically involves setting up Android SDK and Eclipse. Once you have set up your development environment, a good way to test that everything is working is to use Eclipse to create a simple Hello World project and run it in the emulator. If that runs fine, you are almost certain that your system is set up and ready for further development.

## CHAPTER 4

Main Building Blocks

In this chapter, you will learn about the big blocks in Android. We'll give you a high-level overview of what activities are, how intents work, why services are cool, how to use broadcast receivers and content providers to make your app scale, and much more.

By the end of this chapter, you will understand the main Android components for building applications. You should conceptually know when you'd use what component. You will also see how these components relate to a real-world application.

What Are Main Building Blocks?

The main building blocks are components that you use as an application developer to build Android apps. They are the conceptual items that you put together to create a bigger whole. When you start thinking about your application, it is good to take a top-down approach. You design your application in terms of screens, features, and the interactions between them. You start with conceptual drawing, something that you can represent in terms of "lines and circles." This approach to application development helps you see the big picture—how the components fit together and how it all makes sense.

A Real-World Example

Let's say that we want to build a Twitter app. We know that the user should be able to post status updates. We also know the user should be able to see what her friends are up to. Those are basic features. Beyond that, the user should also be able to set her username and password in order to log into her Twitter account. So, now we know we should have these three screens.

Next, we would like this app to work quickly regardless of the network connection or lack thereof. To achieve that, the app has to pull the data from Twitter when it's online and cache the data locally. That will require a service that runs in the background as well as a database.

We also know that we'd like this background service to be started when the device is initially turned on, so by the time the user first uses the app, there's already up-to-date information on her friends.

So, these are some straightforward requirements. Android building blocks make it easy to break them down into conceptual units so that you can work on them independently, and then easily put them together into a complete package.

Activities

An activity is usually a single screen that the user sees on the device at one time. An application typically has multiple activities, and the user flips back and forth among them. As such, activities are the most visible part of your application.

I usually use a website as an analogy for activities. Just like a website consists of multiple pages, so does an Android application consist of multiple activities. Just like a website has a "home page," an Android app has a "main" activity, usually the one that is shown first when you launch the application. And just like a website has to provide some sort of navigation among various pages, an Android app should do the same.

On the Web, you can jump from a page on one website to a page on another. Similarly, in Android, you could be looking at an activity of one application, but shortly after you could start another activity in a completely separate application. For example, if you are in your Contacts app and you choose to text a friend, you'd be launching the activity to compose a text message in the Messaging application.

Activity Life Cycle

Launching an activity can be quite expensive. It may involve creating a new Linux process, allocating memory for all the UI objects, inflating all the objects from XML layouts, and setting up the whole screen. Since we're doing a lot of work to launch an activity, it would be a waste to just toss it out once the user leaves that screen. To avoid this waste, the activity life cycle is managed via Activity Manager.

Activity Manager is responsible for creating, destroying, and managing activities. For example, when the user starts an application for the first time, the Activity Manager will create its activity and put it onto the screen. Later, when the user switches screens, the Activity Manager will move that previous activity to a holding place. This way, if the user wants to go back to an older activity, it can be started more quickly. Older activities that the user hasn't used in a while will be destroyed in order to free more space for the currently active one. This mechanism is designed to help improve the speed of the user interface and thus improve the overall user experience.

Programming for Android is conceptually different than programming for some other environments. In Android, you find yourself responding more to certain changes in the state of your application rather than driving that change yourself. It is a managed, container-based environment similar to programming for Java applets or servlets. So, when it comes to an activity life cycle, you don't get to say what state the activity is in, but you have plenty of opportunity to say what happens during the transitions from state to state. Figure 4-1 shows the states that an activity can go through.

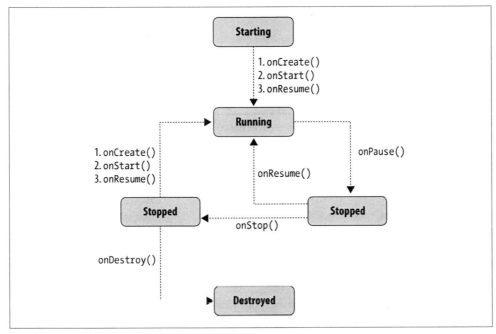

Figure 4-1. Activity life cycle

Starting state

When an activity doesn't exist in memory, it is in a *starting state*. While it's starting up, the activity will go through a whole set of callback methods that you as a developer have an opportunity to fill out. Eventually, the activity will be in a *running state*.

Keep in mind that this transition from starting state to running state is one of the most expensive operations in terms of computing time, and this also directly affects the battery life of the device. This is the exact reason why we don't automatically destroy activities that are no longer shown. The user might want to come back to them, so we keep them around for a while.

Running state

The activity in a running state is the one that is currently on the screen and interacting with the user. We also say this activity is in focus, meaning that all user interactions—such as typing, touching the screen, and clicking buttons—are handled by this one activity. As such, there is only one running activity at any given time.

The running activity is the one that has priority in terms of getting the memory and resources it needs to run as quickly as possible. This is because Android wants to make sure the running activity is zippy and responsive to the user.

Paused state

When an activity is not in focus (i.e., not interacting with the user) but still visible on the screen, we say it's in a *paused state*. This is not a typical scenario, because the device's screen is usually small, and an activity is either taking up the whole screen or none at all. We often see this case with dialog boxes that come up in front of an activity, causing it to become Paused. All activities go through a paused state en route to being stopped.

Paused activities still have high priority in terms of getting memory and other resources. This is because they are visible and cannot be removed from the screen without making it look very strange to the user.

Stopped state

When an activity is not visible, but still in memory, we say it's in a *stopped state*. Stopped activity could be brought back to the front to become a Running activity again. Or, it could be destroyed and removed from memory.

The system keeps activities around in a stopped state because it is likely that the user will still want to get back to those activities some time soon, and restarting a stopped activity is far cheaper than starting an activity from scratch. That is because we already have all the objects loaded in memory and simply have to bring it all up to the foreground.

Stopped activities can be removed from memory at any point.

Destroyed state

A destroyed activity is no longer in memory. The Activity Manager decided that this activity is no longer needed and has removed it. Before the activity is destroyed, it can perform certain actions, such as save any unsaved information. However, there's no guarantee that your activity will be stopped prior to being destroyed. It is possible for a paused activity to be destroyed as well. For that reason, it is better to do important work, such as saving unsaved data, en route to a paused state rather than a destroyed state.

 The fact that an activity is in a running state doesn't mean it's doing much. It could be just sitting there and waiting for user input. Similarly, an activity in a stopped state is not necessarily doing nothing. The state names mostly refer to how active the activity is with respect to user input, in other words, whether an activity is visible, in focus, or not visible at all.

Intents

Intents are messages that are sent among the major building blocks. They trigger an activity to start up, tell a service to start or stop, or are simply broadcasts. Intents are asynchronous, meaning the code that sends them doesn't have to wait for them to be completed.

An intent could be explicit or implicit. In an explicit intent, the sender clearly spells out which specific component should be on the receiving end. In an implicit intent, the sender specifies the type of receiver. For example, your activity could send an intent saying it simply wants someone to open up a web page. In that case, any application that is capable of opening a web page could "compete" to complete this action.

When you have competing applications, the system will ask you which one you'd like to use to complete a given action. You can also set an app as the default. This mechanism works very similarly to your desktop environment, for example, when you downloaded Firefox or Chrome to replace your default Internet Explorer or Safari web browsers.

This type of messaging allows the user to replace any app on the system with a custom one. For example, you might want to download a different SMS application or another browser to replace your existing ones. Figure 4-2 shows how intents may be used to "jump" between various activities, in the same application or in another app altogether.

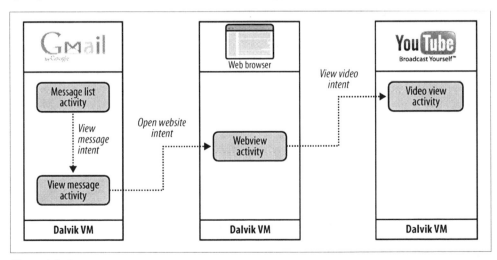

Figure 4-2. Intents

Services

Services run in the background and don't have any user interface components. They can perform the same actions as activities, but without any user interface. Services are useful for actions that we want to perform for a while, regardless of what is on the screen. For example, you might want your music player to play music even as you are flipping between other applications.

 Don't confuse the Android services that are part of an Android app with native Linux services, servers, or daemons, which are a much lower-level component of the operating system.

Services have a much simpler life cycle than activities (see Figure 4-3). You either start a service or stop it. Also, the service life cycle is more or less controlled by the developer, and not so much by the system. Consequently, we as developers have to be mindful to run our services so that they don't consume shared resources unnecessarily, such as the CPU and battery.

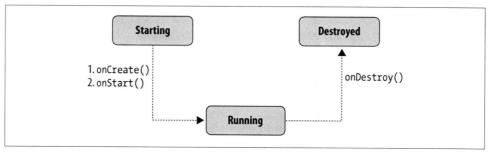

Figure 4-3. Service life cycle

 The fact that a service runs in the background doesn't mean it runs on a separate thread. If a service is doing some processing that takes a while to complete (such as performing network calls), you would typically run it on a separate thread. Otherwise, your user interface will run noticeably slower. In other words, services and activities run on the same main application thread, often called the UI thread.

Content Providers

Content providers are interfaces for sharing data between applications. By default, Android runs each application in its own sandbox so that all data that belongs to an application is totally isolated from other applications on the system. Although small amounts of data can be passed between applications via intents, content providers are much better suited for sharing persistent data between possibly large datasets. As such, the content provider API nicely adheres to the CRUD principle (*http://en.wikipedia.org/ wiki/Create,_read,_update_and_delete*). Figure 4-4 illustrates how the content provider's CRUD interface pierces the application boundaries and allows other apps to connect to it to share data.

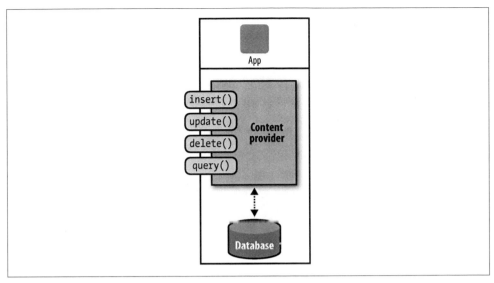

Figure 4-4. Content provider

The Android system uses this mechanism all the time. For example, Contacts Provider is a content provider that exposes all user contact data to various applications. Settings Provider exposes system settings to various applications, including the built-in Settings application. Media Store is responsible for storing and sharing various media, such as photos and music, across various applications. Figure 4-5 illustrates how the Contacts app uses Contacts Provider, a totally separate application, to retrieve data about users' contacts. The Contacts app itself doesn't have any contacts data, and Contacts Provider doesn't have any user interface.

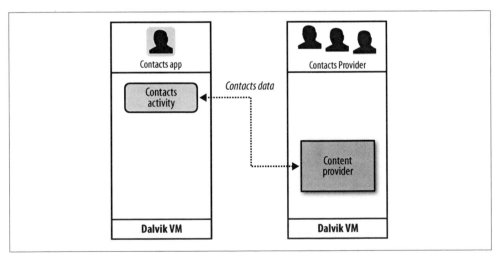

Figure 4-5. Contacts application using Contacts Provider to get the data

This separation of data storage and the actual user interface application offers greater flexibility to mash up various parts of the system. For example, a user could install an alternative address book application that uses the same data as the default Contacts app. Or, he could install widgets on the Home screen that allow for easy changes in the System Settings, such as turning on or off the WiFi, Bluetooth, or GPS features. Many phone manufactures take advantage of content providers to add their own applications on top of standard Android to improve overall user experience, such as HTC Sense (*http://en.wikipedia.org/wiki/HTC_Sense*).

Content providers are relatively simple interfaces, with the standard `insert()`, `update()`, `delete()`, and `query()` methods. These methods look a lot like standard database methods, so it is relatively easy to implement a content provider as a proxy to the database. Having said that, you are much more likely to use content providers than write your own.

Broadcast Receivers

Broadcast receivers are Android's implementation of a system-wide publish/subscribe mechanism (*http://en.wikipedia.org/wiki/Publish/subscribe*), or more precisely, an Observer pattern (*http://en.wikipedia.org/wiki/Observer_pattern*). The receiver is simply dormant code that gets activated once an event to which it is subscribed happens.

The system itself broadcasts events all the time. For example, when an SMS arrives, a call comes in, the battery runs low, or the system gets booted, all those events are broadcasted, and any number of receivers could be triggered by them.

In our Twitter app example, we want to start the update service once the system starts up. To do that, we can subscribe to the broadcast that tells us the system has completed booting up.

You can also send your own broadcasts from one part of your application to another, or to a totally different application.

Broadcast receivers themselves do not have any visual representation, nor are they actively running in memory. But when triggered, they get to execute some code, such as starting an activity, a service, or something else.

Application Context

So far you have seen activities, services, content providers, and broadcast receivers. Together, they make up an application. Another way of saying this is that they live inside the same application context.

Application context refers to the application environment and the process within which all its components are running. It allows applications to share the data and resources between various building blocks.

An application context gets created whenever the first component of this application is started up, regardless of whether that component is an activity, service, or something else. Application context lives as long as your application is alive. As such, it is independent of the activities life cycle. You can easily obtain a reference to the context by calling Context.getApplicationContext() or Activity.getApplication(). Keep in mind that activities and services are already subclasses of context, and as such they inherit all its methods.

Summary

In this chapter, you learned about some of the most important Android application components. We put together these components to create various applications, from a simple Hello World to much more complex creations.

In the next chapter, we'll outline a Yamba application as an example of how all these bits and pieces come together to form a working Android app.

## CHAPTER 5

Yamba Project Overview

The best way to learn is by an example, and that example has to meet certain criteria. After working with thousands of new Android developers and using various example applications to explain some of the unique concepts that this platform has to offer, I concluded that the best example has to be:

Comprehensive
> A good example app should demonstrate most of the aspects of the application framework that are unique to Android. Additionally, there should be a good reason to use a specific feature in order to get the job done. This is important in order to create the right motivation for those new to Android.

Familiar
> The example application should be simple to understand. We want to focus on design and implementation, and not on features and benefits.

The Yamba Application

The application I picked for this book is a Twitter-like application. We call it Yamba, which stands for *Yet Another Micro Blogging App*. Yamba lets a user connect to a service such as Twitter, pull down friends' statuses, and update that user's own status.

Yamba covers most of the main Android building blocks in a natural way. As such, it's a great sample application to illustrate both how various components work individually and how they fit together. Services such as Twitter are more or less familiar to most people, so the features of the application do not require much explanation.

Figures 5-1 through 5-3 show what a finished product could look like.

Figure 5-1. List of status messages from other people, called a timeline

Figure 5-2. Screen where the user can enter a status message

Figure 5-3. User preferences

Figure 5-1 shows how Yamba displays a list of status messages from your friends. Figure 5-2 shows the initial Yamba screen, and Figure 5-3 shows the user preferences.

Design Philosophy

We're going to adopt a certain design philosophy in tackling this project. This philosophy will help guide us in our development and serve as a north star when in doubt about what to do next. Spelling out the design philosophy here should also help eliminate some confusion in the process we're following:

Small increments
> The Yamba application will start out small and will constantly grow in functionality and complexity. Initially, the app will not do much, but it will grow organically one step at a time. Along the way, we'll explain each step so that you're expanding your skills as you go.

Always whole and complete
> The application must always work. In other words, we'll add new features in small, self-contained chunks and pull them back into the main project so that you can see how it fits together as a whole. The application must always work at each stopping point.

Refactoring code
> Once in a while, we'll have to take a step back and refactor the application to remove duplicate code and optimize the design. The goal is to reuse the code and not reinvent the wheel. But we are going to cross those bridges as we get to them, providing the motivation for refactoring along the way. This process will teach you about some general software development best practices as well.

Project Design

If you remember from Chapter 4, an Android application is a loose collection of activities, services, content providers, and broadcast receivers. These are the components from which we put together an application. Figure 5-4 shows the design of the entire Yamba application, which incorporates most of the main Android building blocks.

Part 1: Android User Interface

This part, covered in Chapter 6, will focus on developing the first component of the Yamba application: the Status Update screen. Our tasks are building an activity, networking and multithreading, and debugging.

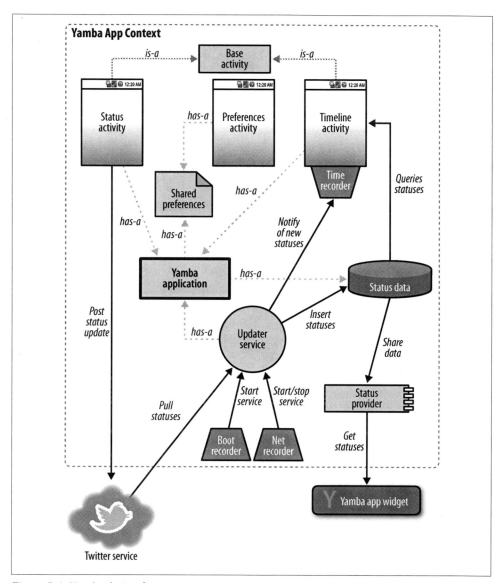

Figure 5-4. Yamba design diagram

Building an Activity

We are going to start by introducing the Android user interface (UI) model. In its UI, Android is quite different from some other paradigms that you might be familiar with. The unique feature is its dual approach to UI via both Java and XML.

In this chapter, you will learn how to develop the user interface for Figure 5-2, where the user updates her status. Through this process, you will use XML and Java to put together a working UI. You will learn about Layouts and Views, units in Android, how to work with images, and how to make the UI look pretty.

Our approach will focus on best practices in UI development so that your application looks good and works well on any Android device, regardless of screen size and resolution.

Networking and Multithreading

Once we have a working screen, we will want to post the user input to the cloud service. For that purpose, we are going to use a third-party library to help us with the Twitter API web service calls.

While making the network calls, you'll notice that the UI starts behaving sluggishly, due to the unpredictable nature of the network. The network latency might even cause our application to stop responding. At that point, we will introduce multithreading in Android and explain how to develop an app that works well regardless of external circumstances.

Debugging Android Apps

A few things are going to go wrong in this section of the book. This is by design, because debugging is a normal part of application development. We'll show you how to use the Android SDK tools to quickly find and fix problems. Debugging will become second nature to you.

Part 2: Preferences, Filesystem, Options Menu, and Intents

This part, covered in Chapter 7, is all about the preferences screen. At the end of this part, your Yamba application will have two screens, one for status updates and the other for setting up the preferences. At this point, Yamba is configurable for various users and starts being a useful app. The elements we'll create at this stage are the activity, the menu system and intents, and the filesystem.

The Activity

First, we'll create the screen, which is an activity, one of Android's basic building blocks. You will see the steps involved and understand what it takes to create new screens.

Menu System and Intents

Next, we'll need a way to get to that screen. For that purpose, we'll introduce a menu system in Android and show how it works. You will also learn about intents and how to send these to open up a specific activity.

Filesystem

Finally, we'll learn about the filesystem on a typical Android device. You will gain a deeper understanding of how the operating system is put together, and you will also learn more about Android security.

Part 3: Android Services

In this part, covered in Chapter 8, introduces background services. By the end of this part, your Yamba application will be able to periodically connect to the cloud and pull down your friends' status updates.

Services

Android services are very useful building blocks. They allow a process to run in the background without requiring any user interface. This is perfect for Yamba, as we'll have an update process connect to the cloud periodically and pull the data. In this section, you will also learn about multithreading considerations as they apply to background services.

Application Object

At this point, we'll notice repetition in the code and recognize that our system is no longer as elegant as it could be. So we are going to introduce the `Application` object as a way to refactor Yamba and make it easier to scale.

Part 4: Working with Databases

We now have the data from our updater service but still need a place to store it. In this part, covered in Chapter 9, we'll introduce you to Android's support for databases. By the end of that chapter, our data from the cloud will be persisted in the database.

SQLite and Android's Support for It

Android ships with a built-in database called SQLite. In addition to this cool little database, the Android framework offers a rich API that makes SQLite easier for us to use. In this section, you will learn how to use SQLite and the API for it. You do not have to be an SQL buff to understand what is going on, but some basic understanding of SQL always helps.

Refactoring the Code Again

At this point, we'll have yet another opportunity to refactor and streamline our code. There will be a strong motivation for refactoring at that moment, and the effort will be further rewarded in later chapters.

Part 5: Lists and Adapters

It might sound like we're back in UI mode, but Lists and Adapters are more organizational aids than user interface elements in Android. They form very powerful components that allow our tiny UI to connect to very large datasets in an efficient and scalable manner. In other words, users will be able to use Yamba in the real world without any performance hits in the long run.

Currently the data is all there in the database, but we have no way to view it. In this part, covered in Chapter 10, the Yamba application will get the much-needed Timeline Activity and a way for the user to see what his friends are chatting about online.

Timeline Activity

We're going to develop this third and final activity in multiple stages. First, we'll use our existing knowledge of the Android UI and put something together. It will work, sort of. Next, we'll improve on that design. The app will look better, but it still won't be ready for the prime time because our design won't be able to handle real-world usage. Finally, we'll get it right by introducing Lists and Adapters to the mix. Finally, we'll get it right by introducing Lists and Adapters to the mix and use them to tie the data to our user interface.

More Refactoring?

We'll have yet another opportunity to refactor our code by introducing a base activity for all our common activity needs. This will give the user a more consistent feel for the app across multiple screens and will make it easier for us to manage the code going forward.

Part 6: Broadcast Receivers

In this part, covered in Chapter 11, we'll equip Yamba with receivers so it can react to events around it in an intelligent way. For that purpose, we'll use broadcast receivers.

Boot and Network Receivers

In our example, we want to start our updates when the device is powered up. We also want to stop pulling the data from the cloud when the network is unavailable, and start it again only when we're back online. This goal will introduce us to one type of broadcast receiver.

Timeline Receiver

This type of receiver will exist only at certain times. Also, it won't receive messages from the Android system, but from other parts of our own Yamba application. This will demonstrate how we can use receivers to put together loosely coupled components in an elegant and flexible way.

Permissions

At this point in the development process you know how to ask for system permissions, such as access to the Internet or filesystem. In this section we'll learn how to define our own permissions and how to enforce them. After all, Yamba components might not want to respond to any other application for some Yamba-specific actions.

Part 7: Content Providers

In this part, covered in Chapter 12, we'll revisit content providers and refactor our database code to use them. To demonstrate that it all works, we'll throw in an Android App Widget.

Status Data

Our status data is OK the way it is if nobody else cares about it. But what if we want to expose some of this data to the rest of the system? After all, other applications might leverage our friends' timelines in new and creative ways. To do that, we'll create a content provider and expose our status data.

Android Widgets

But who will remember to pull up our app? To demonstrate the usefulness of our new status data, we'll put together an app widget. App widgets are those little components that the user can put on the home screen to see weather updates and such. We'll create a widget that will pull the latest status update from the Yamba database via the status data content provider and display it on the home screen.

Part 8: System Services

The Android OS comes with many useful system services, which include processes you can access easily to ask for things such as your location, sensor readings, WiFi hotspots, and much more. In this part, covered in Chapter 13, you will add some cool new features to Yamba, such as the user's current location.

Compass and Location

This example will illustrate how system services work in general, and you will walk away understanding some common patterns for using these services. We'll illustrate building a compass app using sensors, and later, we'll put this knowledge to use by letting Yamba display the user's location when posting status updates.

Intent Service, Alarms, and Notifications

It turns out that some of the cool features provided by Android services can make our Updater service much simpler. So we'll refactor our code yet again. This time, we'll introduce Intent Services that respond to intents. But we're going to need something to fire off these intents on a regular basis, and for that we'll use the Alarm service. We'll also add a feature to notify the user of new updates by putting a notification in the notification bar. For that, we'll use the Notification service. All this refactoring will create a substantially more elegant solution to our Updater service needs.

Summary

This chapter is intended as a road map for the next eight chapters. By the end of all these iterations, you will have built a medium-size Android app from scratch. Even more, you will understand various constructs and how to put them together into a meaningful whole. The hope is that you'll start developing a way of *thinking* in Android.

CHAPTER 6

Android User Interface

In this chapter, you will learn how to build a user interface in Android. You will create your first Activity, learn how to create an XML layout for it, and see how to connect it to Java. You will learn about Views (aka widgets) and Layouts, and learn how to handle Java events, such as button clicks. Additionally, you'll add support for a Twitter-like API into your project as an external *.jar* file so your app can make web service calls to the cloud.

By the end of this chapter, you will have written your own Twitter-like Android app. The app will feature a single screen that will prompt the user for her current status update and post that update online.

Two Ways to Create a User Interface

There are two ways to create a user interface (UI) in Android. One is declarative, and the other one is programmatic. They are quite different but often are used together to get the job done.

Declarative User Interface

The declarative approach involves using XML to declare what the UI will look like, similar to creating a web page using HTML. You write tags and specify elements to appear on your screen. If you have ever handcoded an HTML page, you did pretty much the same work as creating an Android screen.

One advantage of the declarative approach is that you can use what-you-see-is-what-you-get (WYSIWYG) tools. Some of these tools ship with the Eclipse Android Development Tools (ADT) extension, and others come from third parties. Additionally, XML is fairly human-readable, and even people who are unfamiliar with the Android platform and framework can readily determine the intent of the user interface.

The disadvantage of a declarative UI approach is that you can get only so far with XML. XML is great for declaring the look and feel of your user interface, but it doesn't provide a good way of handling user input. That's where the programmatic approach comes in.

Programmatic User Interface

A programmatic user interface involves writing Java code to develop UI. If you have ever done any Java AWT or Java Swing development, Android is pretty much the same in that respect. It is similar to many UI toolkits in other languages as well.

Basically, if you want to create a button programmatically, you have to declare the button variable, create an instance of it, add it to a container and set any button properties that may make sense, such as color, text, text size, background, and so on. You probably also want to declare what the button does once it's clicked, so that's another piece of code. All in all, you end up writing quite a few lines of Java.

Everything you can do declaratively, you can also do programmatically. But Java also allows you to specify what happens when that button is actually clicked. This is the main advantage of a programmatic approach to the user interface.

The Best of Both Worlds

So which approach to use? The best practice is to use both. You would use a declarative (XML) approach to declare everything about the user interface that is static, such as the layout of the screen, all the widgets, etc. You would then switch to a programmatic (Java) approach to define what goes on when the user interacts with the various widgets in the user interface. In other words, you'd use XML to declare what the "button" looks like and Java to specify what it does.

 Note that there are two approaches to developing the actual user interface, but at the end of the day, all the XML is actually "inflated" into Java memory space as if you actually wrote Java code. So, it's only Java code that runs.

Views and Layouts

Android organizes its UI elements into layouts and views. Everything you see, such as a button, label, or text box, is a view. Layouts organize views, such as grouping together a button and label or a group of these elements.

If you have prior experience with Java AWT or Swing, layouts are similar to Java containers and views are similar to Java components. Views in Android are sometimes referred to as widgets.

Don't confuse widgets in the Android UI with App Widgets. The latter are miniature application views that can be embedded in other applications (such as the Home screen application). Here, we are referring to widgets as the views in our activities.

So, a layout can contain other children. Those children can furthermore be layouts themselves, allowing for a complex user interface structure.

A layout is responsible for allocating space for each child. Different layouts use different approaches to laying out their child widgets, as shown in Figure 6-1.

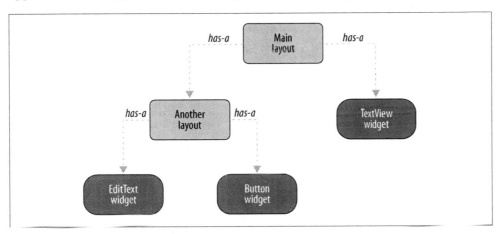

Figure 6-1. Layouts and Views relationship

There are several main layouts that we use more frequently than others, such as `LinearLayout`, `TableLayout`, `FrameLayout`, `RelativeLayout`, and `AbsoluteLayout`.

LinearLayout

LinearLayout is one of the simplest and most common layouts. It simply lays out its children next to each other, either horizontally or vertically. The order of the children matters. As LinearLayout asks its children how much space they need, it allocates the desired space to each child in the order they are added. So, if an "older" child comes along and asks for all the space on the screen, there won't be much left for the subsequent widgets in this layout.

One important property for LinearLayout is `layout_orientation`. Its valid options are `vertical` or `horizontal`.

Although Linear Layout is probably the simplest and most commonly used layout, it is not always the best choice. A good rule of thumb is that if you start to nest multiple Linear Layouts, you should probably use a different layout, such as Relative Layout. Too many nested layouts can have major consequences on the time needed to inflate the UI and on overall CPU and battery consumption.

TableLayout

TableLayout lays out its children in a table and consists of only other TableRow widgets. TableRow represents a row in a table and can contain other UI widgets. TableRow widgets are laid out next to each other horizontally, sort of like LinearLayout with a horizontal orientation.

For those familiar with HTML, Table Layout is similar to the `<table>` element, and Table Row is similar to the `<tr>` element. Whereas in HTML we also have `<td>` to represent each cell in the table, in Android the columns are determined dynamically based on the number of views we add to a table row.

An important property for TableLayout is `stretch_columns`, indicating which column of the table to stretch. You can also use * to stretch all columns.

FrameLayout

FrameLayout places its children on top of each other so that the latest child is covering the previous, like a deck of cards. This layout policy is useful for tabs, for example. FrameLayout is also used as a placeholder for other widgets that will be added programmatically at some later point in time.

RelativeLayout

RelativeLayout lays out its children relative to each other. As such, it is very powerful because it doesn't require you to nest unnecessary layouts to achieve a certain look. At the same time, using RelativeLayout can minimize the total number of widgets that need to be drawn, thus improving the overall performance of your application. Having said that, RelativeLayout requires each of its child views to have an ID set so that we can position it relative to other children.

AbsoluteLayout

AbsoluteLayout positions its children at absolute coordinates on the screen. It is the favorite layout for WYSIWYG tools, and although it is very simple, it is not very flexible. Your user interface would look good on one particular screen, but as soon as the screen size, orientation, or density changed, AbsoluteLayout would not be able to adjust.

Starting the Yamba Project

We are about to start our Yamba project. So, fire up Eclipse and click on File→New→Android Project.

You will get a dialog window asking you about your new Android project (see Figure 6-2). Let's explain again all the significant fields:

Project name
> The name under which Eclipse organizes our project. It is a good idea not to use any spaces in your project name. This makes it easier to access from the command line later. Enter "Yamba" here.

Contents
> Leave this as is—set to creating a new project—since that's what we intend to do.

Build Target
> This field indicates the type of Android system we intend to run this application on. This could be any Android platform, either standard or proprietary. I assume we're working with Android 2.3 (API level 9) and thus will choose the Android 2.3 option.

Application name
> Simply a plain-text name for your application. It can be any text. For our app, feel free to enter "Yamba".

Package name
> This field designates a Java package, and as such it needs to adhere to Java package naming conventions (*http://en.wikipedia.org/wiki/Java_package#Package_naming _conventions*). In a nutshell, you want to use the reverse of your domain name for your package. I'm going to use "com.marakana.yamba" here.

Create Activity
> An option to create an activity as part of this project. You can leave it checked. For the activity name, we must adhere to Java class naming conventions (*http://en .wikipedia.org/wiki/Naming_convention_(programming)#Java*). Doing that simply means using upper CamelCase (*http://en.wikipedia.org/wiki/CamelCase*). I'm going to enter "StatusActivity" here.

Min SDK Version
> Represents the minimum version of Android SDK that must be installed on the device for it to run this particular application. Typically, this number will correspond to the API level that you picked for your target, in our case, Android 9. However, if the app doesn't depend on the latest and greatest API or is capable of scaling gracefully to a lower API, you should rethink this number. In our case, the app will be able to work on API level 4 (Android 1.6), so enter 4 here. This is a good choice because we can distribute our app to way more people than if the minimum were Android 2.3.

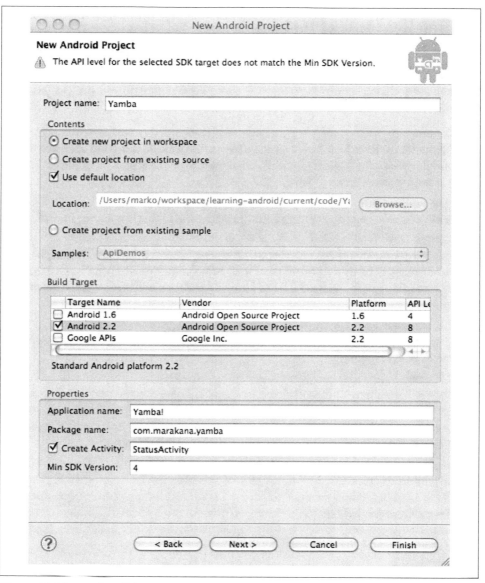

Figure 6-2. New project dialog

Click on Finish. Your Yamba project should now appear in Eclipse's Package Explorer.

The StatusActivity Layout

Let's start by designing the user interface for our screen where we'll enter the new status and click a button to update it.

By default, Eclipse created a file called *main.xml* under the *res/layout* folder. For consistency purposes, we should rename this file to *status.xml* to match our StatusActivity. To rename a file in Eclipse, right-click on it, choose Refactor→Rename…, and enter the new name. Eclipse is somewhat smart about renaming files and does more than just change the name. It also offers to look up all references to this file and update those as well. Although this feature works well when renaming a Java file, it is not fully automatic with XML files. So, renaming this file requires us to change the line in Java where we refer to it via the R class. To do that, in your StatusActivity's onCreate(), change setContentView(R.layout.main); to setContentView(R.layout.status);.

This screen will have four components:

- A title at the top of the screen. This will be a TextView widget.
- A big text area to type our 140-character status update. We'll use an EditText widget for this purpose.
- A button to click to update the status. This will be a Button widget.
- A layout to contain all these widgets and lay them out one after another in a vertical fashion. For this screen, we'll use LinearLayout, one of the more common ones.

Example 6-1 contains the source code for our StatusActivity layout.

Example 6-1. res/layout/status.xml

```
<?xml version="1.0" encoding="utf-8"?>

<!-- Main Layout of Status Activity -->
<LinearLayout xmlns:android="http://schemas.android.com/apk/res/android"
  android:orientation="vertical" android:layout_width="fill_parent"
  android:layout_height="fill_parent">

  <!-- Title TextView-->
  <TextView android:layout_width="fill_parent"
    android:layout_height="wrap_content" android:gravity="center"
    android:textSize="30sp"
    android:layout_margin="10dp" android:text="@string/titleStatus"/>

  <!-- Status EditText  -->
  <EditText android:layout_width="fill_parent"
    android:layout_height="fill_parent" android:layout_weight="1"
    android:hint="@string/hintText" android:id="@+id/editText"
    android:gravity="top|center_horizontal"></EditText>

  <!-- Update Button -->
  <Button android:layout_width="fill_parent"
    android:layout_height="wrap_content" android:text="@string/buttonUpdate"
    android:textSize="20sp" android:id="@+id/buttonUpdate"></Button>

</LinearLayout>
```

This code was generated by Eclipse Graphical Layout, shown in Figure 6-3. Android Development Tools (ADT) for the Eclipse plug-in provides this to help you work with

Android-specific XML files. Since ADT knows that you are working on a UI layout, it opens *status.xml* in Graphical Layout mode. You can also view the raw XML by choosing the status.xml tab at the bottom of this window. That will give you the XML source code for this screen, as displayed in this example.

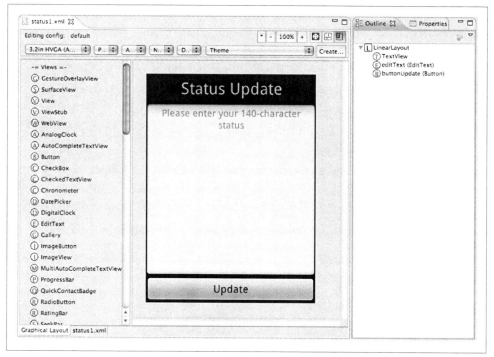

Figure 6-3. Graphical Layout mode for status.xml

Although we discussed the basic meanings of these XML resources in a previous chapter, there are some details in the code that you should know more about, which we'll examine in the following section.

Important Widget Properties

The properties you are most likely to use regularly are:

`layout_height` *and* `layout_width`

Defines how much space this widget is asking from its parent layout to display itself. Although you could enter a value in pixels, inches, or something similar, that is not a good practice. Since your application could run on many different devices with various screen sizes, you want to use relative size for your components, not absolute. So, best practice would be to use either `fill_parent` or `wrap_content` for the value. `fill_parent` means that your widget wants all the available space from its parent. `wrap_content` means that it requires only as much space as it needs to display its own content. Note that in API Level 8 and higher, `fill_parent` has been renamed to `match_parent`.

`layout_weight`

Layout weight is a number between 0 and 1. It implies the weight of our layout requirements. For example, if our `Status EditText` had a default layout weight of 0 and required a layout height of `fill_parent`, then the Update button would be pushed out of the screen because Status and its request for space came before the button. However, when we set the Status widget's layout weight to 1, we are saying we want all available space height-wise, but are yielding to any other widget that also may need space, such as the Update button.

`layout_gravity`

Specifies how this particular widget is positioned within its layout, both horizontally and vertically. Values could be `top`, `center`, `left`, and so on. Notice the difference between this property and `gravity`, explained next. For example, if you have a widget that has its width set to `fill_parent`, trying to center it wouldn't do much, because it's already taking all available space. However, if our `Title Text View` had its width set to `wrap_content`, centering it with `layout_gravity` would generate the desired results.

`gravity`

Specifies how the content of this widget is positioned within the widget itself. It is commonly confused with `layout_gravity`. Which one to use will depend on the size of your widget and the desired look. For example, if our `Title TextView` had the width `fill_parent`, then centering it with `gravity` would work, but centering it with `layout_gravity` wouldn't do anything.

`text`

Not all widgets have this property, but many do, such as `Button`, `EditText`, and `TextView`. It simply specifies the text for the widget. However, it is not a good practice to just enter the text, because then your layout will work in only one locale/language. Best practice is to define all text in a *strings.xml* resource and refer to a particular string using this notation: `@string/titleStatusUpdate`.

`id`

`id` is simply the unique identifier for this particular widget in a particular layout resource file. Not every widget needs an `id`, and I recommend removing unnecessary `ids` to minimize clutter. But widgets that we'll need to manipulate later from Java do need `ids`. `id` has the format `@+id/`*someName*, where *someName* is whatever you want to call your widget. My naming convention is to use the type followed by the name, for example, `@+id/buttonUpdateStatus`.

Strings Resource

Android tries hard to keep data in separate files. So, layouts are defined in their own resources, and all text values (such as button text, title text, etc.) should be defined in their own file called *strings.xml*. This later allows you to provide multiple versions of strings resources for various languages, such as English, Japanese, or Russian.

Example 6-2 shows what our *strings.xml* file looks like at this point.

Example 6-2. res/values/strings.xml

```xml
<?xml version="1.0" encoding="utf-8"?>
<resources>
  <string name="app_name">Yamba 1</string>

  <string name="titleYamba">Yamba</string>
  <string name="titleStatus">Status Update</string>

  <string name="hintText">Please enter your 140-character status</string>
  <string name="buttonUpdate">Update</string>
</resources>
```

The file simply contains sets of name/value pairs.

 I use a certain naming convention for my resource names. Let's look at titleYamba, for example. First, I prefix the resource with the name of what it is, in this case a title of the activity. Second, I give it a name, Yamba. This naming convention helps keep many different resources sorted in an easy-to-find way. Finally, I use CamelCase (*http://en.wiki pedia.org/wiki/CamelCase*) for my names, though some may prefer to use underscores to separate words.

The StatusActivity Java Class

Now that we have our UI designed in XML, we are ready to switch over to Java. Remember from earlier in this chapter that Android provides two ways for building user interfaces. One is by declaring it in XML, which is what we just did, and we got as far as we could (for now). The other one is to build it programmatically in Java. We also said earlier that the best practice is to get as far as possible in XML and then switch over to Java.

Our Java class for this is StatusActivity.java, and the Eclipse New Project dialog has already created the stub for this class. The class is part of the com.marakana.yamba1 Java package, and as such is part of that directory.

Creating Your Application-Specific Object and Initialization Code

As with all main building blocks in Android, such as activities, services, broadcast receivers, and content providers, you usually start by subclassing a base class provided by the Android framework and overriding certain inherited methods. In this case, we subclass Android's Activity class and override its onCreate() method. As you recall, activities have a certain life cycle (see "Activity Life Cycle" on page 28), or state machine through which they go. We as developers do not control what state the activity is in, but we do get to say what happens during a transition to a particular state. In this case, the transition we want to override is the `onCreate()` method that the system's `ActivityManager` invokes when the activity is first created (i.e., when it goes from a starting to a running state). This sort of programming, when we subclass a system class and fill in the blanks, is also known as the Template pattern (*http://en.wikipedia.org/wiki/Template_method_pattern*).

In addition to doing some standard housekeeping, our `onCreate()` will carry out two major tasks that the application needs done just once, at the beginning: set up our button so it responds to clicks and connect to the cloud.

Notice that `onCreate()` takes a `Bundle` as a parameter. This is a small amount of data that can be passed into the activity via the intent that started it. The data provided in a `Bundle` is typically limited to basic data types; more complex ones need to be specially encoded. For the most part, we're not going to be using `Bundle` in our Yamba example, as there's no real need for it.

Keep in mind that whenever you override a method, you first want to make a call to the original method provided by the parent. That's why we have a `super.onCreate()` call here.

So, once you subclass the framework's class, override the appropriate method, and call `super`'s method in it, you are still back where you started: your code does the same thing the original class did. But now we have a placeholder where we can add our own code.

The very first thing we typically do in an activity's `onCreate()` is to load the UI from the XML file and *inflate* it into the Java memory space. In other words, we write some Java code that opens up our XML layout file, parses it, and for each element in XML, creates a corresponding Java object in our memory space. For each attribute of a particular XML element, this code will set that attribute on our Java object. This process is called *inflating from XML,* and the line of code that does all this is `setContentView(R.lay out.status);`.

Remember that the `R` class is the automatically generated set of pointers that helps connect the world of Java to our world of XML and other resources in the */res* folder. Similarly, `R.layout.status` points to our */res/layout/status.xml* file.

This `setContentView()` method does a lot of work, in other words. It reads the XML file, parses it, creates all the appropriate Java objects to correspond to XML elements, sets object properties to correspond to XML attributes, sets up parent/child relationships between objects, and overall inflates the entire view. At the end of this one line, our screen is ready for drawing.

Your objects are not the only ones that define methods and respond to external stimuli. Android's user interface objects do that too. Thus, you can tell your `Button` to execute certain code when its clicked. To do that, you need to define a method named onClick() and put the code there that you want executed. You also have to run the setOnClickListener method on the Button. You pass this as an argument to setOnClick Listener because your object is where you define onClick(). Example 6-3 shows our first version of *StatusActivity.java*, with some additional explanation following the code.

Example 6-3. StatusActivity.java, version 1

```java
package com.marakana.yamba1;

import winterwell.jtwitter.Twitter;
import android.app.Activity;
import android.os.Bundle;
import android.util.Log;
import android.view.View;
import android.view.View.OnClickListener;
import android.widget.Button;
import android.widget.EditText;

public class StatusActivity1 extends Activity implements OnClickListener { // ❶
  private static final String TAG = "StatusActivity";
  EditText editText;
  Button updateButton;
  Twitter twitter;

  /** Called when the activity is first created. */
  @Override
  public void onCreate(Bundle savedInstanceState) {
    super.onCreate(savedInstanceState);
    setContentView(R.layout.status);

    // Find views
    editText = (EditText) findViewById(R.id.editText); // ❷
    updateButton = (Button) findViewById(R.id.buttonUpdate);

    updateButton.setOnClickListener(this); // ❸

    twitter = new Twitter("student", "password"); // ❹
    twitter.setAPIRootUrl("http://yamba.marakana.com/api");
  }

  // Called when button is clicked // ❺
  public void onClick(View v) {
    twitter.setStatus(editText.getText().toString()); // ❻
    Log.d(TAG, "onClicked");
  }
}
```

❶ To make StatusActivity capable of being a button listener, it needs to implement the OnClickListener interface.

❷ Find views inflated from the XML layout and assign them to Java variables.

❸ Register the button to notify this (i.e., StatusActivity) when it gets clicked.

❹ Connect to the online service that supports the Twitter API. At this point, we hard-code the username and password.

❺ The method that is called when button is clicked, as part of the OnClickListener interface.

❻ Make the web service API call to the cloud to update our status.

Compiling Code and Building Your Projects: Saving Files

Once you make changes to your Java or XML files, make sure you save them before moving on. Eclipse builds your project automatically (*http://en.wiktionary.org/wiki/au tomagical*) every time you choose File→Save or press Ctrl-S. So, it is important to save files and make sure you do not move to another file until the current file is fine. You will know your file is fine when there are no little red *x* symbols in your code and the project builds successfully. Because Java depends on XML and vice versa, moving to another file while the current one is broken just makes it even more difficult to find errors.

Java errors typically are easy to find since the little red *x* in the code navigates you straight down to the line number where the error occurred (see Figure 6-4). By putting your mouse right on that error, Eclipse will tell you what the error is and will also offer you some possible fixes. This Eclipse feature is very useful and is analogous to the spellchecker in a word processor.

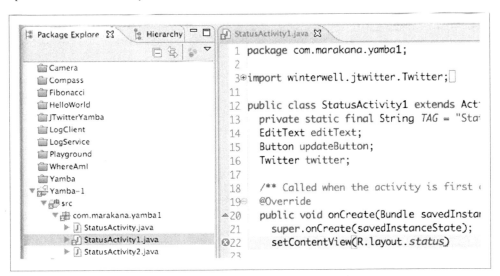

Figure 6-4. Tracing Java errors

Adding the jtwitter.jar Library

We are connecting to the online service that implements the Twitter-compatible API (*http://status.net/wiki/Twitter-compatible_API*) in our application. This connection is done via a series of web service calls (*http://en.wiktionary.org/wiki/web_service*). Since Android uses standard Java networking capabilities, Android doesn't offer much more with respect to web services than we already have in Java. So, as such, there's little value in reinventing the wheel.

To make our life with web services and the Twitter API easier, we're going to use a third-party library, *jtwitter.jar* (*http://www.winterwell.com/software/jtwitter.php*), provided by Winterwell Associates. This library contains a simple Java class that interacts with the online service and abstracts all the intricacies of making network calls and passing the data back and forth. If no one had been kind enough to provide a high-level library for what we need to do, we could always use standard Java networking libraries to get the job done. It just would have been more work.

 The *jtwitter.jar* library provided with this code has been slightly modified from the official Winterwell version to make it work in our Yamba project.

Once you download this library, you can put it inside your project in Eclipse. Simply drag the *jtwitter.jar* file and drop it in the root of your Eclipse project in the Package Manager window. This makes the file part of the project, but our Java code is still unable to locate it.

Java searches for all the classes in its classpath (*http://en.wikipedia.org/wiki/Classpath_(Java)*). To add *jtwitter.jar* to the classpath, right-click on your project, select Properties, and you will get a Properties for Yamba dialog window (see Figure 6-5). Select Java Build Path, and choose the Libraries tab. In there, click on Add JARs... and locate your *jtwitter.jar* file.

Updating the Manifest File for Internet Permission

Before this application can work, we must ask the user to grant us the right to use the Internet. Android manages security by specifying the permissions needed for certain dangerous operations. The user then must explicitly grant those permissions to each application when he first installs the application. The user must grant all or no permissions that the application asks for; there's no middle ground. Also, the user is not prompted about permissions when upgrading an existing app.

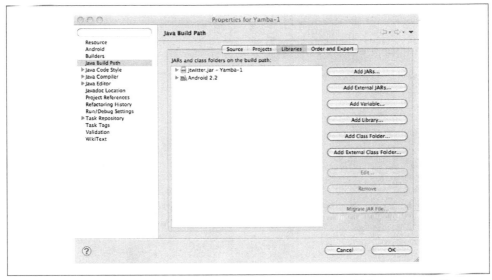

Figure 6-5. Properties for Yamba dialog window in Eclipse, where we add the jtwitter.jar file

 Because we are running this application in debug mode and installing it via a USB cable, Android doesn't prompt us for permissions like it would the end user. However, we still must specify that the application requires certain permissions.

In this case, we want to ask the user to grant this application the INTERNET permission. We need Internet access to connect to the online service. So, open up the *AndroidManifest.xml*

file by double-clicking on it. Note that Eclipse typically opens this file in a WYSIWYG editor with many tabs on the bottom. As always, you can make most of the changes to this file via this interface, but since Eclipse tools are limited and sometimes buggy, we prefer to go straight into the XML view of this file. So, choose the right-most tab at the bottom that says *AnddroidManifest.xml*, and add a `<uses-permission android:name="android.permission.INTERNET" />` element within the `<manifest>` block (see Example 6-4).

Example 6-4. AndroidManifest.xml

```
<?xml version="1.0" encoding="utf-8"?>
<manifest xmlns:android="http://schemas.android.com/apk/res/android"
  android:versionCode="1" android:versionName="1.0" package="com.marakana.yamba1">
  <application android:icon="@drawable/icon" android:label="@string/app_name">

    <activity android:name=".StatusActivity" android:label="@string/titleStatus">
      <intent-filter>
        <action android:name="android.intent.action.MAIN" />
        <category android:name="android.intent.category.LAUNCHER" />
      </intent-filter>
```

```
    </activity>

  </application>
  <uses-sdk android:minSdkVersion="4" />

  <uses-permission android:name="android.permission.INTERNET" /> <!-- ❶ -->
</manifest>
```

❶ Defines the <uses-permission> element for the INTERNET permission.

Logging in Android

Android offers a system-wide logging capability. You can log from anywhere in your code by calling Log.d(TAG, message), where *TAG* and *message* are some strings. TAG should be a tag that is meaningful to you given your code. Typically, a tag would be the name of your app, your class, or some module. Good practice is to define TAG as a Java constant for your entire class, such as:

```
    private static final String TAG = "StatusActivity";
```

 Before your code will compile, you need to import the Log class. Eclipse has a useful feature under Source→Organize Imports, or Ctrl+O for short. Usually, this feature will automatically organize your import statements. However, in the case of Log, often there is a conflict because there are multiple classes named *Log*. This is where you have to use your common sense and figure it out. In this case, the ambiguity is between the Android Log and Apache Log classes, so choice should be easy.

Note that Log takes different severity levels. .d() is for debug level, but you can also specify .e() for error, .w() for warning, or .i() for info. There's also a .wtf() severity level for errors that should never happen. (It stands for What a Terrible Failure, in case you were wondering.) Eclipse color-codes log messages based on their severity level.

 Eclipse's Organize Imports tool can sometimes lead to hard-to-find problems. For example, if your project doesn't have R.java generated (which might happen because there's an earlier problem with one of the XML resources), then Organize Imports will import the android.R class. This other R class is part of the Android framework and has the same name as your local R class, making it hard to notice. So, if you have many compilation errors around your references to R resources, check that android.R is not imported.

LogCat

The Android system log is outputted to LogCat, a standardized system-wide logging mechanism. LogCat is readily available to all Java and C/C++ code. The developer can easily view the logs and filter their output based on severity, such as debug, info, warning, or error, or based on custom-defined tags. As with most things in Android development, there are two ways to view the LogCat: via Eclipse or via the command line.

LogCat from the Eclipse DDMS perspective

To view LogCat in Eclipse, you need to open the LogCat View (see Figure 6-6). You can switch to the DDMS perspective by clicking on the DDMS button in the top-right corner of Eclipse:

or by selecting Window→Open Perspective ›DDMS in the Eclipse menu.

DDMS (*http://developer.android.com/guide/developing/tools/ddms.html*) stands for Dalvik Debug Monitor Server. DDMS is the connection between your application running on the device and your development environment, such as Eclipse.

Figure 6-6. LogCat in Eclipse

You can define filters for LogCat as well. Click on the little green plus button, and the LogCat Filter dialog will come up (see Figure 6-7). You can define a filter based on a tag, severity level, or process ID. This will create another window within LogCat that shows you only the log entries that match your filter.

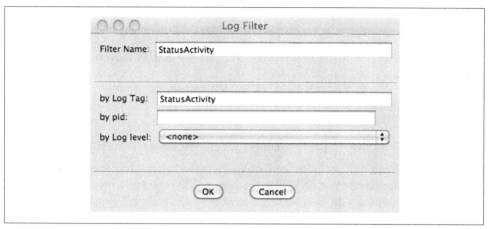

Figure 6-7. LogCat Filter

 DDMS might not show up in the top-right corner if you haven't used it before. If that's the case, go to Window→Open Perspective and choose DDMS there. From there on, it should show up in your window tab as well.

LogCat from the command line

Just like all the tools, anything you can do in Eclipse also can be done from the command line. To view LogCat, open up your terminal window and type:

```
[user:~]> adb logcat
```

This will give you the tail of the current LogCat and will be updated as your device keeps generating log entries. You can also filter log entries on the command line, but the syntax is not the most intuitive. To only see StatusActivity-tagged entries, you specify StatusActivity:*, meaning you want all severity levels for this tag. However, you also have to specify what you don't want to see. To do that, you add *:S, meaning silence all other tags. The following command line illustrates that:

```
[user:~]> adb logcat StatusActivity:* *:S
```

 I find it useful to keep a command-line window open with adb logcat running in it at all times. This makes it easy for me to quickly see what's going on with my app and is certainly much faster than switching to the DDMS perspective in Eclipse.

Threading in Android

A thread is a sequence of instructions executed in order. Although each CPU can process only one instruction at a time, most operating systems are capable of handling multiple threads on multiple CPUs, or interleaving them on a single CPU. Different threads need different priorities, so the operating system determines how much time to give each one if they have to share a CPU.

The Android operating system is based on Linux and as such is fully capable of running multiple threads at the same time. However, you need to be aware of how applications use threads in order to design your application properly.

Single Thread

By default, an Android application runs on a single thread. Single-threaded applications run all commands serially, meaning the next command is not completed until the previous one is done. Another way of saying this is that each call is *blocking*.

This single thread is also known as the UI thread because it's the thread that processes all the user interface commands as well. The UI thread is responsible for drawing all the elements on the screen as well as processing all the user events, such as touches on the screen, clicks of the button, and so on. Figure 6-8 shows the execution of our code on a single UI thread.

Figure 6-8. Single-threaded execution

The problem with running `StatusActivity` on the single thread is our network call to update the status. As with all network calls, the time it takes to execute is outside of our control. Our call to `twitter.updateStatus()` is subject to all the network availability and latency issues. We don't know whether the user is on a super-fast WiFi connection or is using a much slower protocol to connect to the cloud. In other words, our application cannot respond until the network call is completed.

 The Android system will offer to kill any application that is not responding within a certain time period, typically around five seconds for activities. This is known as the Application Not Responding dialog, or ANR for short (see Figure 6-9).

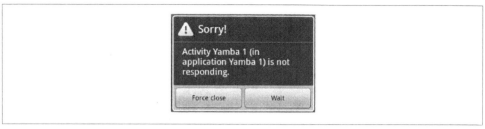

Figure 6-9. Application Not Responding dialog

Multithreaded Execution

A much better solution is to have the potentially long operations run on a separate thread. When multiple tasks run on multiple threads at the same time, the operating system slices the available CPU so that no one task dominates the execution. As a result, it appears that multiple tasks are running in parallel at the same time.

In our example, we could put the actual network call for updating our status in the cloud in a separate thread. That way our main UI thread will not block while we're waiting for the network, and the application will appear much more responsive. We tend to talk of the main thread as running in the foreground and the additional threads as running in the background. They're really all equal in status, alternating their execution on the device's CPU, but from the point of view of the user, the main thread is in the foreground because it deals with the UI. Figure 6-10 shows the execution of our code's two threads—the main UI thread, as well as the auxiliary thread we use to perform potentially long-running network calls.

Figure 6-10. Multithreaded execution

There are multiple ways of accomplishing multithreading. Java has a Thread class that allows for many of these operations. We could certainly use any of the regular Java features to put the network call in the background.

However, using the standard Java Thread class is problematic because another thread is not allowed to update the elements in the main UI thread. This makes sense because to update the UI thread, we would need to synchronize with the current state of its objects, and that would be a job on its own.

In addition to standard Java threading support, Android provides the utility class AsyncTask specifically designed for this purpose.

AsyncTask

AsyncTask is an Android mechanism created to help handle long operations that need to report to the UI thread. To take advantage of this class, we need to create a new subclass of `AsyncTask` and implement the `doInBackground()`, `onProgressUpdate()`, and `onPostExecute()` methods. In other words, we are going to fill in the blanks for what to do in the background, what to do when there's some progress, and what to do when the task completes.

We'll extend our earlier example with an asynchronous posting to the cloud. The first part of Example 6-5 is very similar to the code in Example 6-3, but hands off the posting to the asynchronous thread. A new `AsyncTask` does the posting in the background.

Example 6-5. StatusActivity.java, version 2

```
package com.marakana.yamba1;

import winterwell.jtwitter.Twitter;
import winterwell.jtwitter.TwitterException;
import android.app.Activity;
import android.os.AsyncTask;
import android.os.Bundle;
import android.util.Log;
import android.view.View;
import android.view.View.OnClickListener;
import android.widget.Button;
import android.widget.EditText;
import android.widget.Toast;

public class StatusActivity2 extends Activity implements OnClickListener {
  private static final String TAG = "StatusActivity";
  EditText editText;
  Button updateButton;
  Twitter twitter;

  /** Called when the activity is first created. */
  @Override
  public void onCreate(Bundle savedInstanceState) {
    super.onCreate(savedInstanceState);
    setContentView(R.layout.status);

    // Find views
    editText = (EditText) findViewById(R.id.editText);
    updateButton = (Button) findViewById(R.id.buttonUpdate);
    updateButton.setOnClickListener(this);

    twitter = new Twitter("student", "password");
    twitter.setAPIRootUrl("http://yamba.marakana.com/api");
  }

  // Asynchronously posts to twitter
  class PostToTwitter extends AsyncTask<String, Integer, String> { // ❶
    // Called to initiate the background activity
```

```
@Override
protected String doInBackground(String... statuses) { // ❷
  try {
    Twitter.Status status = twitter.updateStatus(statuses[0]);
    return status.text;
  } catch (TwitterException e) {
    Log.e(TAG, e.toString());
    e.printStackTrace();
    return "Failed to post";
  }
}

// Called when there's a status to be updated
@Override
protected void onProgressUpdate(Integer... values) { // ❸
  super.onProgressUpdate(values);
  // Not used in this case
}

// Called once the background activity has completed
@Override
protected void onPostExecute(String result) { // ❹
  Toast.makeText(StatusActivity2.this, result, Toast.LENGTH_LONG).show();
}
}

// Called when button is clicked
public void onClick(View v) {
  String status = editText.getText().toString();
  new PostToTwitter().execute(status); // ❺
  Log.d(TAG, "onClicked");
}

}
```

❶ The PostToTwitter class in this case is an inner class of StatusActivity. It also sub-classes AsyncTask. Notice the use of Java generics (*http://en.wikipedia.org/wiki/Generics_in_Java*) to describe the data types that this AsyncTask will use in its methods. I'll explain these three types next. The first data type is used by doInBackground, the second by onProgressUpdate, and the third by onPostExecute.

❷ doInBackground() is the callback that specifies the actual work to be done on the separate thread, as if it's executing in the background. The argument String... is the first of the three data types that we defined in the list of generics for this inner class. The three dots indicate that this is an array of Strings, and you have to declare it that way, even though you want to pass only a single status.

❸ onProgressUpdate() is called whenever there's progress in the task execution. The progress should be reported from the doInBackground() call. In this case, we do not have any meaningful progress to report. If this example were instead a file download, for instance, this could report the percentage of completion or amount of data downloaded thus far. The actual data type—in this case, Integer—refers to the second argument in the generics definition of this class.

❹ onPostExecute() is called when our task completes. This is our callback method to update the user interface and tell the user that the task is done. In this particular case, we are using a Toast feature of the Android UI to display a quick message on the screen. Notice that Toast uses the makeText() static method to make the actual message. Also, do not forget to include show(); otherwise, your message will never be displayed, and there won't be any errors—a hard bug to find. The argument that this method gets is the value that doInBackground() returns, in this case a String. This also corresponds to the third generics datatype in the class definition.

❺ Once we have our AsyncTask set up, we can use it. To use it, we simply instantiate it and call execute() on it. The argument that we pass in is what goes into the doInBackground() call. Note that in this case we are passing a single string that is being converted into a string array in the actual method later on, which is an example of Java's variable number of arguments feature (*http://en.wikipedia.org/wiki/Variadic _function*).

At this point, when the user clicks on the Update Status button, our activity will create a separate thread using AsyncTask and place the actual network operation on that thread. When done, the AsyncTask will update the main UI thread by popping up a Toast message to tell the user that the operation either succeeded or failed. This approach makes our application much more responsive, and users should never get the "Application Not Responding: Force Close or Wait" message shown in Figure 6-9. At this point, our application looks like Figure 6-11 when running.

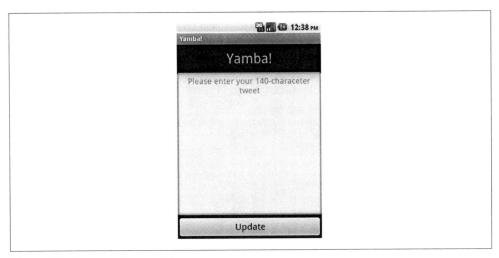

Figure 6-11. StatusActivity, part 1

Other UI Events

So far, you have seen how to handle the click events by implementing `OnClick Listener` and providing the `onClick()` method, which is invoked when the button is clicked. Imagine that we want to provide a little counter telling the user how many characters of input are still available out of the maximum of 140. To do that, we need another type of listener.

Android provides many different listeners for various events, such as touch, click, and so on. In this case, we're going to use `TextWatcher` to watch for text changes in the edit text field. Steps for this listener are similar to the steps for `OnClickListener` and many other listeners.

From the user's standpoint, we'll add another `TextView` to our layout to indicate how many characters are still available. This text will change color, from green to yellow to red, as the user approaches the 140-character limit.

In Java, we'll implement `TextWatcher` and attach it to the field where the user is typing the actual text. The `TextWatcher` methods will be invoked as the user changes the text, and based on the amount of text entered, we'll update the counter. See Example 6-6.

Example 6-6. res/layout/status2.xml

```xml
<?xml version="1.0" encoding="utf-8"?>
<!-- Main Layout of Status Activity -->
<LinearLayout xmlns:android="http://schemas.android.com/apk/res/android"
  android:orientation="vertical" android:layout_width="fill_parent"
  android:layout_height="fill_parent">

  <!-- Title TextView-->
  <TextView android:layout_width="fill_parent"
    android:layout_height="wrap_content" android:gravity="center"
    android:text="@string/titleStatus" android:textSize="30sp"
    android:layout_margin="10dp" />

  <!-- Text Counter TextView ❶ -->
  <TextView android:layout_width="wrap_content"
    android:layout_height="wrap_content" android:layout_gravity="right"
    android:id="@+id/textCount" android:text="000"
    android:layout_marginRight="10dp" />

  <!-- Status EditText  -->
  <EditText android:layout_width="fill_parent"
    android:layout_height="fill_parent" android:layout_weight="1"
    android:hint="@string/hintText" android:id="@+id/editText"
    android:gravity="top|center_horizontal"></EditText>

  <!-- Update Button -->
  <Button android:layout_width="fill_parent"
    android:layout_height="wrap_content" android:text="@string/buttonUpdate"
    android:textSize="20sp" android:id="@+id/buttonUpdate"></Button>
```

```
</LinearLayout>
```

❶ New `TextView` that represents how many characters are still available for the user to type. We start at 140 and then go down as the user enters text.

The version of `StatusActivity` shown in Example 6-7 implements the `TextWatcher` interface, and the new methods in this example appear at the end of the class. Initially the text of the counter is in green to indicate we can keep on typing. As we approach the maximum, the text turns yellow and eventually changes to red to indicate we are beyond the maximum message size.

Example 6-7. StatusActivity.java, final version

```java
package com.marakana.yamba1;

import winterwell.jtwitter.Twitter;
import winterwell.jtwitter.TwitterException;
import android.app.Activity;
import android.graphics.Color;
import android.os.AsyncTask;
import android.os.Bundle;
import android.text.Editable;
import android.text.TextWatcher;
import android.util.Log;
import android.view.View;
import android.view.View.OnClickListener;
import android.widget.Button;
import android.widget.EditText;
import android.widget.TextView;
import android.widget.Toast;

public class StatusActivity extends Activity implements OnClickListener,
    TextWatcher { // ❶
  private static final String TAG = "StatusActivity";
  EditText editText;
  Button updateButton;
  Twitter twitter;
  TextView textCount; // ❷

  /** Called when the activity is first created. */
  @Override
  public void onCreate(Bundle savedInstanceState) {
    super.onCreate(savedInstanceState);
    setContentView(R.layout.status);

    // Find views
    editText = (EditText) findViewById(R.id.editText);
    updateButton = (Button) findViewById(R.id.buttonUpdate);
    updateButton.setOnClickListener(this);

    textCount = (TextView) findViewById(R.id.textCount); // ❸
    textCount.setText(Integer.toString(140)); // ❹
    textCount.setTextColor(Color.GREEN); // ❺
```

```
    editText.addTextChangedListener(this); // ❻

    twitter = new Twitter("student", "password");
    twitter.setAPIRootUrl("http://yamba.marakana.com/api");
}

// Called when button is clicked
public void onClick(View v) {
  String status = editText.getText().toString();
  new PostToTwitter().execute(status);
  Log.d(TAG, "onClicked");
}

// Asynchronously posts to twitter
class PostToTwitter extends AsyncTask<String, Integer, String> {
  // Called to initiate the background activity
  @Override
  protected String doInBackground(String... statuses) {
    try {
      Twitter.Status status = twitter.updateStatus(statuses[0]);
      return status.text;
    } catch (TwitterException e) {
      Log.e(TAG, e.toString());
      e.printStackTrace();
      return "Failed to post";
    }
  }

  // Called when there's a status to be updated
  @Override
  protected void onProgressUpdate(Integer... values) {
    super.onProgressUpdate(values);
    // Not used in this case
  }

  // Called once the background activity has completed
  @Override
  protected void onPostExecute(String result) {
    Toast.makeText(StatusActivity.this, result, Toast.LENGTH_LONG).show();
  }
}

// TextWatcher methods
public void afterTextChanged(Editable statusText) { // ❼
  int count = 140 - statusText.length(); // ❽
  textCount.setText(Integer.toString(count));
  textCount.setTextColor(Color.GREEN); // ❾
  if (count < 10)
    textCount.setTextColor(Color.YELLOW);
  if (count < 0)
    textCount.setTextColor(Color.RED);
}

public void beforeTextChanged(CharSequence s, int start, int count, int after) { // ❿
}
```

```
    public void onTextChanged(CharSequence s, int start, int before, int count) { // ⓫
    }
}
```

❶ We declare that `StatusActivity` now implements `TextWatcher`. This means we need to actually provide the implementation for this interface, which we do later on in this class.

❷ `textCount` is our text view, defined in Example 6-6.

❸ First, we need to find the `textCount` in the inflated layout.

❹ We set the initial text to `140` because that's the maximum length of a status message in our app. Note that `TextView` takes text as value, so we convert a number to text here.

❺ The `textCount` field will change color dynamically based on the number of remaining characters. In this case, we start with green. Notice that the `Color` class is part of the Android framework and not Java. In other words, we're using `android.graph ics.Color` and not `java.awt.Color`. `Color.GREEN` is one of the few colors defined as a constant in this class (more on colors in the next section).

❻ Here we attach `TextWatcher` to our `editText` field. In other words, `editText` will call the `TextWatcher` instance, in this case `this`, which refers to this object itself.

❼ `afterTextChanged()` is one of the methods provided by the `TextWatcher` interface. This method is called whenever the text changes in the view that this `TextWatcher` is watching. In our case, whenever the user changes the underlying text in `editText`, this method is invoked with the current text.

❽ Here we do some math to figure out how many characters are left, given the 140-character limit.

❾ Next, based on the availability of the text, we update the color of the counter. So, if more than 10 characters are available, we are still in the green. Fewer than 10 means we are approaching the limit, thus the counter turns yellow. If we are past the limit of 140 characters, the counter turns red.

❿ This method is called just before the actual text replacement is completed. In this case, we don't need this method, but as part of implementing the `TextWatcher` interface, we must provide its implementation, event though it's empty.

⓫ Similarly, we are not using `onTextChanged()` in this case, but must provide its blank implementation. Figure 6-12 shows what the TextWatcher looks like in our application when running.

Figure 6-12. StatusActivity, part 1

Adding Color and Graphics

Our application works well, but it's a bit dull looking. A little bit of color and some graphics could go a long way. Android offers a lot of support to make your application snazzy. We're going to see some basics here.

Adding Images

For starters, we want to add a background to our screen. This background is going to be some kind of graphics file. In Android, most images go to a resource folder called *drawable*. You may notice that you already have three folders with this name:

- */res/drawable-hdpi* for devices with high-density screens
- */res/drawable-mdpi* for devices with medium-density screens
- */res/drawable-ldpi* for devices with low-density screens

We are going to create another *drawable* folder called simply */res/drawable*. To do that, right-click on the *res* folder and choose New→Folder. For the name, enter *drawable*. You can now put your graphics that are independent of screen density in this folder. We're going to assume you found some cool background graphics and that you saved the file in this new folder under the name *background.png*. Although Android supports many different file formats, PNG (*http://en.wikipedia.org/wiki/Portable_Network _Graphics*) is preferred to the GIF standard because PNG is lossless and doesn't require any patent licenses.

Although PNG officially stands for Portable Network Graphics, it is also commonly known as PNG's Not Gif, to reflect its departure from the controversial GIF standard.

Remember that all resources are being "watched" by Eclipse, and the moment we put something in there, Eclipse will use its Android SDK tools to update the R class automatically. So at this point, we'll have a reference to `R.drawable.background` and could use this resource from Java. But we won't.

We are going to update the status activity layout file *res/layout/status.xml* next. Our goal is to make this background file the background graphic for the entire screen. To do that, we'll update the top layout in our file and set its background to point to this new background PNG file, which means we have to open the *status.xml* layout. Now we have two ways of adding the background to the top layout.

Using the WYSIWYG editor in Eclipse

One way is to use Eclipse's WYSIWYG tool, as shown in Figure 6-13. In this tool, we need to first select the main layout, which might be difficult since many other components are in front of it. The red border indicates which view or layout is selected.

Another way of making your selection is to open up your Outline view in Eclipse and select the top element there. This view might not be currently visible in your Eclipse, depending on how you arranged the many available windows. One sure way to get the Outline view is to go to Window→Show View→Outline and open it up that way. Once you open this view, you can select the top layout, in this case our LinearLayout. You will know it's selected if a red border is around your entire activity.

Next, you want to open up the Properties view in Eclipse. Again, this view might already be opened, but if it's not visible as a window in Eclipse, go to Window→Show View→Other, and under the General section, pick Properties. This will open up a view in which you can change various properties for this particular view.

The property we want to modify is *background*. You can now click on the little ... button, which will bring up the Reference Chooser dialog (see Figure 6-14). In this dialog, choose Drawable→Background.

This will set the background of your top layout to `@drawable/background`. As you recall, this is the way that one XML resource refers to another resource. In this case, our *status.xml* layout is referring to the *background.png* drawable. Notice that we do not use extensions when referring to other file resources. Android figures out the best file format automatically, in case there are files with the same name but different extensions.

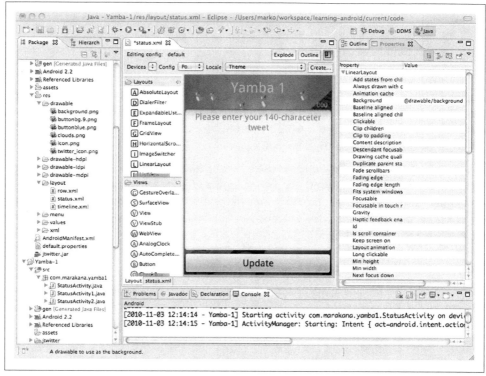

Figure 6-13. Eclipse Graphical Layout Editor

Updating directly in XML code

Another approach is to go straight into the XML code and make changes there. Remember that everything you can do with Eclipse tools, you can also do in a plain-text editor. To switch to the XML code view, select the status.xml tab at the bottom of the window, next to the Layout tab. This will open up the file with your standard XML editor.

In this case, to add the background resource to our entire activity, we simply add `android:background="@drawable/background"` to our `<LinearLayout>` element.

From now on, we're going to be making changes directly in the XML code because it's much simpler to explain. Also, the WYSIWYG editor can do only so much, and often you run into its limitations.

Adding Color

We now have the background for the entire screen, but what about the actual text box that users type the text into? The current design is stock. We could improve on it by adding some color and transparency.

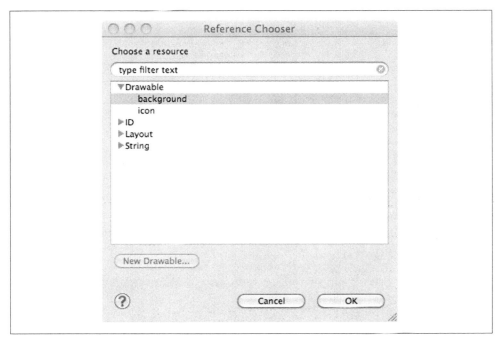

Figure 6-14. Reference Chooser

Android uses the standard RGB (*http://en.wikipedia.org/wiki/Rgb*) color set, but it also optionally expands it with an Alpha channel (*http://en.wikipedia.org/wiki/alpha_chan nel*). So, you can express color as RGB or ARGB, where A is the amount of transparency, R is the amount of red, G is for green, and B stands for blue. The combination of these three colors and optional transparency gives you every conceivable color from white to black, and from opaque to fully transparent! That's the whole point of ARGB. Of course, the granularity isn't exactly what Monet would be happy with; each value has only 256 possibilities.

Amounts of each channel can be represented either as values between 0 and 255 or by using the hexadecimal system (*http://en.wikipedia.org/wiki/Hexadecimal*) values between 0 and FF. So, the actual values could be AARRGGBB, where each letter can be replaced with a value between 0 and F. There's also a shorter version of ARGB, where each value is repeated. For example, #3A9F is the same as #33AA99FF and corresponds to #33 for alpha, #AA for red, #99 for green, and #FF for blue. Notice that we use the # symbol in front of hexadecimal values to distinguish them from decimal values.

So, we could update the background of our `EditText` element to be `#cfff`, which is a somewhat transparent white color.

Next, we can update the color of the title text by changing the `textColor` property for that `TextView`. A good color would be white, for example. One way to specify white is

#fff, but alternatively we could enter @android:color/white. The android: part of that statement refers to the Android operating system's set of resources, in this case a predefined color white. Example 6-8 shows these new additions to our *status.xml* code.

Example 6-8. res/layout/status.xml

```xml
<?xml version="1.0" encoding="utf-8"?>

<!-- Main Layout of Status Activity -->
<LinearLayout xmlns:android="http://schemas.android.com/apk/res/android"
  android:orientation="vertical" android:layout_width="fill_parent"
  android:layout_height="fill_parent" android:background="@drawable/background"><!--❶-->

  <!-- Title TextView-->
  <TextView android:layout_width="fill_parent"
    android:layout_height="wrap_content" android:gravity="center"
    android:text="@string/titleStatus" android:textSize="30sp"
    android:layout_margin="10dp" android:textColor="@android:color/white" /><!--❷-->

  <!-- Text Counter TextView -->
  <TextView android:layout_width="wrap_content"
    android:layout_height="wrap_content" android:layout_gravity="right"
    android:id="@+id/textCount" android:text="000"
    android:layout_marginRight="10dp" />

  <!-- Status EditText  -->
  <EditText android:layout_width="fill_parent"
    android:layout_height="fill_parent" android:layout_weight="1"
    android:hint="@string/hintText" android:id="@+id/editText"
    android:gravity="top|center_horizontal" android:background="#cfff" /><!--❸-->

  <!-- Update Button -->
  <Button android:layout_width="fill_parent"
    android:layout_height="wrap_content" android:text="@string/buttonUpdate"
    android:textSize="20sp" android:id="@+id/buttonUpdate" />

</LinearLayout>
```

❶ We set the background of the main layout to point to the *background.png* file in our */res/drawable/* directory.

❷ We set the color of the title text to point to the color defined in the system color resource white.

❸ We set the background of the EditText area to a transparent white by specifying #cfff, a hexadecimal ARGB value.

At this point you've seen multiple ways to specify colors for different properties of various views in your activity. Android offers many properties and many different widgets. You should be able to extrapolate from this how to set other properties and make your application UI look exactly the way you want.

Alternative Resources

Android supports multiple competing sets of resources. For example, you could have multiple versions of a *strings.xml* file, *status.xml* layout, or *background.png* image. You might want multiple versions of same resource so that the best version can be used under different circumstances. We touched on this in "Adding Images" on page 74.

Imagine that your application is used in another country with a different language. In that case, you could provide a *strings.xml* version specifically for that language. Or imagine that a user runs your application on a different device, with a different screen that has more pixels. In that case, you'd want versions of your images specifically for this screen's pixel density. Similarly, users might simply rotate the device from portrait to landscape mode. Our application will redraw properly, but there are further enhancements we could make to the layout of the UI given the orientation of the screen.

Android provides for all these cases in an elegant way. Basically, you simply need to create alternative folders for specific constraints. For example, our standard layout files go into the */res/layout* folder, but if we wanted to provide an alternative layout specifically for landscape mode, we'd simply create a new file called */res/layout-land/ status.xml*. And if you wanted to provide a translated version of your *strings.xml* file for users who are in a French-speaking part of Canada, you'd put it in file called *res/ values-fr-rCA/strings.xml*.

As you see from these examples, alternative resources work by specifying the qualifiers in the names of their resource folders. In the case of the French Canadian strings, Android knows that the first qualifier -fr refers to language, and the second qualifier -rCA specifies that the region is Canada. In both cases, we use two-letter ISO codes (*http://www.loc.gov/standards/iso639-2/php/code_list.php*) to specify the country. So in this case, if the user is in Quebec and her device is configured to favor the French language, Android will look for string resources in the */res/values-fr-rCA/strings.xml file*. If it doesn't find a specific resource, it will fall back to the default */res/values/ strings.xml* file. Also, if the user in France, in this case Android will use the default resource, because our French Canadian qualifiers do not match French for France.

Using qualifiers, you can create alternative resources for languages and regions, screen sizes and orientations, device input modes (touch screen, stylus), keyboard or no keyboard, and so on. But how do you figure out this naming convention for resource folder names? The easiest solution is to use Eclipse's New Android XML File dialog (see Figure 6-15). To open the New Android XML File dialog, choose File→New...→Android XML File from the Eclipse menu.

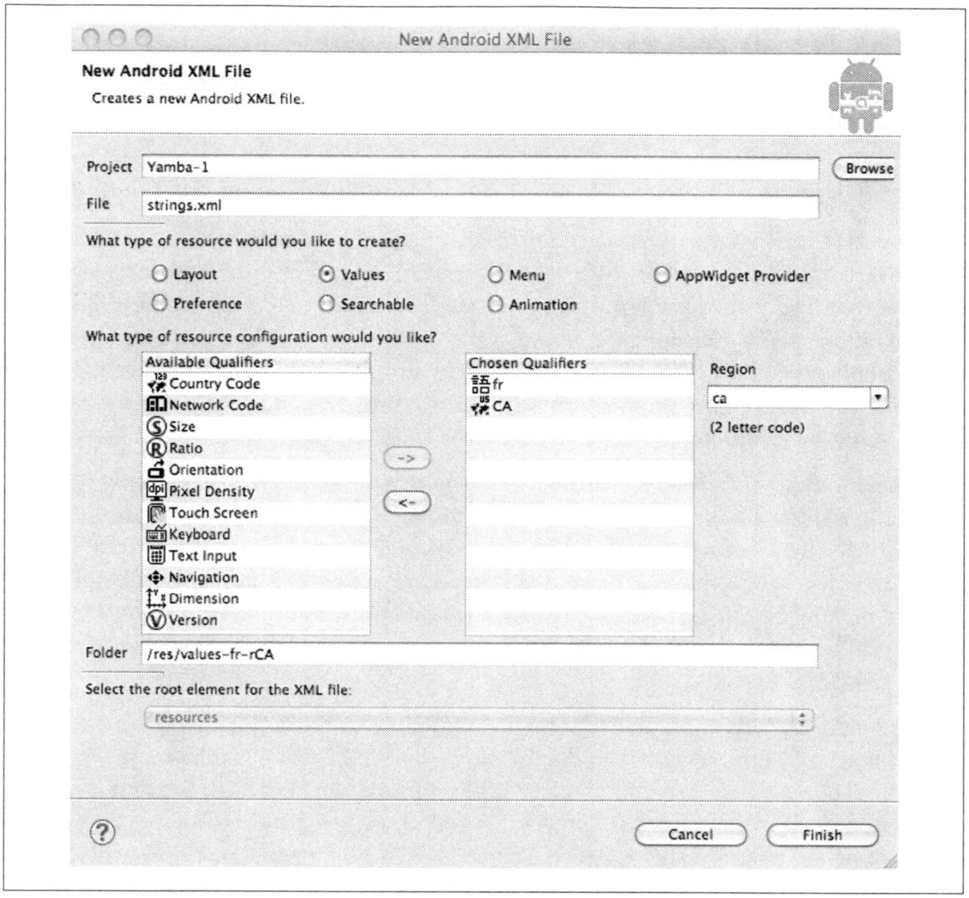

Figure 6-15. Alternative resources with New Android XML File dialog

Optimizing the User Interface

The user interface is one of the most expensive parts of a typical Android application. To create a simple screen, your application has to inflate the XML from resources. For each element, it has to create a new Java object and assign its properties to it. Then, it needs to draw each widget on the screen. All this takes many computing cycles.

Given this, it is worth keeping in mind few optimization points. You may want to try to limit the number of widgets you have on the screen. This is specially true when you are using nested layouts to achieve a desired look. This layout approach can sometimes get out of control, and if you are nesting unnecessary objects in a loop (say, displaying rows of data on the screen), then the number of widgets quickly explodes, and your user interface becomes sluggish.

Generally, you want your structure to be flat instead of deep. You can accomplish this by replacing nested layouts with relative layouts.

Hierarchy Viewer

There's a very useful tool that ships with the Android SDK called Hierarchy Viewer (see Figure 6-16). Go ahead and start it; it is in your *SDK/tools* directory.

Hierarchy Viewer allows you to attach to any Android device, emulator, or physical phone and then introspect the structure of the current view. It shows you all the widgets currently loaded in memory, their relationships to each other, and all their properties. You can introspect not just your screens, but the screens of any application on your device. This is also a good way to see how some other applications are structured.

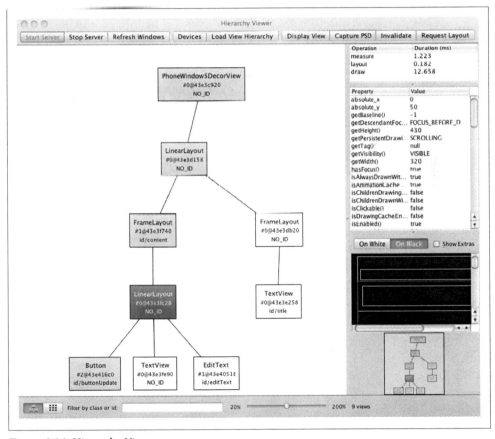

Figure 6-16. Hierarchy Viewer

Summary

By the end of this section, your application should run and should look like Figure 6-17. It should also successfully post your tweets to your Twitter account. You can verify it is working by logging into an online service of your choice that supports the Twitter API, such as *http://yamba.marakana.com*, using the same username and password that are hardcoded in the application.

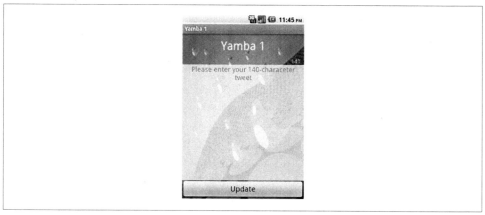

Figure 6-17. StatusActivity

Figure 6-18 illustrates what we have done so far as part of the design outlined in Figure 5-4.

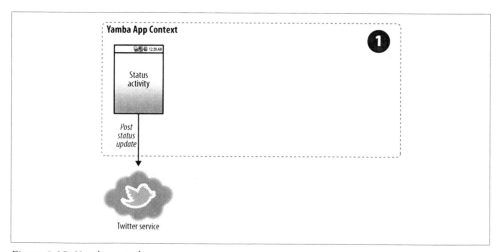

Figure 6-18. Yamba completion

Preferences, the Filesystem, the Options Menu, and Intents

In this chapter, you will learn how to create preferences for your application, how the filesystem is organized, and how to use intents and the options menu to jump from one activity to another.

Preferences

Preferences are user-specific settings for an application. Preferences usually consist of some configuration data as well as a user interface to manipulate that data.

From the user interface point of view, preferences can be simple text values, check-boxes, selections from a pull-down menu, or similar items. From a data point of view, preferences are a collection of name-value pairs (*http://en.wikipedia.org/wiki/Attribute-value_pair*), also known as key-value or attribute-value pairs. The values are basic data types, such as integers, booleans, and strings.

Our micro-blogging application needs to connect to a specific server in the cloud using specific user account information. For that, Yamba needs to know the username and password for that account as well as the URL of the server it's connecting to. This URL is also known as the API root. So, in our case, we'll have three fields where the user can enter and edit his username, password, and the API root. This data will be stored as strings.

To enable our app to handle user-specific preferences, we need to build a screen to enter the information, Java code to validate and process that information, and some kind of mechanism to store this information.

All this sounds like a lot of work, but Android provides a framework to help streamline working with user preferences. First, we'll define what our preference data looks like in a Preference resource file.

To create preferences for our application, we need to:

1. Create a Preference resource file called *prefs.xml*.
2. Implement the *PrefsActivity.java* file that inflates that resource file.
3. Register this new activity with the *AndroidManifest.xml* file.
4. Provide a way to start that activity from the rest of the application.

Prefs Resource

We are going to start by creating *prefs.xml*, a resource file that outlines what our preference screen will look like. The easiest way to create it is to use the New Android XML File tool in Eclipse, as shown in Figure 7-1. To start the New Android XML File dialog, go to File→New→Android XML File, or click on the little *a+* icon in Eclipse's top menu bar:

The key is to give the new file a name, in this case *prefs.xml*, and to choose Preference for the type of resource. The tool should automatically suggest creating this new file in the */res/xml* folder and that the root element for the XML file should be `PreferenceScreen`. As discussed before in "Alternative Resources" on page 79, we could create alternative versions of this same resource by applying various qualifiers, such as screen size and orientation, language and region, etc.

> We're using Eclipse tools where applicable to get the job done more quickly. If you were to use another tool, you'd have to create this file manually and put it in the correct folder.

Once you click on Finish, Eclipse will create a new file for you and open it up. Eclipse typically opens the XML files it knows about in its developer-friendly view.

In this view, you can create the username preference entry by selecting PreferenceScreen on the left, and then choosing Add→EditTextPreference. On the right-hand side, expand the "Attributes from Preferences" section. Eclipse will offer you a number of attributes to set for this `EditTextPreference`.

Not all attributes are equally important. Typically, you will care about the following:

Key
A unique identifier for each preference item. This is how we'll look up a particular preference later.

Title
The preference name that the user will see. It should be a short name that fits on a single line of the preference screen.

Summary
A short description of this preference item. This is optional, but using it is highly recommended.

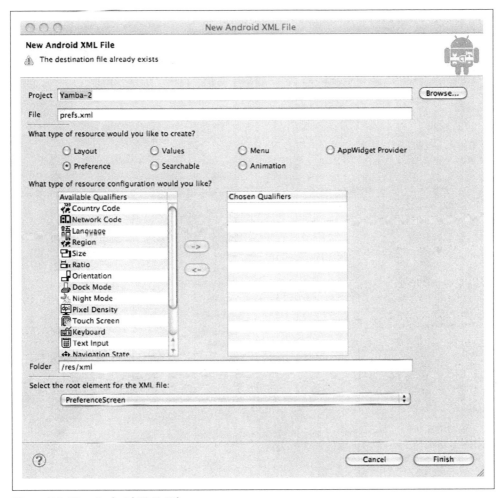

Figure 7-1. New Android XML File

For the username preference, we'll put "username" for its key. We will define the Title and Summary in *strings.xml*, as this is the best practice.

Instead of modifying the *strings.xml* file directly, you can use an Eclipse shortcut. Here's how it goes:

1. Click on Browse and select New String.... This will open a dialog to create a new string resource.
2. Enter `titleUsername` for the R.string. value and `Username` for the String value.
3. Click OK, and this will insert a new string resource in *strings.xml*.
4. You can now pick that value from the list of resources.

Using these instructions for adding the Username preference item, you can now repeat the same steps for Password and API Root items.

You can switch to the actual XML code by clicking on the tab at the bottom of the window, shown in Figure 7-2.

Figure 7-2. Prefs.xml in developer-friendly view

The raw XML for the preference resource looks like the code shown in Example 7-1.

Example 7-1. res/xml/prefs.xml

```xml
<?xml version="1.0" encoding="utf-8"?>
<PreferenceScreen xmlns:android="http://schemas.android.com/apk/res/android">

  <EditTextPreference android:title="@string/titleUsername"
    android:summary="@string/summaryUsername" android:key="username"></EditTextPreference>

  <EditTextPreference android:title="@string/titlePassword"
    android:password="true" android:summary="@string/summaryPassword"
    android:key="password"></EditTextPreference>

  <EditTextPreference android:title="@string/titleApiRoot"
    android:summary="@string/summaryApiRoot" android:key="apiRoot"></EditTextPreference>

</PreferenceScreen>
```

`<PreferenceScreen>` is the root element that defines our main preference screen. It has three children, all `<EditTextPreference>`. This is simply a piece of editable text. Other common elements here could be `<CheckBoxPreference>`, `<ListPreference>`, and so on.

The main property of any of these elements is the key. The key is how we'll look up these values later on. Remember, preferences is just a set of name-value pairs at the end of the day.

Like we said a couple of times earlier, although Eclipse does provide developer-friendly tools to manage XML files, you often run into certain limitations with Eclipse. For example, we would like to hide the actual text that the user types in the password field, which is a common practice. Android does provide support for that, but Eclipse tools haven't yet integrated this function. Since we can always edit the XML directly, in this case we add an `android:password="true"` property to our password property. This will cause the password to be masked while the user types it in.

PrefsActivity

Now that we have the preferences defined in their own XML resource file, we can create the activity to display these preferences. You may recall from <<Activities> that every screen in an Android app is an activity. So, to display the screen where a user enters the username and password for his online account, we'll create an activity to handle that screen. This will be a special preference-aware activity.

To create an activity, we create a new Java class. In Eclipse, select your package under your *src* folder, right-click on the package, and select New→Class. A New Java Class window will pop up. You just need to enter `PrefsActivity` for the Name and click Finish. This will create a *PrefsActivity.java* file under your package in your source folder.

Our `PrefsActivity` class, shown in Example 7-2, is a very simple Java file. This is because we inherit from `PreferenceActivity`, an Android framework class that knows how to handle preferences.

Example 7-2. PrefsActivity.java

```
package com.marakana.yamba2;

import android.os.Bundle;
import android.preference.PreferenceActivity;

public class PrefsActivity extends PreferenceActivity { // ❶

  @Override
  protected void onCreate(Bundle savedInstanceState) { // ❷
    super.onCreate(savedInstanceState);
    addPreferencesFromResource(R.xml.prefs); // ❸
  }

}
```

❶ Unlike regular activities, `PrefsActivity` will subclass (i.e., extend) the `Preference Activity` class.

❷ Just like any other activity, we override the `onCreate()` method to initialize the activity.

❸ Unlike regular activities that usually call `setContentView()`, our preference activity will set its content from the *prefs.xml* file via a call to `addPreferencesFromResource()`.

If you don't want to type the long signature of `onCreate()` and other methods that we often have to implement or override, you could use an Eclipse tool to help you with that. While in your *PrefsActivity.java* file and after you add `...extends PreferenceActivity...`, you can choose Source→Override/Implement Methods.... This will bring up a dialog box with an appropriate selection of methods you could override or implement, given that you are subclassing the `PreferenceActivity` class. In here, you can choose `onCreate()`, and Eclipse will insert the stub for this method into your code.

Update the Manifest File

Whenever we create one of these main building blocks (Activities, Services, Broadcast Receivers, or Content Providers), we need to define them in the *AndroidManifest.xml* file. In this case, we have a new `PrefsActivity` and must add it to the manifest file.

Just like with any Android XML file, opening *AndroidManifest.xml* in Eclipse typically will bring up the developer-friendly view of that file. In this file view, you could choose the Application tab, and then under Application Nodes, choose Add→Activity and name it `.PrefsActivity`.

However, we can also do this straight from the raw XML by clicking on the Android-Manifest.xml tab on the bottom of this window. I find that Eclipse is useful when it comes to creating XML files, but often editing the raw XML is faster and gives you much more control.

When editing code in Eclipse, you can use the Ctrl-space bar key shortcut to invoke the type-ahead feature of Eclipse. This is very useful for both XML and Java code and is context-sensitive, meaning Eclipse is smart enough to know what could possibly be entered at that point in the code. Using Ctrl-space bar makes your life as a programmer much easier because you don't have to remember long method names and tags, and it helps avoid typos.

So our manifest file now looks like the code shown in Example 7-3.

Example 7-3. AndroidManifest.xml

```xml
<?xml version="1.0" encoding="utf-8"?>
<manifest xmlns:android="http://schemas.android.com/apk/res/android"
  android:versionCode="1" android:versionName="1.0" package="com.marakana.yamba2">
  <application android:icon="@drawable/icon" android:label="@string/app_name">

    <activity android:name=".StatusActivity" android:label="@string/titleStatus">
      <intent-filter>
        <action android:name="android.intent.action.MAIN" />
        <category android:name="android.intent.category.LAUNCHER" />
      </intent-filter>
    </activity>

    <activity android:name=".PrefsActivity"
              android:label="@string/titlePrefs" /> <!-- ❶ -->

  </application>
  <uses-sdk android:minSdkVersion="4" />

  <uses-permission android:name="android.permission.INTERNET" />
</manifest>
```

❶ Defines the new `PrefsActivity`.

We now have a new preference activity, but there's no good way of getting to it yet. We need a way to launch this new activity. For that, we use the options menu.

The Options Menu

The options menu is an Android user interface component that provides standardized menus to applications. The menus appear at the bottom of the screen when the user presses the Menu button on the device.

To add support for the options menu to an application, we need to do the following:

1. Create the *menu.xml* resource where we specify what the menu consists of.
2. Add `onCreateOptionsMenu()` to the activity that should have this menu. This is where we inflate the *menu.xml* resource.
3. Provide handling of menu events in `onOptionsItemSelected()`.

The Menu Resource

We start by defining the menus in an XML resource for the options menu. Just like with other Android XML files, we can use the little *a+* icon in the Eclipse toolbar or choose File→New...→Android XML to launch the New Android XML File dialog. In this dialog, enter "menu.xml" in the file field, and for Type, select Menu. Click the Finish button, and Eclipse will create a new folder called */res/menu* that contains the *menu.xml* file and will open this file in the developer-friendly view (see Figure 7-3).

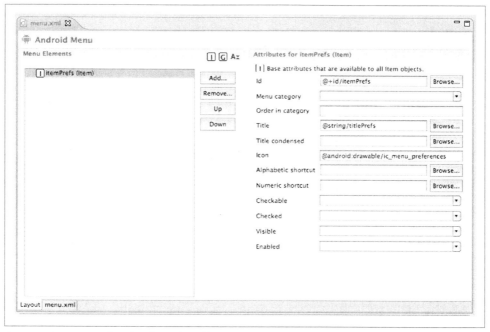

Figure 7-3. Menu.xml in developer-friendly view

In this view, you can click on Add→Item, which will add a new menu item to your menu. In the Attributes section on the right, you can see over a dozen attributes that we can set for this menu item. Just like before, not all attributes are equally important:

Id

> The unique identifier of this resource. Just as when we designed the layout in Chapter 6, this identifier is typically of the form @+id/*someId* , where *someId* is the name that you give it. This name should contain only letters, numbers, and the underscore character.

Title

> The title of this menu as it will appear on the display. Keep in mind that screen space typically is limited, so keep the title short. Additionally, you can provide a "Title condensed" attribute to specify a shorter version of the title that will be shown instead if space is limited. Just like before, best practice is to define the actual text value of the title in the *strings.xml* resource and just reference it here.

Icon

> The icon that displays along with the menu item's title. Although not required, it is a very useful visual cue from a usability point of view. In this case it also illustrates how to point to Android system resources.

The next section describes these resources in more detail.

Android System Resources

Just like your application can have resources, so can the Android system. Like most other operating systems, Android comes with some preloaded images, graphics, sound clips, and other types of resources. Recall that our app resources are in /res/. To refer to Android system resources, prefix them with the `android:` keyword in XML, for example, `@android:drawable/ic_menu_preferences`. If you are referring to an Android system resource from Java, then you use `android.R` instead of the usual `R` reference.

 The actual resource files are in your SDK, inside a specific platform folder. For example, if you are using Android 9 (Gingerbread), the resource folder would be `android-sdk/platforms/android-9/data/res/`.

The raw XML of *menu.xml* is shown in Example 7-4.

Example 7-4. res/menu/menu.xml

```
<?xml version="1.0" encoding="utf-8"?>
<menu xmlns:android="http://schemas.android.com/apk/res/android">
  <item android:id="@+id/itemPrefs" android:title="@string/titlePrefs"
    android:icon="@android:drawable/ic_menu_preferences"></item>
</menu>
```

As you can see, there's just one `<item>` element within our `<menu>` element, making this a single-item menu.

Update StatusActivity to Load the Menu

Recall that the options menu is loaded by your activity when the user clicks on her device's Menu button. The first time the Menu button is pressed, the system will call the activity's `onCreateOptionsMenu()` method to inflate the menu from the *menu.xml* resource. This process is similar to inflating the user interface from layout resources, discussed in "The StatusActivity Java Class" on page 56. Basically, the *inflater* reads the XML code, creates a corresponding Java object for each element, and sets each XML object's properties accordingly.

From that point on, the menu is in memory, and `onCreateOptionsMenu()` doesn't get called again until the activity is destroyed. Each time the user selects a menu item, though, `onOptionsItemSelected()` gets called to process that click. We'll talk about this in the next section.

We need to update the `StatusActivity` to load up the options menu. To do that, add an `onCreateOptionsMenu()` method to `StatusActivity`. This method gets called only the first time the user clicks on the menu button:

```
// Called first time user clicks on the menu button
@Override
```

```
public boolean onCreateOptionsMenu(Menu menu) {
  MenuInflater inflater = getMenuInflater();    // ❶
  inflater.inflate(R.menu.menu, menu);          // ❷
  return true; // ❸
}
```

❶ We get the `MenuInflater` object from the context.

❷ Use the inflater to inflate the menu from the XML resource.

❸ We must return `true` for this menu to be displayed.

Update StatusActivity to Handle Menu Events

We also need a way to handle various clicks on the menu items. To do that, we add
another callback method, `onOptionsItemSelected()`. This method is called every time
the user clicks on a menu item:

```
// Called when an options item is clicked
@Override
public boolean onOptionsItemSelected(MenuItem item) {
  switch (item.getItemId()) {                                  // ❶
  case R.id.itemPrefs:
    startActivity(new Intent(this, PrefsActivity.class));      // ❷
  break;
  }

  return true;  // ❸
}
```

❶ Since the same method is called regardless of which item the user clicks, we need to
figure out the ID of that item, and based on that, switch to a specific case to handle
each item. At this point, we have only one menu item, but that might change in the
future. Switching an item ID is a very scalable approach and will adapt nicely as our
application grows in complexity.

❷ The `startActivity()` method in context allows us to launch a new activity. In this
case, we are creating a new intent that specifies starting the `PrefsActivity` class.

❸ Return `true` to consume the event here.

 Just like before, you could use the Eclipse shortcut Source→Override/
Implement Methods to add both `onCreateOptionsMenu()` and
`onOptionsItemSelected()`.

Strings Resource

Our updated *strings.xml* now looks like the code shown in Example 7-5.

Example 7-5. res/values/strings.xml

```xml
<?xml version="1.0" encoding="utf-8"?>
<resources>
  <string name="app_name">Yamba 2</string>
  <string name="titleYamba">Yamba 2</string>

  <string name="hintText">Please enter your 140-character status</string>
  <string name="buttonUpdate">Update</string>

  <string name="titleStatus">Status Update</string>
  <string name="titlePrefs">Prefs</string>
  <string name="titleUsername">Username</string>
  <string name="titlePassword">Password</string>
  <string name="titleApiRoot">API Root</string>

  <string name="summaryUsername">Please enter your username</string>
  <string name="summaryPassword">Please enter your password</string>
  <string name="summaryApiRoot">URL of Root API for your service</string>
</resources>
```

You should be able to run your application at this point and see the new Prefs Activity by clicking on Menu→Prefs in StatusActivity (see Figure 7-4). Try changing your username and password, then reboot your phone, restart the app, and verify that the information is still there.

Figure 7-4. PrefsActivity

Shared Preferences

Now that we have a preference activity and a way to save our username, password, and API root, it is time to make use of it. To programmatically access your preferences, we'll use the SharedPreference class provided by the Android framework.

This class is called `SharedPreference` because this preference is easily accessible from any component of this application (activities, services, broadcast receivers, and content providers).

In `StatusActivity`, add a definition for the `prefs` object globally to the class:

```
SharedPreferences prefs;
```

Now, to get the preference object, add the following to `onCreate()`:

```
@Override
        public void onCreate(Bundle savedInstanceState) {
                ...
                // Setup preferences
                prefs = PreferenceManager.getDefaultSharedPreferences(this); // ❶
                prefs.registerOnSharedPreferenceChangeListener(this);    // ❷
        }
```

❶ Each application has its own shared preferences available to all components of this application context. To get the instance of this `SharedPreferences`, we use `PreferenceManager.getDefaultSharedPreferences()` and pass it `this` as the current context for this app. The name "shared" could be confusing. To clarify, it means that this preference object contains data shared by various parts of this application only; it is not shared with any other application.

❷ The user can and will change preferences. So we need a mechanism to notify this activity that the old values are stale. To do that, we register `this`, meaning our `StatusActivity` with our shared preferences. For this to work, we'll need to add `...implements OnSharedPreferenceChangeListener` to our class definition as well as implement the required `onSharedPreferenceChanged()` method. This method will be explained in a bit.

Now that we have the username, password, and API root coming from user-defined preferences, we can refactor our Twitter code so it no longer hardcodes them. To do that, we add a private method to `StatusActivity` responsible for returning a valid `twitter` object. This method lazily initializes `twitter`, which means that if `twitter` exists, it returns it as-is; otherwise, the method creates it:

```
private Twitter getTwitter() {
  if (twitter == null) { // ❶
    String username, password, apiRoot;
    username = prefs.getString("username", "");     // ❷
    password = prefs.getString("password", "");
    apiRoot = prefs.getString("apiRoot", "http://yamba.marakana.com/api");

    // Connect to twitter.com
    twitter = new Twitter(username, password);       // ❸
    twitter.setAPIRootUrl(apiRoot); // ❹
  }
  return twitter;
}
```

❶ Only if `twitter` is null (i.e., undefined), we create it.

❷ Get the username and password from the shared preference object. The first parameter in `getString()` is the key we assigned to each preference item, such as `username` and `password`. The second argument is the default value in case such a preference is not found. Keep in mind that the first time a user runs your application, the preference file doesn't exist, so defaults will be used. So, if the user hasn't set up her preferences in `PrefsActivity`, this code will attempt to log in with an empty username and password, and thus fail. However, the failure will happen when the user tries to do the actual status update because that's how the *jtwitter* library is designed.

❸ We log into the Twitter service with user-defined preferences.

❹ Remember that we need to update the actual service that we are using by updating the API root URL for that service.

Now we don't use the `twitter` object directly anymore, but instead call `getTwitter()` to get it. So, `onClick()` becomes like this:

```
public void onClick(View v) {

        // Update twitter status
        try {
                getTwitter().setStatus(editText.getText().toString());
        } catch (TwitterException e) {
                Log.d(TAG, "Twitter setStatus failed: " + e);
        }
}
```

Note that although we moved the code where we initialize our connection to the cloud, we still need the `AsyncTask` to deal with the fact that this call is still blocking and may take a while to complete, as it's subject to network availability and latency.

As we mentioned before when updating `onCreate()` and registering for preference updates, we need to handle what happens when the user changes his username or password. By registering `prefs.registerOnSharedPreferenceChangeListener(this)` in `onCreate()` and implementing `OnSharedPreferenceChangeListener`, we got a callback method `onSharedPreferenceChanged()` that the system will invoke whenever preferences change. In this method, we simply invalidate the `twitter` object, so the next time it is needed, `getTwitter()` will recreate it:

```
public void onSharedPreferenceChanged(SharedPreferences prefs, String key) {
        // invalidate twitter object
        twitter = null;
}
```

The Filesystem Explained

So, where does the device store these preferences? How secure is my username and password? To answer that, we need to look at how the Android filesystem is organized.

Exploring the Filesystem

There are two ways for you to access the filesystem on an Android device: via Eclipse or the command line.

In Eclipse, we use the File Explorer view to access the filesystem. To open up the File Explorer view, go to Window→Show View→Other...→Android→File Explorer. You can also access the File Explorer view via the DDMS perspective (*http://developer.android .com/guide/developing/tools/ddms.html*). Select the DDMS perspective icon in the top-right corner of Eclipse:

or go to Window→Open Perspective→Other...→DDMS. If you have multiple devices connected to your workstation, make sure you select which one you are working with in the Devices view. You should now be able to navigate through the device's filesystem.

If you prefer the command line, you can always use `adb shell` to get to the shell of the device. From there you can explore the filesystem like you would on any other Unix platform.

Filesystem Partitions

There are three main parts of the filesystem on every Android device. As shown in Figure 7-5, they are:

- The system partition (*/system/*)
- The SDCard partition (*/sdcard/*)
- The user data partition at (*/data/*)

System Partition

Your entire Android operating system is located in the system partition. This is the main partition that contains all your preinstalled applications, system libraries, Android framework, Linux command-line tools, and so on.

The system partition is mounted read-only, meaning that you as developer have very little influence over it. As such, this partition is of limited interest to us.

The system partition in the Emulator corresponds to the *system.img* file in your platform images directory, located in the *android-sdk/platforms/android-8/images/* folder.

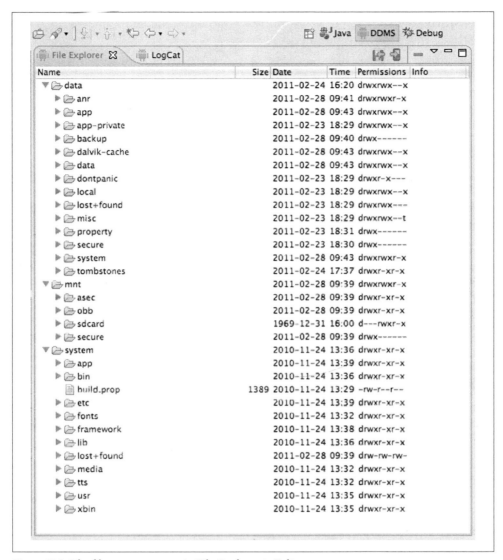

Name	Size	Date	Time	Permissions	Info
▼ 📂 data		2011-02-24	16:20	drwxrwx--x	
▶ 📂 anr		2011-02-28	09:41	drwxrwxr-x	
▶ 📂 app		2011-02-28	09:43	drwxrwx--x	
▶ 📂 app-private		2011-02-23	18:29	drwxrwx---x	
▶ 📂 backup		2011-02-28	09:40	drwx------	
▶ 📂 dalvik-cache		2011-02-28	09:43	drwxrwx--x	
▶ 📂 data		2011-02-28	09:43	drwxrwx--x	
▶ 📂 dontpanic		2011-02-23	18:29	drwxr-x---	
▶ 📂 local		2011-02-23	18:29	drwxrwx--x	
▶ 📂 lost+found		2011-02-23	18:29	drwxrwx---	
▶ 📂 misc		2011-02-23	18:29	drwxrwx--t	
▶ 📂 property		2011-02-23	18:31	drwx------	
▶ 📂 secure		2011-02-23	18:30	drwx------	
▶ 📂 system		2011-02-28	09:43	drwxrwxr-x	
▶ 📂 tombstones		2011-02-24	17:37	drwxr-xr-x	
▼ 📂 mnt		2011-02-28	09:39	drwxrwxr-x	
▶ 📂 asec		2011-02-28	09:39	drwxr-xr-x	
▶ 📂 obb		2011-02-28	09:39	drwxr-xr-x	
▶ 📂 sdcard		1969-12-31	16:00	d---rwxr-x	
▶ 📂 secure		2011-02-28	09:39	drwx------	
▼ 📂 system		2010-11-24	13:36	drwxr-xr-x	
▶ 📂 app		2010-11-24	13:39	drwxr-xr-x	
▶ 📂 bin		2010-11-24	13:36	drwxr-xr-x	
📄 build.prop	1389	2010-11-24	13:29	-rw-r--r--	
▶ 📂 etc		2010-11-24	13:39	drwxr-xr-x	
▶ 📂 fonts		2010-11-24	13:32	drwxr-xr-x	
▶ 📂 framework		2010-11-24	13:38	drwxr-xr-x	
▶ 📂 lib		2010-11-24	13:36	drwxr-xr-x	
▶ 📂 lost+found		2011-02-28	09:39	drw-rw-rw-	
▶ 📂 media		2010-11-24	13:32	drwxr-xr-x	
▶ 📂 tts		2010-11-24	13:32	drwxr-xr-x	
▶ 📂 usr		2010-11-24	13:35	drwxr-xr-x	
▶ 📂 xbin		2010-11-24	13:35	drwxr-xr-x	

Figure 7-5. The filesystem as seen via File Explorer in Eclipse

SDCard Partition

The SDCard partition is a free-for-all mass storage area. Your app can read files from this partition as well as write files to it if it holds WRITE_TO_EXTERNAL_STORAGE permission. This is a great place to store large files, such as music, photos, videos, and similar items.

Note that since the FroYo version of Android, the */sdcard* mount point appears in the Eclipse File Explorer under the */mnt/sdcard* location. This is due to the new feature in FroYo that allows for storing and running applications on the SDCard as well.

As an app developer, the SDCard partition is very useful and important to you. At the same time, this partition is not very structured.

This partition typically corresponds to *sdcard.img* in your Android Virtual Device (AVD) directory. This directory is in your *~/.android/avd/* folder and will have a subdirectory for each specific virtual device. On the physical device, it is an actual SD card (*http://en.wikipedia.org/wiki/Secure_Digital*).

The User Data Partition

As user and app developer, the most important partition is the user data partition. This is where all your user data is stored, all the downloaded apps are located, and most importantly, all the applications' data. This includes both preinstalled apps as well as user-downloaded apps.

So, while user apps are stored in the */data/app/* folder, the most important folder to us as app developers is the */data/data/* folder. More specifically, within this folder there's a subfolder corresponding to each app. This folder is identified by the Java package that this app used to sign itself. Again, this is why Java packages are important to Android security.

The Android framework provides a number of handy methods as part of its context that help you access the user data filesystem from within your application. For example, take a look at getFilesDir() (*http://developer.android.com/reference/android/content/ContextWrapper.html#getFilesDir()*).

This partition typically corresponds to *user-data.img* in your Android Virtual Device (AVD) directory. As before, this directory is in your *~/.android/avd/* folder and will have a subdirectory for each specific virtual device.

When you create a new app, you assign your Java code to a specific package. Typically, this package follows the Java convention of reverse domain name plus app name. For example, the Yamba app is in the com.marakana.yamba package. So, once installed, Android creates a special folder just for this app under */data/data/com.marakana.yamba/*. This folder is the cornerstone of our private, secured filesystem dedicated to each app.

There will be subfolders in */data/data/com.marakana.yamba2/*, but they are well-defined. For example, the preferences are in */data/data/com.marakana.yamba2/shared_prefs/*. As a matter of fact, if you open up the DDMS perspective in Eclipse and select File Explorer, you can navigate to this partition. You will probably see the *com.marakana.yamba2_preferences.xml* file in there. You could pull this file and examine it, or you could use adb shell.

adb shell is another one of those common adb subcommands to access the shell of your device (either physical or virtual). For instance, you could just open up your command-line terminal and type:

```
[user:~]> adb shell
# cd /data/data/com.marakana.yamba2/shared_prefs
# cat com.marakana.yamba2_preferences.xml
<?xml version='1.0' encoding='utf-8' standalone='yes' ?>
<map>
<string name="password">password</string>
<string name="apiRoot">http://yamba.marakana.com/api</string>
<string name="username">student</string>
</map>
#
```

This XML file represents the storage for all our preference data for this application. As you can see, our username, password, and API root are all stored in there.

Filesystem Security

So, how secure is this? This is a common question posed by security folks. Storing usernames and passwords in clear text always raises eyebrows.

To answer this question, I usually compare it to finding someone's laptop on the street. Although we can easily gain access to the "hard drive" via the adb tool, that doesn't mean we can read its data. Each folder under */data/data/* belongs to a separate user account managed by Linux. Unless our app is that app, it won't have access to that folder. So, short of us reading byte-by-byte on the physical device, even clear-text data is secure.

On the Emulator, we have root permissions, meaning we can explore the entire file-system. This is useful for development purposes.

Summary

At this point, the user can specify her username and password for the micro-blogging site. This makes the app usable to way more people than the previous version in which this information was hardcoded.

Figure 7-6 illustrates what we have done so far as part of the design outlined earlier in Figure 5-4.

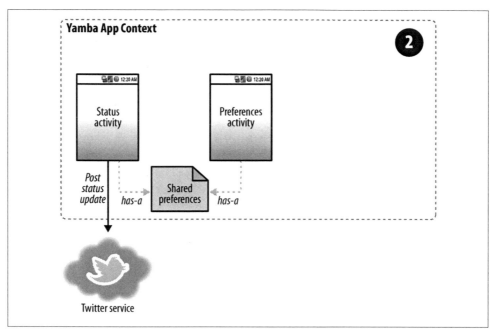

Figure 7-6. Yamba completion

Services

Services are among the main building blocks in Android. Unlike an activity, a service doesn't have a user interface; it is simply a piece of code that runs in the background of your application.

Services are used for processes that should run independently of activities, which may come and go. Our Yamba application, for example, needs to create a service to periodically connect to the cloud and check for new statuses from the user's friends. This service will be always on and always running, regardless of whether the user ever starts the activity.

Just like an activity, a service has a well-defined life cycle. You as the developer get to define what happens during transitions between states. Whereas an activity's state is managed by the runtime's ActivityManager, service state is controlled more by intents. Essentially, whenever an activity needs your service, it will invoke it through an intent that starts the service. An already running service can receive the start message repeatedly and at unanticipated times. You can also stop a service, which is also called destroying it.

A service can be bound or unbound. Bound services can provide more specific APIs to other applications via an interface called AIDL (Android Interface Definition Language; see Chapter 14). For now, we'll focus on unbound services, where the life cycle of a service is not tied to the life cycle of the activities that started them. The only states for bound services are started and stopped (destroyed).

In this chapter, you will create a service. The purpose of this service is to run in the background and update your app with the latest timeline from the user's Twitter account. Initially, the service will just print your friends' timeline to the logfile. The service will create a separate thread, so you will learn about concurrency in this chapter as well. You will also learn about Toasts and understand the context in which services and activities run.

By the end of this chapter, you will have a working app that can both post to Twitter and periodically check what friends are up to.

The Yamba Application Object

We now have support for preferences in our `StatusActivity`. We also have the utility method `getTwitter()` to help us get the actual `Twitter` object that we use to connect to the online service.

It is likely that we'll need some of these features in other parts of our application. Instead of copying them from file to file, it would be useful if we could put this code in a separate place that is accessible by most parts of our app. Android provides just a place for that in the form of an `Application` object.

An `Application` object represents the common state of your entire application. As long as any part of your application is running, the application object will be created. Most applications use the default `android.app.Application` class that the framework provides. However, you can implement your own instance of this object and add the common app features to it.

We are going to create our own instance of this object and call it `YambaApplication`. The steps for creating the `YambaApplication` class are:

1. Create the Java class representing `YambaApplication`.
2. Register the new class with the *AndroidManifest.xml* file.

The YambaApplication Class

First, we are going to create a new Java class in the same package as the rest of our classes. We'll call this class `YambaApplication`, and it will extend the `Application` base class from the framework.

Next, we're going to move common tasks into this base object. We anticipate that more parts of our application are going to need to connect to the online service as well as read the preference data.

Notice in Example 8-1 that the `Application` object has the usual `onCreate()` method, but it also provides the `onTerimante()` callback as a place to implement any cleanup that we might want to do. At this point we don't have anything to clean up, but this is a good opportunity to create some logging information so we can see when the application actually shuts down. We might expand on this later.

Example 8-1. YambaApplication.java

```
package com.marakana.yamba3;

import winterwell.jtwitter.Twitter;
import android.app.Application;
import android.content.SharedPreferences;
import android.content.SharedPreferences.OnSharedPreferenceChangeListener;
import android.preference.PreferenceManager;
import android.text.TextUtils;
```

```
import android.util.Log;

public class YambaApplication1 extends Application implements
    OnSharedPreferenceChangeListener { // ❶
  private static final String TAG = YambaApplication1.class.getSimpleName();
  public Twitter twitter; // ❷
  private SharedPreferences prefs;

  @Override
  public void onCreate() { // ❸
    super.onCreate();
    this.prefs = PreferenceManager.getDefaultSharedPreferences(this);
    this.prefs.registerOnSharedPreferenceChangeListener(this);
    Log.i(TAG, "onCreated");
  }

  @Override
  public void onTerminate() { // ❹
    super.onTerminate();
    Log.i(TAG, "onTerminated");
  }

  public synchronized Twitter getTwitter() { // ❺
    if (this.twitter == null) {
      String username = this.prefs.getString("username", "");
      String password = this.prefs.getString("password", "");
      String apiRoot = prefs.getString("apiRoot",
          "http://yamba.marakana.com/api");
      if (!TextUtils.isEmpty(username) && !TextUtils.isEmpty(password)
          && !TextUtils.isEmpty(apiRoot)) {
        this.twitter = new Twitter(username, password);
        this.twitter.setAPIRootUrl(apiRoot);
      }
    }
    return this.twitter;
  }

  public synchronized void onSharedPreferenceChanged(
      SharedPreferences sharedPreferences, String key) { // ❻
    this.twitter = null;
  }

}
```

❶ For YambaApplication to be a valid application object, it must subclass the frame-work-provided Application class. Notice that we also moved responsibility for being the OnSharedPreferenceChangeListener from StatusActivity to YambaApplication.

❷ Twitter and SharedPreferences are now part of this common object and no longer part of StatusActivity.

❸ onCreate() is called when the application is first created. The application is created whenever any of its parts, such as an activity or a service, is first needed.

❹ onTerminate() is a placeholder for us to do some cleanup when the application is about to shut down. At this point, we just use it for logging purposes.

❺ We also moved getTwitter() from StatusActivity to YambaApplication because it's going to be used by other parts of our application and we want to maximize the code reuse. Notice the use of the synchronized keyword here. A synchronized method in Java means that only one thread can be inside of such a method at one time (*http://download.oracle.com/javase/tutorial/essential/concurrency/syncmeth.html*). This is now important because this method could be used by different threads that our application might have.

❻ onSharedPreferenceChanged() is now also part of YambaApplication instead of StatusActivity.

Now that we have YambaApplication and have moved some responsibilities from StatusActivity to this new class, we can simplify StatusActivity even further, as shown in Example 8-2.

Example 8-2. StatusActivity using YambaApplication

```
...
Twitter.Status status = ((YambaApplication) getApplication())
    .getTwitter().updateStatus(statuses[0]);  // ❶
...
```

❶ We now use the getTwitter() method from YambaApplication instead of keeping it locally. This way, the same method can be reused by other parts of the application that need access to the cloud service.

Update the Manifest File

The final step is to tell our application to use the YambaApplication class instead of the default Application class. To do that, we need to update the Android manifest file and add an attribute to the <application> element:

```
<?xml version="1.0" encoding="utf-8"?>
<manifest xmlns:android="http://schemas.android.com/apk/res/android"
    android:versionCode="1" android:versionName="1.0" package="com.marakana.yamba2">
    <application android:icon="@drawable/icon" android:label="@string/app_name"
        android:name=".YambaApplication"> <!--❶-->
        ...
    </application>
    ...
</manifest>
```

❶ The attribute android:name=".YambaApplication" in the <application> element tells the Android system to instantiate our YambaApplication object as the application.

So, at this point we have successfully moved common functionality from StatusActivity to YambaApplication. This process is also known as code refactoring (*http://en.wikipedia.org/wiki/Code_refactoring*) and is a good practice as we keep on adding new features to our application.

Simplifying StatusActivity

Now that the functionality for getting the Twitter object has been moved to YambaApplication, we can simplify StatusActivity to refer to that functionality there. Here's what our new PostToTwitter AsyncTask would look like:

```
class PostToTwitter extends AsyncTask<String, Integer, String> {
  // Called to initiate the background activity
  @Override
  protected String doInBackground(String... statuses) {
    try {
    YambaApplication yamba = ((YambaApplication) getApplication()); // ❶
    Twitter.Status status = yamba.getTwitter().updateStatus(statuses[0]); // ❷
      return status.text;
    } catch (TwitterException e) {
      Log.e(TAG, "Failed to connect to twitter service", e);
      return "Failed to post";
    }
  }
  ...
}
```

❶ We get the reference to the Application object via the getApplication() call in the current context. Since we have a custom YambaApplication object, we need to cast the generic Application into YambaApplication.

❷ Once we have the reference to our application object, we can call its methods, such as the getTwitter() method.

You have seen how we have refactored our StatusActivity to move some of the common functionality into a shared Application object. Now that we have done that, we can create our UpdaterService, which will use some of this common functionality.

UpdaterService

As mentioned in the introduction to this chapter, we need a service to run as an always-on background process pulling the latest Twitter statuses into a local database. The purpose of this pull mechanism is to cache updates locally so our app can have data even when it's offline. We'll call this service UpdaterService.

Steps to creating a service are:

1. Create the Java class representing your service.
2. Register the service in the Android manifest file.
3. Start the service.

Creating the UpdaterService Java Class

The basic procedure for creating a service, as with activities and other main building blocks, is to subclass a `Service` class provided by the Android framework.

To create the new service, we need to create a new Java file. Go ahead and select your Java package in the *src* folder, right-click and choose New→Class, and type in "UpdaterService" as the class name. This will create a new *UpdaterService.java* file as part of your package.

You may recall from "Services" on page 31 that a typical service goes through the life cycle illustrated in Figure 8-1.

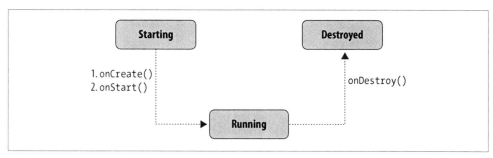

Figure 8-1. Service life cycle

Next, we want to override some of the main life cycle methods:

`onCreate()`
> Called when the service is created for the first time

`onStartCommand()`
> Called when the service is started

`onDestroy()`
> Called when the service is terminated

To do that, you can use Eclipse tool Source→Override/Implement Methods and select those three methods.

At this point, in the spirit of producing a minimally working app at each stage of learning, we'll write just a little code that logs a note in each of the overridden methods. So the shell of our service looks like the code in Example 8-3.

Example 8-3. UpdaterService.java, version 1

```
package com.marakana.yamba3;

import android.app.Service;
import android.content.Intent;
import android.os.IBinder;
import android.util.Log;
```

```
public class UpdaterService1 extends Service {
  static final String TAG = "UpdaterService"; // ❶

  @Override
  public IBinder onBind(Intent intent) { // ❷
    return null;
  }

  @Override
  public void onCreate() { // ❸
    super.onCreate();
    Log.d(TAG, "onCreated");
  }

  @Override
  public int onStartCommand(Intent intent, int flags, int startId) { // ❹
    super.onStartCommand(intent, flags, startId);
    Log.d(TAG, "onStarted");
    return START_STICKY;
  }

  @Override
  public void onDestroy() { // ❺
    super.onDestroy();
    Log.d(TAG, "onDestroyed");
  }
}
```

❶ As in all major classes, I like to add the TAG constant because I use Log.d() quite a bit.

❷ onBind() is used in bound services to return the actual implementation of something called a *binder*. Since we are not using a bound service, we can just return null here.

❸ onCreate() is called when the service is initially created. It is not called for subsequent startService() calls, so it is a good place to do work that needs to be done only once during the life of a service.

❹ onStartCommand() is called each time the service receives a startService() intent. A service that is already stated could get multiple requests to start again, and each will cause onStartCommand() to execute.

❺ onDestroy() is called just before the service is destroyed by the stopService() request. This is a good place to clean up things that might have been initialized in onCreate().

Update the Manifest File

Now that we have the shell of our service, we have to define it in the manifest file, just like any other main building block; otherwise, we won't be able to call our service. Simply open *AndroidManifest.xml*, click on the right-most tab to see the raw XML code, and add the following within the <application> element:

```
...
    <application android:icon="@drawable/icon" android:label="@string/app_name">
        ...
        <service android:name=".UpdaterService" /> <!-- ❶ -->
        ...
    </application>
    ...
```

❶ UpdaterService definition.

Services are equal to activities as Android building blocks, so they appear at the same level in the manifest file.

Add Menu Items

Now that we have the service defined and declared, we need a way to start and stop it. The easiest way would be to add a menu button to our options menu that we have already created. Later on, we'll have a more intelligent way of starting services, but for now this manual approach is easier to understand.

To add start/stop menu buttons, we'll add two more menu items to our *menu.xml* resource, just as we created the Prefs menu item before in "The Menu Resource" on page 89. The updated *menu.xml* now looks like the code in Example 8-4.

Example 8-4. menu.xml

```
<?xml version="1.0" encoding="utf-8"?>
<menu xmlns:android="http://schemas.android.com/apk/res/android">
  <item android:id="@+id/itemPrefs" android:title="@string/titlePrefs"
    android:icon="@android:drawable/ic_menu_preferences"></item>  <!-- ❶ -->
  <item android:title="@string/titleServiceStart" android:id="@+id/itemServiceStart"
    android:icon="@android:drawable/ic_media_play"></item>  <!-- ❷ -->
  <item android:title="@string/titleServiceStop" android:id="@+id/itemServiceStop"
    android:icon="@android:drawable/ic_media_pause"></item> <!-- ❸ -->
</menu>
```

❶ This is the item we defined in the previous chapter.

❷ The ServiceStart item has the usual id, title, and icon attributes. This icon is another Android system resource.

❸ The ServiceStop item is similar to the ServiceStart item.

Now that the menu resource has been updated, it's time to handle those items when the user clicks on them.

Update the Options Menu Handling

To handle new menu items, we need to update the onOptionsItemSelected() method in StatusActivity, just as we did in "Update StatusActivity to Handle Menu Events" on page 92. So open your *StatusActivity.java* file and locate the onOptionsItem Selected() method. We now have a framework in this method to support any number of menu items. To add support for starting and stopping our service, we launch intents pointing to our UpdaterService via startService() and stopService() calls. The final code looks like this:

```
// Called when an options item is clicked
@Override
public boolean onOptionsItemSelected(MenuItem item) {
  switch (item.getItemId()) {
  case R.id.itemServiceStart:
    startService(new Intent(this, UpdaterService.class)); // ❶
    break;
  case R.id.itemServiceStop:
    stopService(new Intent(this, UpdaterService.class));  // ❷
    break;
  case R.id.itemPrefs:
    startActivity(new Intent(this, PrefsActivity.class));
    break;
  }

  return true;
}
```

❶ Creates an intent to start UpdaterService. If the service doesn't already exist, the runtime calls the service's onCreate() method. Then onStartCommand() is called, regardless of whether this service is new or already running.

❷ Similarly, this uses the stopService() call to send an intent intended for Updater Service. This will cause onDestroy() to be called on the service if the service is running. If it isn't, nothing happens, and this intent is simply ignored.

In this example, we are using explicit intents to specify exactly which class the intents are intended for, namely UpdaterService.class.

Testing the Service

At this point, you can restart your application. Note that you do not need to restart the emulator. When your application starts up, click on the menu, and your new buttons should appear in the menu options. You can now freely click on the start and stop service buttons.

To verify that your service is working, open up your LogCat and look for the appropriate log messages that you generated in your service code. Remember from "Logging in Android" on page 62 that you can view the LogCat both in Eclipse and via the command line.

Another way to verify that the service is running is to go to the Android Settings app and see whether it is listed. To do that, go to the Home screen, press Menu, and choose Settings. Then go to Applications→Running services. You should see your service listed, as shown in Figure 8-2.

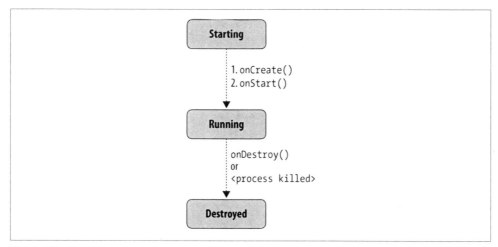

Figure 8-2. Running services

Your service is now working, although it's not doing much at this point.

Looping in the Service

By design, our service is supposed to wake up every so often, check the online service for new status updates, an then go back to "sleep" for some time. And this work needs to keep on happening forever, until the service is stopped. A good way to implement this is to have our service run in a loop and pause execution between iterations. Java provides a `Thread.sleep()` method that we can use to make the currently running thread pause and relinquish CPU for some number of milliseconds.

Another consideration to keep in mind is that the service could require a good deal of time to make its connection to Twitter and pull in friends' status data. The behavior of networking calls depends on the type of network connection we have at the moment, the responsiveness of the server, and all sorts of other factors that collectively make up the network latency.

If we run our update operation on the default thread, any delay caused by the network update will cause our user interface to block. This in turn will make our application appear sluggish to the user and may even lead to the Android system offering to kill our application by bringing up the "Force Close or Wait" dialog window, as discussed in "Threading in Android" on page 65.

The best solution to this problem is to put the actual work of the network update in a separate thread. To do this, we can use standard Java threading support, as shown in Example 8-5. The work of a service should often be in a separate thread from the main UI thread, regardless of how little time you expect the service to take. You always need to separate the noninteractive processing from user interaction. When you have network activity, as in Yamba, it's even more important to keep it separate, but the principle applies to any service.

Example 8-5. UpdaterService.java, version 2

```java
package com.marakana.yamba3;

import android.app.Service;
import android.content.Intent;
import android.os.IBinder;
import android.util.Log;

public class UpdaterService2 extends Service {
  private static final String TAG = "UpdaterService";

  static final int DELAY = 60000; // a minute ❶
  private boolean runFlag = false;  // ❷
  private Updater updater;

  @Override
  public IBinder onBind(Intent intent) {
    return null;
  }

  @Override
  public void onCreate() {
    super.onCreate();

    this.updater = new Updater(); // ❸

    Log.d(TAG, "onCreated");
  }

  @Override
  public int onStartCommand(Intent intent, int flags, int startId) {
    super.onStartCommand(intent, flags, startId);

    this.runFlag = true; // ❹
    this.updater.start();

    Log.d(TAG, "onStarted");
    return START_STICKY;
  }

  @Override
  public void onDestroy() {
    super.onDestroy();

    this.runFlag = false; // ❺
```

```
      this.updater.interrupt(); // ❻
      this.updater = null;

      Log.d(TAG, "onDestroyed");
   }

   /**
    * Thread that performs the actual update from the online service
    */
   private class Updater extends Thread {  // ❼

      public Updater() {
         super("UpdaterService-Updater");  // ❽
      }

      @Override
      public void run() { // ❾
         UpdaterService2 updaterService = UpdaterService2.this;  // ❿
         while (updaterService.runFlag) {  // ⓫
            Log.d(TAG, "Updater running");
            try {
               // Some work goes here...
               Log.d(TAG, "Updater ran");
               Thread.sleep(DELAY);  // ⓬
            } catch (InterruptedException e) {  // ⓭
               updaterService.runFlag = false;
            }
         }
      }
   } // Updater
}
```

❶ Specifies the constant for the delay between network updates. We could make this configurable via preferences as well.

❷ This flag helps us know whether the service is currently running.

❸ Updater is the separate thread that performs the actual network update. Because the thread needs to be created only once, we do so in the service's onCreate() method.

❹ When the service is to start, its onStartCommand() method is called. This is also a good place to start our Updater thread and update the flag identifying it as running.

❺ Similarly, onDestroy() is a good place to stop our network update thread and update the flag to show that it is no longer running.

❻ To stop the actual thread from running, we invoke interrupt() on it. We also set it to null to help the garbage collection process clean it up.

❼ This is where we define the Updater class. It is a thread, so it extends Java's Thread class.

❽ The purpose of this is to simply give our thread a name. Having a name helps identify various running threads and aids in debugging.

❾ A Java thread must provide a run() method. This is where the actual work is done.

❿ This simply creates a reference to our service, of which this thread is an inner class.

⓫ This is the loop that keeps this network update going as long as the service is not stopped. Remember that runFlag is set in the service's onStartCommand() and onDestroy() methods.

⓬ The call to Thread.sleep() pauses the execution of this particular Updater thread for some number of milliseconds. Earlier we set our DELAY constant to one minute.

⓭ When we signal interrupt() to a running thread, it will cause an InterruptedExcep tion in the run() method. We handle the exception simply by setting the runFlag to false so the thread doesn't keep trying to run again until it is restarted.

Testing the Service

At this point, you can run the application and start the service. If you observe the logfile, you'll notice that every minute or so the service logs that it ran our job. Also, stopping the service will stop further execution of the job.

Here's the LogCat output of what is going on with our service:

```
D/UpdaterService( 3494): onCreated
D/UpdaterService( 3494): onStarted
D/UpdaterService( 3494): Updater running
D/UpdaterService( 3494): Updater ran
D/UpdaterService( 3494): Updater running
D/UpdaterService( 3494): Updater ran
...
D/UpdaterService( 3494): onDestroyed
```

As you can see, the service was created and started. It also ran couple of times before it finally got destroyed.

Pulling Data from Twitter

We now have a framework and are ready to make the actual connection to the online Twitter-like service, pull the status data, and display that data in our application. Twitter and Twitter-like services offer many different APIs to retrieve our friends' updates. The *jtwitter.jar* library exposes most of them to us via the Twitter class. Perhaps one of the most appropriate methods is getFriendsTimeline(), which returns the 20 most recent posts made over the past 24 hours from the user and her friends.

To use this Twitter API feature, we need to connect to the online service. And to do that, we need the username, password, and root API for our online service. As you recall from the previous chapter, we have already refactored most of this functionality into the YambaApplication object (see "The Yamba Application Object" on page 102). We can reuse all those features here because our service is part of the same application and as such has access to the same `Application` object.

However, we do need to make a minor update to `YambaApplication`, because we would also like to know whether our service is running. To do that, we'll add a flag to `YambaApplication` and provide setter and getter methods to access and update that flag:

```
public class YambaApplication extends Application
  implements OnSharedPreferenceChangeListener {
  private boolean serviceRunning; // ❶
  ...

  public boolean isServiceRunning() { // ❷
    return serviceRunning;
  }

  public void setServiceRunning(boolean serviceRunning) { // ❸
    this.serviceRunning = serviceRunning;
  }
}
```

❶ The flag that indicates whether the service is running. Note that this flag is private to this class, so nobody else can directly access it and change it.

❷ The public method to check the status of the `serviceRunning` flag.

❸ Another public method to set the state of the `serviceRunning` flag.

Now we can write new code for `UpdaterService` and have it connect to the online API to pull the latest status updates from our friends. Example 8-6 shows the final version.

Example 8-6. UpdaterService.java, final version

```
package com.marakana.yamba3;

import java.util.List;
import winterwell.jtwitter.Twitter;
import winterwell.jtwitter.TwitterException;
import android.app.Service;
import android.content.Intent;
import android.os.IBinder;
import android.util.Log;

public class UpdaterService extends Service {
  private static final String TAG = "UpdaterService";

  static final int DELAY = 60000; // wait a minute
  private boolean runFlag = false;
  private Updater updater;
  private YambaApplication yamba; // ❶

  @Override
  public IBinder onBind(Intent intent) {
    return null;
  }
```

```
@Override
public void onCreate() {
  super.onCreate();
  this.yamba = (YambaApplication) getApplication(); // ❷
  this.updater = new Updater();

  Log.d(TAG, "onCreated");
}

@Override
public int onStartCommand(Intent intent, int flags, int startId) {
  super.onStartCommand(intent, flags, startId);

  this.runFlag = true;
  this.updater.start();
  this.yamba.setServiceRunning(true); // ❸

  Log.d(TAG, "onStarted");
  return START_STICKY;
}

@Override
public void onDestroy() {
  super.onDestroy();

  this.runFlag = false;
  this.updater.interrupt();
  this.updater = null;
  this.yamba.setServiceRunning(false); // ❹

  Log.d(TAG, "onDestroyed");
}

/**
 * Thread that performs the actual update from the online service
 */
private class Updater extends Thread {
  List<Twitter.Status> timeline; // ❺

  public Updater() {
    super("UpdaterService-Updater");
  }

  @Override
  public void run() {
    UpdaterService updaterService = UpdaterService.this;
    while (updaterService.runFlag) {
      Log.d(TAG, "Updater running");
      try {
        // Get the timeline from the cloud
        try {
          timeline = yamba.getTwitter().getFriendsTimeline(); // ❻
        } catch (TwitterException e) {
          Log.e(TAG, "Failed to connect to twitter service", e);  // ❼
```

```
        }

        // Loop over the timeline and print it out
        for (Twitter.Status status : timeline) { // ❽
          Log.d(TAG, String.format("%s: %s", status.user.name, status.text)); // ❾
        }

        Log.d(TAG, "Updater ran");
        Thread.sleep(DELAY);
      } catch (InterruptedException e) {
        updaterService.runFlag = false;
      }
    }
  }
 } // Updater
}
```

❶ This variable allows access to the YambaApplication object that contains our shared features, such as a way to read preferences and connect to the online service.

❷ We get the reference to our YambaApplication object by using the getApplication() call.

❸ Once we start the service, we update the serviceRunning flag in the shared application object, YambaApplication.

❹ Similarly, when the service stops, we update the flag in the application object.

❺ We are using Java generics (*http://en.wikipedia.org/wiki/Generics_in_Java*) to define the timeline variable as a List of Twitter.Status instances.

❻ We call getTwitter() in YambaApplication to get the twitter object, and then call getFriendsTimeline() on it to get the last 20 status posts from the past 24 hours. Note that this is the actual method that implements the web service call to our cloud service. As such, it could take some time to complete, depending on the network latency. Because we run this in our dedicated thread, we won't affect the main user interface thread while we wait for the network operation to complete.

❼ A network call can fail for any number of reasons. Here we handle failure by printing the stack trace of what went wrong. The actual printout will be visible in LogCat.

❽ Now that we have initialized the timeline list, we can loop over it. The easiest approach is to use Java's "for each" loop, which automatically iterates over our list, assigning each element in turn to the status variable.

❾ For now, we simply print out the statuses of who said what to the LogCat output.

Testing the Service

Now we can run our application, start the service, and see the list of our friends' statuses in the LogCat:

```
D/UpdaterService(  310): Marko Gargenta: it is great that you got my message
D/UpdaterService(  310): Marko Gargenta: hello this is a test message from my phone
D/UpdaterService(  310): Marko Gargenta: Test
D/UpdaterService(  310): Marko Gargenta: right!
...
```

Summary

We now have a working service, which we start and stop and in a relatively crude, manual way. The service connects to the cloud service and pulls down the status posts from our friends. For now, we just print this data in the LogCat, but in the next chapter we'll insert the data into the database.

Figure 8-3 illustrates what we have done so far as part of the design outlined earlier in Figure 5-4.

Figure 8-3. Yamba completion

The Database

The Android system uses databases to store useful information that needs to be persisted even when the user kills the app or even shuts down the device and powers it back on. The data includes contacts, system settings, bookmarks, and so on.

So, why use a database in a mobile application? After all, isn't it better to keep our data in a cloud where it's always backed up instead of storing it in a mobile device that is easily lost or damaged?

A database in a mobile device is very useful as a supplement to the online world. Although in many cases it is much better to count on the data living in the cloud, it is useful to store it locally in order to access it more quickly and have it available even when the network is not available. In this case, we are using a local database as a cache. This is also how we use it in our Yamba application.

In this chapter, you will learn how Android supports databases. You will learn to create and use a database inside the Yamba application to store our status updates locally. Local data will help Yamba display statuses to the user quickly, without having to wait for the network to provide the data. Our service will run in the background and periodically update the database so that the data is relatively fresh. This will improve the overall user experience of the application.

About SQLite

SQLite is an open source database that has been around for a long time, is quite stable, and is popular on many small devices, including Android. There are couple of good reasons why SQLite is a great fit for Android app development:

- It's a zero-configuration database. That means there's absolutely no database configuration for you as the developer. This makes it relatively simple to use.
- It doesn't have a server. There's no SQLite database process running. It is basically a set of libraries that provide the database functionality. Not having a server to worry about is also a good thing.

- It's a single-file database. This makes database security straightforward, as it boils down to filesystem security. We already know that Android sets aside a special, secure sandbox for each application.
- It's open source.

The Android framework offers several ways to use SQLite easily and effectively, and we'll look at the basic usage in this chapter. You may be pleased to find that, although SQLite uses SQL, Android provides a higher-level library with an interface that is much easier to integrate into an application.

 Although SQLite support is built into Android, it is by no means your only option when it comes to data persistence for your app. You can always use another database system, such as JavaDB or MongoDB, but you'd have to bundle the required libraries with your app and would not be able to rely on Android's built-in database support. SQLite is not an alternative to a full SQL server; instead, it is an alternative to using a local file with an arbitrary format.

DbHelper

Android provides an elegant interface for your app to interact with an SQLite database. To access the database, you first need a helper class that provides a "connection" to the database, creating the connection if it doesn't already exist. This class, provided to you by the Android framework, is called `SQLiteOpenHelper`. The database class it returns is an instance of `SQLiteDatabase`.

In the following subsections I'll explain some of the background concepts you should understand when working with `DbHelper`. I'm not going to explain SQL or basic database concepts such as normalization, because there are hundreds of good places to find that information, and I expect most of my readers already know it. However, this chapter should give you enough to get started, even if your knowledge of databases is spotty.

The Database Schema and Its Creation

A schema is just a description of what's in a database. In our Yamba database, for instance, we want fields for the following information about each tweet we retrieve from Twitter:

created_at
 The date when the tweet was sent
txt
 The text of the tweet

user
> The user who sent the tweet

So each row in our table will contain the data for one tweet, and these four items will be the columns in our schema, along with a unique ID for each tweet. We need the ID so we can easily refer to a tweet. SQLite, like most databases, allows us to declare the ID as a primary key and even assigns a unique number automatically to each tweet for us.

The schema has to be created when our application starts, so we'll do it in the onCreate() method of DbHelper. We might add new fields or change existing ones in a later version of our application, so we'll assign a version number to our schema and provide an onUpgrade() method that we can call to alter the schema.

onCreate() and onUpgrade() are the only methods in our application when we need to use SQL. We'll execute CREATE TABLE in onCreate() to create a table in our database. In a production application, we'd use ALTER TABLE in onUpgrade() when the schema changes, but that requires a lot of complex introspection of the database, so for now we'll use DROP TABLE and recreate the table. Of course, DROP TABLE destroys any data currently in the table, but that's not a problem for our Yamba application. It always refills the table with tweets from the past 24 hours, which are the only ones our users will care about.

Four Major Operations

The DbHelper class offers you a high-level interface that's much simpler than SQL. The developers realized that most applications use databases for only four major operations, which go by the appealing acronym CRUD: create, read (query), update, and delete (*http://en.wikipedia.org/wiki/Create,_read,_update_and_delete*). To fulfill these requirements, DbHelper offers:

insert()
> Inserts one or more rows into the database

query()
> Requests rows matching the criteria you specify

update()
> Replaces ones or more rows that match the criteria you specify

delete()
> Deletes rows matching the criteria you specify

Each of these methods has variants that enhance it with other functions. To use one of the methods, create a ContentValues container and place in it the information you want inserted, updated, etc. This chapter will show you the process for an insert, and the other operations work in similar ways.

So, why not use SQL directly? There are three good reasons why.

First, from a security point of view, an SQL statement is a prime candidate for a security attack on your application and data, known as an SQL injection attack (*http://en.wiki pedia.org/wiki/SQL_injection*). That is because the SQL statement takes user input, and unless you check and isolate it very carefully, this input could embed other SQL statements with undesirable effects.

Second, from a performance point of view, executing SQL statements repeatedly is highly inefficient because you'd have to parse the SQL every time the statement runs.

Finally, the DbHelper methods are more robust and less likely to pass through the compiler with undetected errors. When you include SQL in a program, it's easy to create errors that turn up only at runtime.

Android's database framework only supports prepared statements for standard CRUD operations: INSERT, UPDATE, DELETE, and SELECT. For other SQL statements, we pass them directly to SQLite. That's why we used execSQL() to run the code to CREATE TABLE.... This is OK because that code doesn't depend on any user input, and as such SQL injection is not possible. Additionally, that code runs very rarely, so there's no need to worry about the performance implications.

Cursors

A query returns a set of rows along with a pointer called a *cursor*. You can retrieve results one at a time from the cursor, causing it to advance each time to the next row. You can also move the cursor around in the result set. An empty cursor indicates that you've retrieved all the rows.

In general, anything you do with SQL could lead to an SQL exception because it's code is interacting with a system that's outside of our direct control. For example, the database could be running out of space or somehow corrupted. So, it is a good practice to handle all the SQLExceptions by surrounding your database calls in try/catch blocks.

It's easy to do this using the Eclipse shortcut:

1. Select the code for which you'd like to handle exceptions. Typically this would be most of your SQL calls.
2. In the Eclipse menu, choose Source→Surround With→Try/catch Block. Eclipse will generate the appropriate try/catch statements around your code for the proper exception class.
3. Handle this exception in the catch block. This might be a simple call to Log.e() to pass the tag, message, and the exception object itself.

First Example

So now we're going to create our own helper class to help us open our Yamba database (see Example 9-1). We'll call the class DbHelper. It will create the database file if one doesn't already exist, or it will upgrade the user's database if the schema has changed between versions.

Like many other classes in Android, we usually start by subclassing a framework class, in this case SQLiteOpenHelper. We then need to implement the class's constructor, as well as onCreate() and onUpgrade() methods.

Example 9-1. DbHelper.java, version 1

```java
package com.marakana.yamba4;

import android.content.Context;
import android.database.sqlite.SQLiteDatabase;
import android.database.sqlite.SQLiteOpenHelper;
import android.provider.BaseColumns;
import android.util.Log;

public class DbHelper1 extends SQLiteOpenHelper { // ❶
  static final String TAG = "DbHelper";
  static final String DB_NAME = "timeline.db"; // ❷
  static final int DB_VERSION = 1; // ❸
  static final String TABLE = "timeline"; // ❹
  static final String C_ID = BaseColumns._ID;
  static final String C_CREATED_AT = "created_at";
  static final String C_SOURCE = "source";
  static final String C_TEXT = "txt";
  static final String C_USER = "user";
  Context context;

  // Constructor
  public DbHelper1(Context context) { // ❺
    super(context, DB_NAME, null, DB_VERSION);
    this.context = context;
  }

  // Called only once, first time the DB is created
  @Override
  public void onCreate(SQLiteDatabase db) {
    String sql = "create table " + TABLE + " (" + C_ID + " int primary key, "
    + C_CREATED_AT + " int, " + C_USER + " text, " + C_TEXT + " text)"; // ❻

    db.execSQL(sql);  // ❼

    Log.d(TAG, "onCreated sql: " + sql);
  }

  // Called whenever newVersion != oldVersion
  @Override
  public void onUpgrade(SQLiteDatabase db, int oldVersion, int newVersion) { // ❽
    // Typically do ALTER TABLE statements, but...we're just in development,
    // so:

    db.execSQL("drop table if exists " + TABLE); // drops the old database
    Log.d(TAG, "onUpdated");
    onCreate(db); // run onCreate to get new database
```

```
    }
}
```

❶ Start by subclassing SQLiteOpenHelper.

❷ This is the database filename.

❸ This is the version of our database. The version number is important so that later, when you change the schema, you can provide existing users with a way to upgrade their database to the latest schema.

❹ The following are some database constants specific to our application. It is handy to define these as constants to that we can refer to them from other classes.

❺ We override SQLiteOpenHelper by passing the constants to super and retaining the local reference to the context.

❻ This is the actual SQL that we'll pass on to the database to have it create the appropriate SQL schema that we need.

❼ Once we have our SQL to create the database, run execSQL () on the database object that was passed into onCreate().

❽ onUpgrade() is called whenever the user's database version is different than the application version. This typically happens when you change the schema and release the application update to users who already have older version of your app.

 As mentioned earlier, you would typically execute ALTER TABLE ... SQL statements in onUpgrade(). Since we don't have an old database to alter, we are assuming this application is still in prerelease mode and are just deleting any user data when recreating the database.

Next, we need to update the service in order to have it open up the database connection, fetch the data from the network, and insert it into the database.

Update UpdaterService

Remember that our UpdaterService connects to the cloud and gets the data. So UpdaterService also is responsible for inserting this data into the local database.

In Example 9-2, we update the UpdaterService to pull the data from the cloud and store it in the database.

Example 9-2. UpdaterService.java, version 1

```
package com.marakana.yamba4;

import java.util.List;
```

```java
import winterwell.jtwitter.Twitter;
import winterwell.jtwitter.TwitterException;
import android.app.Service;
import android.content.ContentValues;
import android.content.Intent;
import android.database.sqlite.SQLiteDatabase;
import android.os.IBinder;
import android.util.Log;

public class UpdaterService1 extends Service {
  private static final String TAG = "UpdaterService";

  static final int DELAY = 60000; // wait a minute
  private boolean runFlag = false;
  private Updater updater;
  private YambaApplication yamba;

  DbHelper1 dbHelper; // ❶
  SQLiteDatabase db;

  @Override
  public IBinder onBind(Intent intent) {
    return null;
  }

  @Override
  public void onCreate() {
    super.onCreate();
    this.yamba = (YambaApplication) getApplication();
    this.updater = new Updater();

    dbHelper = new DbHelper1(this); // ❷

    Log.d(TAG, "onCreated");
  }

  @Override
  public int onStartCommand(Intent intent, int flag, int startId) {
    if (!runFlag) {
      this.runFlag = true;
      this.updater.start();
      ((YambaApplication) super.getApplication()).setServiceRunning(true);

      Log.d(TAG, "onStarted");
    }
    return Service.START_STICKY;
  }

  @Override
  public void onDestroy() {
    super.onDestroy();

    this.runFlag = false;
    this.updater.interrupt();
    this.updater = null;
```

```
    this.yamba.setServiceRunning(false);

  Log.d(TAG, "onDestroyed");
}

/**
 * Thread that performs the actual update from the online service
 */
private class Updater extends Thread {
  List<Twitter.Status> timeline;

  public Updater() {
    super("UpdaterService-Updater");
  }

  @Override
  public void run() {
    UpdaterService1 updaterService = UpdaterService1.this;
    while (updaterService.runFlag) {
      Log.d(TAG, "Updater running");
      try {
        // Get the timeline from the cloud
        try {
          timeline = yamba.getTwitter().getFriendsTimeline(); // ❸
        } catch (TwitterException e) {
          Log.e(TAG, "Failed to connect to twitter service", e);
        }

        // Open the database for writing
        db = dbHelper.getWritableDatabase(); // ❹

        // Loop over the timeline and print it out
        ContentValues values = new ContentValues(); // ❺
        for (Twitter.Status status : timeline) { // ❻
          // Insert into database
          values.clear(); // ❼
          values.put(DbHelper1.C_ID, status.id);
          values.put(DbHelper1.C_CREATED_AT, status.createdAt.getTime());
          values.put(DbHelper1.C_SOURCE, status.source);
          values.put(DbHelper1.C_TEXT, status.text);
          values.put(DbHelper1.C_USER, status.user.name);
          db.insertOrThrow(DbHelper1.TABLE, null, values); // ❽

          Log.d(TAG, String.format("%s: %s", status.user.name, status.text));
        }

        // Close the database
        db.close(); // ❾

        Log.d(TAG, "Updater ran");
        Thread.sleep(DELAY);
      } catch (InterruptedException e) {
        updaterService.runFlag = false;
      }
    }
  }
```

```
    }
  } // Updater

}
```

❶ Because we likely need db and dbHelper objects throughout the class, we declare them globally to the class.

❷ Create the instance of DbHelper and pass this as its context. This works because the Android Service class is a subclass of Context. DbHelper will figure out whether the database needs to be created or upgraded.

❸ We need to connect to the online service, get the latest updates, and insert them into the database. getTwitter() in YambaApplication is our lazy initialization of the Twitter object. Then, we call the actual Twitter API call getFriendsTimeline() to get the last 20 statuses from friends posted in the last 24 hours.

❹ Get the writable database so we can insert new statuses into it. The first time we make this call, onCreate() in DbHelper will run and create the database file for this user.

❺ ContentValues is a simple name-value pair data structure that maps database table names to their respective values.

❻ We loop over all the status data that we received. In this case, we are using a Java for-each loop to make the iteration simple.

❼ For each record, we create a content value. We are reusing the same Java object, clearing it each time we start the loop and populating appropriate values for the status data.

❽ We insert the content value into the database via an insert() call to the SQLiteData base object. Notice that we are not piecing together an SQL statement here, but rather using a *prepared statement* approach to inserting into the database.

❾ Finally, remember to close the database. This is important because another activity could be trying to read or write from this shared resource.

We are now ready to run our code and test it to make sure everything works.

Testing the Service

At this point, we can test whether the database was created properly and whether the service has populated it with some data. We're going to do this step by step.

Verify that the database was created

If the database file was created successfully, it will be located in the */data/data/com.marakana.yamba/databases/timeline.db* file. You can use the Eclipse DDMS perspective and File Explorer view to look at the filesystem of the device, or you can use

`adb shell` on your command line, and then run `ls /data/data/com.marakana.yamba/`
`databases/timeline.db` to make sure the file is there.

To use File Explorer in Eclipse, either open the DDMS perspective in the top-right corner of your Eclipse or go to Windows→Show View→Other...→Android→File Explorer. This will open the view of the filesystem of the device you are currently looking at.

So far, you know that the database file is there, but don't really know whether the database schema was created properly. The next section addresses that.

Using sqlite3

Android ships with the command-line tool `sqlite3`. This tool gives you access to the database itself.

To see whether your database schema was created properly:

1. Open up your terminal or command-line window.
2. Type `adb shell` to connect to your running emulator or physical phone.
3. Change the directory to the location of your database file by typing `cd /data/data/`
   `com.marakana.yamba/databases/`.
4. Connect to the database with the `sqlite3 timeline.db` command.

At this point, you should be connected to the database. Your prompt should be `sqlite>`, indicating that you are inside the SQLite:

```
[user:~]> adb shell
# cd /data/data/com.marakana.yamba/databases/
# ls
timeline.db
# sqlite3 timeline.db
SQLite version 3.6.22
Enter ".help" for instructions
Enter SQL statements terminated with a ";"
sqlite>
```

At this point, you can send two types of commands to your SQLite database:

- Standard SQL commands, such as `insert ...`, `update ...`, `delete ...`, and `select ...`, as well as `create table ...`, `alter table ...`, and so on. Note that SQL (*http://en.wikipedia.org/wiki/SQL*) is another language altogether, and as such is not covered in this book. We assume here that you have a very basic knowledge of SQL. Also note that in `sqlite3`, you must terminate your SQL statements with a semi-colon (;).

- `sqlite3` commands. These are commands that are specific to SQLite. You can see the list of all commands by typing `.help` at the `sqlite3>` prompt. For now, we'll just use `.schema` to verify that the schema was created:

```
# sqlite3 timeline.db
SQLite version 3.6.22
Enter ".help" for instructions
Enter SQL statements terminated with a ";"
sqlite> .schema
CREATE TABLE android_metadata (locale TEXT);
CREATE TABLE timeline ( _id integer primary key,created_at integer, source text,
        txt text, user text );
```

The last line tells us that our database table timeline indeed was created and looks like
we expected, with the columns _id, created_at, source, txt, and user.

> New Android developers often execute the sqlite3 timeline.db com-
> mand in a wrong folder, and then wonder why the database table wasn't
> created. SQLite will not complain if the file you are referring to doesn't
> exist; it will simply create a brand-new database. So, make sure you
> are either in the correct folder (/data/data/com.marakana.yamba/data-
> bases/) when you execute sqlite3 timeline.db, or run the command
> specifying the full path to your file: sqlite3 /data/data/com.mara
> kana.yamba/databases/timeline.db.

Now that we have a way to create and open up our database, we are ready to update
the service that will insert the data into the database.

At this point we should be getting the data from the online service as well as inserting
that data in the database. We can also verify that the data is indeed in the database by
using sqlite3.

Database Constraints

When your service runs for the second time, you'll notice that it fails and that you get
many SQLExceptions in the LogCat. You will also notice that it complains about the
database constraint failing.

This happens because we have duplicate IDs. If you remember, we are fetching all the
data from the online service, including the IDs used online. We are then inserting this
in to our local database. But we get the data via the getFriendsTimeline() call, which
returns the 20 most recent posts made in the past 24 hours, and we do this every minute
or so. So, unless you have friends who post more than 20 posts a minute, you'll likely
get duplicates. That means we're attempting to insert duplicate IDs into a database that
is set up with _id as the primary key, which means they must be unique. This fails for
duplicate entries, and that's why the database complains and throws an SQLException.

We could check with the database that there are no duplicates before performing an
insert, but that would mean writing that logic. Since the database is already good at
database stuff, it is more efficient to attempt to insert duplicate entries, fail at it, and
ignore that failure.

To do that, we need to change db.insert() to db.insertOrThrow(), catch the SQL Exception, and ignore it:

```
...
try {
  db.insertOrThrow(DbHelper.TABLE, null, values);  // ❶
  Log.d(TAG, String.format("%s: %s", status.user.name, status.text));
} catch (SQLException e) {  // ❷
  // Ignore exception
}
...
```

❶ Attempts to insert into the database, but if it fails, it throws an exception.

❷ We catch this exception and ignore it. We will improve on this later in the next section.

At this point, our code works, but it's not ideal. There's an opportunity to refactor it further.

Refactoring Status Data

The work we did previously for the UpdaterService is not ideal for supporting our next user of this data: the TimelineActivity. Since TimelineActivity will also need to access the same database and fetch the same data, it would be better if we would share some of the same functionality between the UpdaterService and the TimelineActivity.

In order to do that, we'll create a new Java class, StatusData, and make it the common container for database-related functionality (see Example 9-3). It will be hiding (encapsulating) SQLite in a higher-level class accessible to other parts of the Yamba application. The rest of our app will then just ask for StatusData and will not be concerned with how that data is generated. This is a better design and later will allow us to improve it even further with Content Providers, as explained in Chapter 12.

Example 9-3. StatusData.java

```
package com.marakana.yamba4;

import android.content.ContentValues;
import android.content.Context;
import android.database.Cursor;
import android.database.sqlite.SQLiteDatabase;
import android.database.sqlite.SQLiteOpenHelper;
import android.util.Log;

public class StatusData { // ❶
  private static final String TAG = StatusData.class.getSimpleName();

  static final int VERSION = 1;
  static final String DATABASE = "timeline.db";
  static final String TABLE = "timeline";
```

```java
public static final String C_ID = "_id";
public static final String C_CREATED_AT = "created_at";
public static final String C_TEXT = "txt";
public static final String C_USER = "user";

private static final String GET_ALL_ORDER_BY = C_CREATED_AT + " DESC";

private static final String[] MAX_CREATED_AT_COLUMNS = { "max("
    + StatusData.C_CREATED_AT + ")" };

private static final String[] DB_TEXT_COLUMNS = { C_TEXT };

// DbHelper implementations
class DbHelper extends SQLiteOpenHelper {

  public DbHelper(Context context) {
    super(context, DATABASE, null, VERSION);
  }

  @Override
  public void onCreate(SQLiteDatabase db) {
    Log.i(TAG, "Creating database: " + DATABASE);
    db.execSQL("create table " + TABLE + " (" + C_ID + " int primary key, "
        + C_CREATED_AT + " int, " + C_USER + " text, " + C_TEXT + " text)");
  }

  @Override
  public void onUpgrade(SQLiteDatabase db, int oldVersion, int newVersion) {
    db.execSQL("drop table " + TABLE);
    this.onCreate(db);
  }
}

private final DbHelper dbHelper; // ❷

public StatusData(Context context) {  // ❸
  this.dbHelper = new DbHelper(context);
  Log.i(TAG, "Initialized data");
}

public void close() { // ❹
  this.dbHelper.close();
}

public void insertOrIgnore(ContentValues values) {  // ❺
  Log.d(TAG, "insertOrIgnore on " + values);
  SQLiteDatabase db = this.dbHelper.getWritableDatabase();  // ❻
  try {
    db.insertWithOnConflict(TABLE, null, values,
        SQLiteDatabase.CONFLICT_IGNORE);  // ❼
  } finally {
    db.close(); // ❽
  }
}
```

```
/**
 *
 * @return Cursor where the columns are _id, created_at, user, txt
 */
public Cursor getStatusUpdates() {  // ❾
  SQLiteDatabase db = this.dbHelper.getReadableDatabase();
  return db.query(TABLE, null, null, null, null, null, GET_ALL_ORDER_BY);
}

/**
 *
 * @return Timestamp of the latest status we ahve it the database
 */
public long getLatestStatusCreatedAtTime() {  // ❿
  SQLiteDatabase db = this.dbHelper.getReadableDatabase();
  try {
    Cursor cursor = db.query(TABLE, MAX_CREATED_AT_COLUMNS, null, null, null,
        null, null);
    try {
      return cursor.moveToNext() ? cursor.getLong(0) : Long.MIN_VALUE;
    } finally {
      cursor.close();
    }
  } finally {
    db.close();
  }
}

/**
 *
 * @param id of the status we are looking for
 * @return Text of the status
 */
public String getStatusTextById(long id) {  // ⓫
  SQLiteDatabase db = this.dbHelper.getReadableDatabase();
  try {
    Cursor cursor = db.query(TABLE, DB_TEXT_COLUMNS, C_ID + "=" + id, null,
        null, null, null);
    try {
      return cursor.moveToNext() ? cursor.getString(0) : null;
    } finally {
      cursor.close();
    }
  } finally {
    db.close();
  }
}

}
```

❶ Most of the StatusData code is a direct cut-and-paste from *DbHelper.java*. This is because it now makes sense to make DbHelper an inner class (*http://en.wikipedia.org/wiki/Inner_class*) because DbHelper now exists only in the context of StatusData and is private to it. In other words, outside of StatusData, no other part of the system is concerned with the fact that we are using a database to store our data. That also makes our system flexible, which we will see later with the use of Content Providers.

❷ This is the private and final reference to the dbHelper instance. Making it final (*http://en.wikipedia.org/wiki/Final_(Java)*) ensures that this object is created only once, whichever part of the system requests it first.

❸ The constructor simply constructs a new instance of DbHelper.

❹ We need to expose close() for the dbHelper so users of it close it properly.

❺ This is the new and improved version of the db.insert...() method that we had in DbHelper previously.

❻ We open the database only when we need it, which is right before writing to it.

❼ In this case, we use insertWithOnConflict() and pass SQLiteDatabase.CONFLICT_IGNORE as the final parameter to indicate that when there's a conflict, the exception should be ignored. Remember that we did have a conflict with the duplicate IDs, as explained in "Database Constraints" on page 129.

❽ Notice that we close the database right after we are done. We do this in the finally (*http://en.wikipedia.org/wiki/Exception_handling*) section of our exception handling. This ensures the database is shut down properly, regardless of whether something went wrong. This theme is something we repeat in getLatestStatus CreatedAtTime() and getStatusTextById().

❾ This method simply returns all the statuses in the database, with the latest first.

❿ getLatestStatusCreatedAtTime() returns the timestamp of the latest status in the database. Having a way to determine the newest locally cached status is useful later, to ensure we add only new statuses into the database.

⓫ For a given ID, getStatusTextById() returns the actual text of this status.

Now that we have a new common place to handle status data, we can have it hang off of our common Application object so that any part of the application can access the data easily (see Example 9-4). Consequently, the UpdaterService and TimelineActivity classes are in a has-a (*http://en.wikipedia.org/wiki/Has-a*) relationship to StatusData via the YambaApplication object.

Example 9-4. YambaApplication.java

```
...
private StatusData statusData; // ❶
...

public StatusData getStatusData() { // ❷
  return statusData;
}

// Connects to the online service and puts the latest statuses into DB.
```

```java
// Returns the count of new statuses
public synchronized int fetchStatusUpdates() {  // ❸
  Log.d(TAG, "Fetching status updates");
  Twitter twitter = this.getTwitter();
  if (twitter == null) {
    Log.d(TAG, "Twitter connection info not initialized");
    return 0;
  }
  try {
    List<Status> statusUpdates = twitter.getFriendsTimeline();
    long latestStatusCreatedAtTime = this.getStatusData()
        .getLatestStatusCreatedAtTime();
    int count = 0;
    ContentValues values = new ContentValues();
    for (Status status : statusUpdates) {
      values.put(StatusData.C_ID, status.getId());
      long createdAt = status.getCreatedAt().getTime();
      values.put(StatusData.C_CREATED_AT, createdAt);
      values.put(StatusData.C_TEXT, status.getText());
      values.put(StatusData.C_USER, status.getUser().getName());
      Log.d(TAG, "Got update with id " + status.getId() + ". Saving");
      this.getStatusData().insertOrIgnore(values);
      if (latestStatusCreatedAtTime < createdAt) {
        count++;
      }
    }
    Log.d(TAG, count > 0 ? "Got " + count + " status updates"
        : "No new status updates");
    return count;
  } catch (RuntimeException e) {
    Log.e(TAG, "Failed to fetch status updates", e);
    return 0;
  }
}
```

...

❶ The Yamba application now encapsulates the status data as a private StatusData object.

❷ This object is available to the rest of the application for viewing only via this accessor method.

❸ This is where we moved most of the code from the previous version of the Updater Service. This was the code that was running on the Updater thread, connecting to the online service to get the data, and then saving that data in the database.

We can now simplify the UpdaterService so it uses the refactored code in the YambaApplication to get the latest data (see Example 9-5). Note that most of the Updater's run() method has been moved to YambaApplication's fetchStatusUpdates() method. In addition, the Updater doesn't need any access to the StatusData object, which is totally hidden from it.

Example 9-5. UpdaterService.java

...

```java
private class Updater extends Thread {

  public Updater() {
    super("UpdaterService-Updater");
  }

  @Override
  public void run() {
    UpdaterService updaterService = UpdaterService.this;
    while (updaterService.runFlag) {
      Log.d(TAG, "Running background thread");
      try {
        YambaApplication yamba = (YambaApplication) updaterService
            .getApplication(); // ❶
        int newUpdates = yamba.fetchStatusUpdates(); // ❷
        if (newUpdates > 0) { // ❸
          Log.d(TAG, "We have a new status");
        }
        Thread.sleep(DELAY);
      } catch (InterruptedException e) {
        updaterService.runFlag = false;
      }
    }
  }
} // Updater
```

...

❶ We get the reference to the YambaApplication object, which is readily available to the Android Service and thus our own UpdaterService instance.

❷ We use the newly created fetchStatusUpdates() method in YambaApplication, which now houses most of the functionality that was previously part of this run() method.

❸ One feature of fetchStatusUpdates() is that it returns the number of new records that were fetched. We can use this info for debugging for now, but later will use it for an additional purpose.

Summary

At this point, Yamba can pull the statuses of our friends from the cloud and post them into the local database. We still don't have a way to view this data, but we can verify that the data is there in the database.

Figure 9-1 illustrates what we have done so far as part of the design outlined earlier in Figure 5-4.

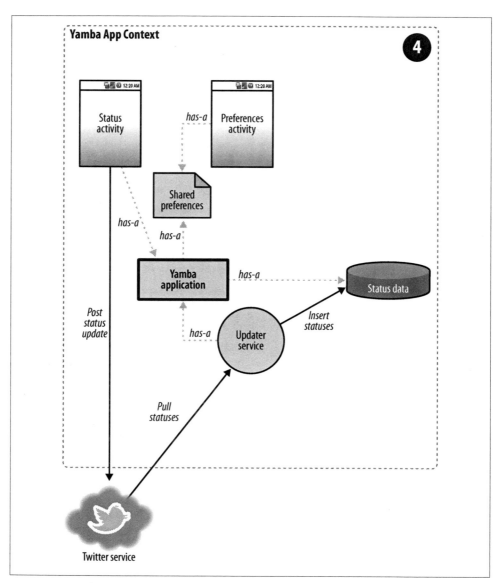

Figure 9-1. Yamba completion

Lists and Adapters

In this chapter, you will learn how to create selection widgets, such as a `ListView`. But this isn't just a chapter about user interface elements. We are deepening our understanding of data from the previous chapter by learning how to read data from the status database and first simply output it to the screen as scrollable text. You will then learn about adapters in order to connect your database directly with the list and create a custom adapter to implement some additional functionality. You will link this new activity with your main activity so that the user can both post and read tweets.

By the end of this chapter, your app will be able to post new tweets, as well as pull them from Twitter, store them in the local database, and let the user read the statuses in a nice and efficient UI. At that point, your app will have three activities and a service.

TimelineActivity

We're going to create a new activity called `TimelineActivity` to display all the statuses from our friends. This activity pulls the data from the database and displays it on the screen. Initially, we do not have a lot of data in the database, but as we keep on using the application, the amount of statuses might explode. Our application needs to account for that.

We are going to build this activity in a few steps, keeping the application whole and complete as we make each improvement:

1. The first iteration of `TimelineActivity` uses a `TextView` to display all the output from the database. Since there may be quite a bit of data, we will use `ScrollView` to wrap our text and provide scroll bars.

2. The second iteration uses the much more scalable and efficient `ListView` and `Adapter` approach. In this step, you will learn how adapters and lists work.

3. Finally, we will create a custom `Adapter` to handle some additional business logic. At this point, we are going under the hood of an adapter and adding custom processing. You'll understand the purpose and usage of adapters better after this exercise.

Basic TimelineActivity Layout

In this first iteration, we are creating a new layout for the `TimelineActivity`. This layout initially uses a `TextView` to display all the data that we have in the database. This is fine initially when we don't have too many statuses to show.

Introducing ScrollView

Since it's unlikely that all our data will fit on a single page, we need a way to scroll the text. To do that, we use `ScrollView`. `ScrollView` is like a window that uses scroll bars to display part of a larger component that takes more space than the screen provides. To make some potentially large views scrollable, you wrap them with this `Scroll View`. For example, we have a printout of friends' statuses in the form of a `TextView`. As more statuses are added, this `TextView` could become large. In order to make it scrollable on a small screen, we put it into a `ScrollView`.

A `ScrollView` can contain only one direct child. If you want to combine multiple views into a single view that scrolls, you first need to organize those views into another layout, like you did previously in "The StatusActivity Layout" on page 52, and than add that layout into the `ScrollView`.

Typically you want `ScrollView` to take all the available space on the screen, so you will specify its layout width and height as `fill_parent`.

A `ScrollView` usually is not manipulated from Java, so it doesn't require an `id`.

In Example 10-1, we wrap our `TextView` with a `ScrollView` so that when there's a lot of text to display, `ScrollView` automatically adds scroll bars.

Example 10-1. res/layout/timeline_basic.xml

```
<?xml version="1.0" encoding="utf-8"?>
<LinearLayout xmlns:android="http://schemas.android.com/apk/res/android"
  android:orientation="vertical" android:layout_height="fill_parent"
  android:layout_width="fill_parent" android:background="@drawable/background">

  <!-- Title ❶ -->
  <TextView android:layout_width="wrap_content"
    android:layout_height="wrap_content" android:layout_gravity="center"
    android:layout_margin="10dp" android:text="@string/titleTimeline"
    android:textColor="#fff" android:textSize="30sp" />

  <!-- Text output wrapper ❷ -->
  <ScrollView android:layout_height="fill_parent"
```

```
      android:layout_width="fill_parent">

      <!-- Text output ❸ -->
      <TextView android:layout_height="fill_parent"
        android:layout_width="fill_parent" android:id="@+id/textTimeline"
        android:background="#6000" />
  </ScrollView>

</LinearLayout>
```

❶ This is the title that we show at the top of this activity's screen. Notice that we defined the `titleTimeline` string resource in the */res/values/strings.xml* file, just like we did before in "Strings Resource" on page 55.

❷ The `ScrollView` that wraps our `TextView` and adds scroll bars as needed.

❸ The `TextView` that shows the actual text, in this case our friends' statuses from the database.

Creating the TimelineActivity Class

Now that we have the layout file, we need to create the `TimelineActivity` class. Just as with any other Java file, go to the Eclipse Package Explorer, right-click on your `com.marakana.yamba` package, choose New→Class, and name it `TimelineActivity`.

And just as before, whenever we create a new Java class that is also a main building block—an activity, service, broadcast receiver, or content provider—we first subclass a base class provided by the Android framework. In the case of activities, that class is `Activity`.

The method we almost universally override in any activity is `onCreate()`. This is a great place for us to initialize the database. The flip side of the coin is `onDestroy()`, a good place to clean up anything that we create in `onCreate()`. In this case, we close the database in `onDestroy()`. Because we'd like the data to be as fresh as possible, we put the code for querying the database and outputting the data in `onResume()`, the method called every time this activity is brought up front. Example 10-2 shows our code.

Example 10-2. TimelineActivity.java, version 1

```
package com.marakana.yamba5;

import android.app.Activity;
import android.database.Cursor;
import android.database.sqlite.SQLiteDatabase;
import android.os.Bundle;
import android.widget.TextView;

public class TimelineActivity1 extends Activity { // ❶
    DbHelper dbHelper;
    SQLiteDatabase db;
    Cursor cursor;
    TextView textTimeline;
```

```
@Override
protected void onCreate(Bundle savedInstanceState) {
  super.onCreate(savedInstanceState);
  setContentView(R.layout.timeline);

  // Find your views
  textTimeline = (TextView) findViewById(R.id.textTimeline);

  // Connect to database
  dbHelper = new DbHelper(this);  // ❷
  db = dbHelper.getReadableDatabase();  // ❸
}

@Override
public void onDestroy() {
  super.onDestroy();

  // Close the database
  db.close(); // ❹
}

@Override
protected void onResume() {
  super.onResume();

  // Get the data from the database
  cursor = db.query(DbHelper.TABLE, null, null, null, null, null,
      DbHelper.C_CREATED_AT + " DESC"); // ❺
  startManagingCursor(cursor);  // ❻

  // Iterate over all the data and print it out
  String user, text, output;
  while (cursor.moveToNext()) {  // ❼
    user = cursor.getString(cursor.getColumnIndex(DbHelper.C_USER));  // ❽
    text = cursor.getString(cursor.getColumnIndex(DbHelper.C_TEXT));
    output = String.format("%s: %s\n", user, text); // ❾
    textTimeline.append(output); // ❿
  }
}
```

}

❶ This is an activity, so we start by subclassing the Android framework's Activity class.

❷ We need access to the database to get the timeline data. onCreate() is a good place to connect to the database.

❸ Once dbHelper opens the database file, we need to ask it for the actual database object. To do that, we can use either getReadableDatabase() or getWritableData base(). In this case, we are only reading the data from the timeline, so we open the database for reading only.

❹ At some point we need to close the database and release that resource. If the database was opened in onCreate(), the counterpart to that would be onDestroy(). So, we close the database there. Remember that onDestroy() is called only when the system has to free up resources.

❺ To query the data from the database, we use the query() method. This method seems to contain almost endless parameters, but most of them map nicely to various parts of the SQL SELECT statement. So this line is equivalent to SQL's SELECT * FROM time line ORDER BY created_at DESC. The various null values refer to parts of the SELECT statement we are not using, such as WHERE, GROUPING, and HAVING. The data returned to us is of type Cursor, which is an iterator (*http://en.wikipedia.org/wiki/Iterator*).

❻ startManagingCursor() is a convenience method that tells the activity to start managing the cursor's life cycle the same way it manages its own. This means that when this activity is about to be destroyed, it will make sure to release any data referred to by the cursor, thus helping Java's garbage collector clean up memory more quickly. The alternative is for us to add code manually in various override methods and worry about cursor management ourselves.

❼ cursor, if you recall from "Cursors" on page 122, represents all the data we received from the database SELECT statement that was effectively executed by our query() method. This data is generally in the form of a table, with many rows and columns. Each row represents a single record, such as a single status in our timeline. Each row also has columns that we predefined, such as _id, created_at, user, and txt. As we mentioned before, cursor is an iterator (*http://en.wikipedia.org/wiki/Iterator*), meaning we can step through all its data one record at a time. The first call to cursor's moveToNext() positions the cursor at the start. moveToNext() stops when there's no more data to process.

❽ For each record that the cursor currently points to, we can ask for its value by type and column index. So cursor.getString(3) returns a string value of the status, and cursor.getLong(1) gives us the timestamp indicating when this record was created. Refer back to Chapter 9 to see how we define strings such as C_USER and C_TEXT in our program that map to column names in the database. However, having hardcoded column indices is not a good practice, because if we ever change the schema, we'll have to remember to update this code. Also, the code is not very readable in this form. A better practice is to ask the database for the index of each column. We do that with the cursor.getColumnIndex() call.

❾ We use String.format() to format each line of the output. Because we chose the TextView widget to display the data, we can only display text, or in other words, formatted strings. In a later iteration of this code, we'll improve on this.

❿ We finally append that new line of output to our text view textTimeline so the user can see it on the screen.

Although this approach works for smaller data sets, it is not optimal or recommended. The better approach is to use a `ListView` to represent the list of statuses stored in the database. `ListView`, which we'll use in the next version of our `TimelineActivity`, is much more scalable and efficient.

About Adapters

A `ScrollView` will work for a few dozen records. But what if your status database has hundreds or even thousands of records? Waiting to get and print them all would be highly inefficient. The user probably doesn't even care about all of the data anyhow.

To address this issue, Android provides adapters. These are a smart way to connect a `View` with some kind of data source (see Figure 10-1). Typically, your view would be a `ListView` and the data would come in the form of a `Cursor` or `Array`. So adapters come as subclasses of `CursorAdapter` or `ArrayAdapter`.

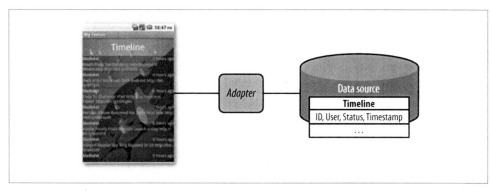

Figure 10-1. Adapter

Adding a ListView to TimelineActivity

As before, our first stop in upgrading our applications is our resources file. We'll add a `ListView` to the timeline layout by editing *timeline.xml*, shown in Example 10-3.

Example 10-3. res/layout/timeline.xml

```
<?xml version="1.0" encoding="utf-8"?>
<LinearLayout xmlns:android="http://schemas.android.com/apk/res/android"
  android:orientation="vertical" android:layout_height="fill_parent"
  android:layout_width="fill_parent" android:background="@drawable/background">
  <TextView android:layout_width="wrap_content"
    android:layout_height="wrap_content" android:layout_gravity="center"
    android:layout_margin="10dp" android:text="@string/titleTimeline"
    android:textColor="#fff" android:textSize="30sp" />

  <!-- ❶ -->
  <ListView android:layout_height="fill_parent"
```

```
      android:layout_width="fill_parent" android:id="@+id/listTimeline"
      android:background="#6000" />

</LinearLayout>
```

❶ Adding ListView to your layout is like adding any other widget. The main attributes are id, layout_height, and layout_width.

ListView versus ListActivity

We could have used ListActivity as the parent class for our TimelineActivity. ListActivity is an activity that has a ListView. Either approach would work, but we chose to subclass Activity and create ListView separately to provide step-by-step, incremental learning.

ListActivity is slightly easier to use in cases where the built-in ListView is the only widget in the activity. ListActivity also makes it very easy to assign an existing array of elements to its list via the XML binding. However, we are using a Cursor for data and not an array (because our data comes from the database), and we do have an additional TextView for the scrollview's title, so the simplicity of ListActivity in this case is outweighed by the customization we require.

Creating a Row Layout

There's one more XML file to take care of. Although *timeline.xml* describes the entire activity, we also need to specify what a single row of data looks like—that is, a single line item on the screen that will show information such as who said what and when.

The easiest way to do that is to create another XML file just for that row. As for any new XML file, we use the Android New XML File dialog window: File→New→Android New XML File. Let's name this file *row.xml* and select Layout for the type.

For this layout, we chose one LinearLayout with two lines arranged vertically. The first line consists of the user and timestamp, and the second contains the actual status message. Notice that the first line uses another LinearLayout to position the user and timestamp horizontally next to each other.

The row of data in the ListView is represented by a custom layout defined in the *row.xml* file, shown in Example 10-4.

Example 10-4. res/layout/row.xml

```
<?xml version="1.0" encoding="utf-8"?>
  <!-- ❶ -->
<LinearLayout xmlns:android="http://schemas.android.com/apk/res/android"
  android:layout_height="wrap_content" android:orientation="vertical"
  android:layout_width="fill_parent">

  <!-- ❷ -->
```

```
<LinearLayout android:layout_height="wrap_content"
    android:layout_width="fill_parent">

    <!-- ❸ -->
    <TextView android:layout_height="wrap_content"
        android:layout_width="fill_parent" android:layout_weight="1"
        android:id="@+id/textUser" android:text="Slashdot"
        android:textStyle="bold" />

    <!-- ❹ -->
    <TextView android:layout_height="wrap_content"
        android:layout_width="fill_parent" android:layout_weight="1"
        android:gravity="right" android:id="@+id/textCreatedAt"
        android:text="10 minutes ago" />
</LinearLayout>

<!-- ❺ -->
<TextView android:layout_height="wrap_content"
    android:layout_width="fill_parent" android:id="@+id/textText"
    android:text="Firefox comes to Android" />

</LinearLayout>
```

❶ The main layout for the entire row. It is vertical because our row consists of two lines.

❷ A layout that runs horizontally and represents the first line of data, namely the user and timestamp.

❸ The user who posted this update.

❹ The timestamp indicating when it was posted. It should be a relative time (e.g., 10 minutes ago).

❺ The actual status.

Creating an Adapter in TimelineActivity.java

Now that we have the XML files sorted out, we are ready to update the Java code, shown in Example 10-5. First, we need to create the adapter. Adapters generally come in two flavors: those that represent array data and those that represent cursor data. Since our data is coming from the database, we are going to use the cursor-based adapter. One of the simplest of those is SimpleCursorAdapter.

SimpleCursorAdapter requires us to describe a single row of data (which we do in *row.xml*), the data (a cursor in our case), and the mapping for a single record of data to the single row in the list. The last parameter maps each cursor column to a view in the list.

Example 10-5. TimelineActivity.java, version 2

```
package com.marakana.yamba5;

import android.app.Activity;
```

```
import android.database.Cursor;
import android.database.sqlite.SQLiteDatabase;
import android.os.Bundle;
import android.widget.ListView;
import android.widget.SimpleCursorAdapter;

public class TimelineActivity2 extends Activity {
  DbHelper dbHelper;
  SQLiteDatabase db;
  Cursor cursor;  // ❶
  ListView listTimeline;  // ❷
  SimpleCursorAdapter adapter;  // ❸
  static final String[] FROM = { DbHelper.C_CREATED_AT, DbHelper.C_USER,
      DbHelper.C_TEXT };  // ❹
  static final int[] TO = { R.id.textCreatedAt, R.id.textUser, R.id.textText };  // ❺

  @Override
  protected void onCreate(Bundle savedInstanceState) {
    super.onCreate(savedInstanceState);
    setContentView(R.layout.timeline);

    // Find your views
    listTimeline = (ListView) findViewById(R.id.listTimeline);  // ❻

    // Connect to database
    dbHelper = new DbHelper(this);
    db = dbHelper.getReadableDatabase();
  }

  @Override
  public void onDestroy() {
    super.onDestroy();

    // Close the database
    db.close();
  }

  @Override
  protected void onResume() {
    super.onResume();

    // Get the data from the database
    cursor = db.query(DbHelper.TABLE, null, null, null, null, null,
        DbHelper.C_CREATED_AT + " DESC");
    startManagingCursor(cursor);

    // Set up the adapter
    adapter = new SimpleCursorAdapter(this, R.layout.row, cursor, FROM, TO);  // ❼
    listTimeline.setAdapter(adapter);  // ❽
  }

}
```

❶ Cursor to all the status updates that we have in the database.

---

❷ `listTimeline` is our `ListView` that displays the data.

❸ `adapter` is our custom adapter, explained in the text that follows this example.

❹ `FROM` is a string array specifying which columns in the cursor we're binding from. We use the same strings already used to refer to columns in our program.

❺ `TO` is an array of integers representing IDs of views in the *row.xml* layout to which we are binding data. The number of elements in `FROM` and `TO` must be the same, so that element at index 0 in `FROM` maps to element 0 in `TO`, and so on.

❻ We get the `ListView` from the XML layout.

❼ Once we have the data as a cursor, the layout of a single row from the *row.xml* file, and the `FROM` and `TO` constants for mapping the data, we are ready to create the `SimpleCursorAdapter`.

❽ Finally, we need to tell our `ListView` to use this adapter.

At this point, `TimelineActivity` is complete, but not yet registered with the manifest file. We'll do that in the next section. However, if we were to run this activity, you'd quickly notice that the timestamp doesn't look quite the way we imagined it.

Remember that we are storing the status creation time in the database as a `long` value representing the number of milliseconds since January 1st, 1970. And since that's the value in the database, that's the value we show on the screen as well. This is the standard Unix time (*http://en.wikipedia.org/wiki/Unix_time*), which is very useful for representing actual points in time. But the value is not very meaningful to users. Instead of showing value `1287603266359`, it would be much nicer to represent it to the user as "10 Minutes Ago." This friendly time format is known as *relative time*, and Android provides a method to convert from one format to the other.

The question is where to inject this conversion. As it stands right now, the `SimpleCursorAdapter` is capable only of mapping straight from a database value to layout view. This doesn't work for our needs, because we need to add some business logic in between the data and the view. To do this, we'll create our own adapter.

TimelineAdapter

`TimelineAdapter` is our custom adapter, shown in Example 10-6. Although `SimpleCursor Adapter` did a straightforward mapping of data in the database to views on the screen, we had an issue with the timestamp. The job of `TimelineAdapter` is to inject some business logic to convert the Unix timestamp to relative time. The method in `SimpleCursorAdapter` that creates a displayable view from input data is `bindView()`, so we'll override that method and ask it to massage the data before it is displayed.

Typically, if you are not sure which method to override, look at the online documentation for the particular system class that you are modifying (in this case, *http://developer .android.com/reference/android/widget/SimpleCursorAdapter.html*).

Example 10-6. TimelineAdapter.java

```java
package com.marakana.yamba5;

import android.content.Context;
import android.database.Cursor;
import android.text.format.DateUtils;
import android.view.View;
import android.widget.SimpleCursorAdapter;
import android.widget.TextView;

public class TimelineAdapter extends SimpleCursorAdapter { // ❶
  static final String[] FROM = { DbHelper.C_CREATED_AT, DbHelper.C_USER,
      DbHelper.C_TEXT }; // ❷
  static final int[] TO = { R.id.textCreatedAt, R.id.textUser, R.id.textText }; // ❸

  // Constructor
  public TimelineAdapter(Context context, Cursor c) { // ❹
    super(context, R.layout.row, c, FROM, TO);
  }

  // This is where the actual binding of a cursor to view happens
  @Override
  public void bindView(View row, Context context, Cursor cursor) { // ❺
    super.bindView(row, context, cursor);

    // Manually bind created at timestamp to its view
    long timestamp = cursor.getLong(cursor
        .getColumnIndex(DbHelper.C_CREATED_AT)); // ❻
    TextView textCreatedAt = (TextView) row.findViewById(R.id.textCreatedAt); // ❼
    textCreatedAt.setText(DateUtils.getRelativeTimeSpanString(timestamp)); // ❽
  }

}
```

❶ To create our own custom adapter, we subclass one of the Android standard adapters, in this case the same `SimpleCursorAdapter` we used in the previous section.

❷ This constant defines the columns of interest to us in the database, as in the previous example.

❸ This constant specifies the IDs of views that we'll map those columns to.

❹ Because we're defining a new class, we need a constructor. It simply calls the parent constructor using `super`.

❺ The only method we override is `bindView()`. This method is called for each row to map its data to its views, and it's where the gist of the adapter work happens. In order to reuse most of the data-to-views mapping provided by `SimpleCursor` `Adapter`, we call `super.bindView()` first.

❻ To override default mapping for the timestamp, we first get the actual timestamp value from the database.

❼ Next, we find the specific `TextView` in the *row.xml* file.

❽ Finally, we set the value of `textCreatedAt` to the relative time since the timestamp. To do this, we use the Android SDK method `DateUtils.getRelativeTimeSpan String()`.

At this point, we can further simplify our `TimelineActivity` class because we moved some of the adapter details to `TimelineAdapter`. Example 10-7 shows this simplified code.

Example 10-7. TimelineActivity.java, version 3

```java
package com.marakana.yamba5;

import android.app.Activity;
import android.database.Cursor;
import android.database.sqlite.SQLiteDatabase;
import android.os.Bundle;
import android.widget.ListView;

public class TimelineActivity3 extends Activity {
  DbHelper dbHelper;
  SQLiteDatabase db;
  Cursor cursor;
  ListView listTimeline;
  TimelineAdapter adapter;  // ❶

  @Override
  protected void onCreate(Bundle savedInstanceState) {
    super.onCreate(savedInstanceState);
    setContentView(R.layout.timeline);

    // Find your views
    listTimeline = (ListView) findViewById(R.id.listTimeline);

    // Connect to database
    dbHelper = new DbHelper(this);
    db = dbHelper.getReadableDatabase();
  }

  @Override
  public void onDestroy() {
    super.onDestroy();

    // Close the database
    db.close();
  }

  @Override
  protected void onResume() {
    super.onResume();

    // Get the data from the database
    cursor = db.query(DbHelper.TABLE, null, null, null, null, null,
        DbHelper.C_CREATED_AT + " DESC");
    startManagingCursor(cursor);
```

```
  // Create the adapter
  adapter = new TimelineAdapter(this, cursor);  // ❷
  listTimeline.setAdapter(adapter); // ❸
}

}
```

❶ We change `SimpleCursorAdapter` to `TimelineAdapter`.

❷ Create a new instance of the `TimelineAdapter`, and pass it the context and the data.

❸ Set our `ListView` to connect to the data via the adapter.

One of the shortcomings of overriding `bindView()` is that we use `super.bindView()` to bind all views first, and then replace its behavior for one particular element. This is somewhat wasteful. The final version of our application in this chapter will optimize the process.

ViewBinder: A Better Alternative to TimelineAdapter

Instead of creating a new `TimelineAdapter` that is a subclass of `SimpleCursorAdapter` and overriding its `bindView()` method, we could attach the business logic directly to the existing `SimpleCursorAdapter`. This approach is more efficient because we are not overriding `bindView()` and we do not require a separate custom adapter class.

To attach business logic to an existing `SimpleCursorAdapter`, use its `setViewBinder()` method. We will need to supply the method with an implementation of `ViewBinder`. `ViewBinder` is an interface that specifies `setViewValue()`, where the actual binding of a particular date element to a particular view happens.

Again, we discovered the `setViewBinder()` feature of this `SimpleCursorAdapter` framework class by reading its reference documentation.

In our final iteration of `TimelineAdapter`, we create a custom `ViewBinder` as a constant and attach it to the stock `SimpleCursorAdapter`, as shown in Example 10-8.

Example 10-8. TimelineActivity.java with ViewBinder

```
...

@Override
protected void onResume() {
  ...
  adapter.setViewBinder(VIEW_BINDER); // ❶
  ...
}

// View binder constant to inject business logic that converts a timestamp to
// relative time
static final ViewBinder VIEW_BINDER = new ViewBinder() { // ❷
```

```
    public boolean setViewValue(View view, Cursor cursor, int columnIndex) { // ❸
      if (view.getId() != R.id.textCreatedAt)
        return false; // ❹

      // Update the created at text to relative time
      long timestamp = cursor.getLong(columnIndex); // ❺
      CharSequence relTime = DateUtils.getRelativeTimeSpanString(view
          .getContext(), timestamp); // ❻
      ((TextView) view).setText(relTime); // ❼

      return true; // ❽
    }

  };

  ...
```

❶ We attach a custom `ViewBinder` instance to our stock adapter. `VIEW_BINDER` is defined later in our code.

❷ The actual implementation of a `ViewBinder` instance. Notice that we are implementing it as an inner class. There's no reason for any other class to use it, and thus it shouldn't be exposed to the outside world. Also notice that it is `static final`, meaning that it's a constant.

❸ The only method that we need to provide is `setViewValue()`. This method is called for each data element that needs to be bound to a particular view.

❹ First we check whether this view is the view we care about, i.e., our `TextView` representing when the status was created. If not, we return `false`, which causes the adapter to handle the bind itself in the standard manner. If it is our view, we move on and do the custom bind.

❺ We get the raw timestamp value from the cursor data.

❻ Using the same Android helper method we used in our previous example, `DateUtils.getRelativeTimeSpanString()`, we convert the timestamp to a human-readable format. This is that business logic that we are injecting.

❼ Update the text on the actual view.

❽ Return `true` so that `SimpleCursorAdapter` does not process `bindView()` on this element in its standard way.

Updating the Manifest File

Now that we have the `TimelineActivity`, it would make sense to make it the "main" activity for our Yamba application. After all, users are more likely to check what their friends are doing than to update their own status.

To do that, we need to update the manifest file. As usual, we'll list `TimelineActivity` within the `<activity>` element in the *AndroidManifest.xml* file, just as we added the preference activity to the manifest file in "Update the Manifest File" on page 88:

```
<activity android:name=".TimelineActivity" />
```

Now, in order to make `TimelineActivity` the main entry point into our application, we need to register it to respond to certain *intents*. Basically, when the user clicks to start your application, the system sends an intent. You have to define an activity to "listen" to this intent. The activity does that by filtering the intents with an `IntentFilter`. In XML, this is within the `<intent-filter>` element, and it usually contains at least an `<action>` element representing the actual intent action we're interested in.

You might have noticed that `StatusActivity` had some extra XML compared to `PrefsActivity`. The extra code is the intent filter block, along with the action that it's filtering for.

There is a special action named `android.intent.action.MAIN` that simply indicates this is the main component that should be started when the user wants to start your application. Additionally, the `<category>` element tells the system that this application should be added to the main Launcher application so that the user can see its app icon along with all the other icons, click on it, and start it. This category is defined as `android.intent.category.LAUNCHER`.

So, to make `TimelineActivity` the main entry point, we simply list it and move the code from the `StatusActivity` declaration over to the `TimelineActivity` declaration, as shown in Example 10-9.

Example 10-9. AndroidManifest.xml

```
<?xml version="1.0" encoding="utf-8"?>
<manifest xmlns:android="http://schemas.android.com/apk/res/android"
  android:versionCode="1" android:versionName="1.0" package="com.marakana.yamba5">
  <application android:icon="@drawable/icon" android:label="@string/app_name"
    android:name=".YambaApplication">

    <activity android:name=".TimelineActivity" android:label="@string/titleTimeline">
      <intent-filter> <!-- ❶ -->
        <action android:name="android.intent.action.MAIN" /> <!-- ❷ -->
        <category android:name="android.intent.category.LAUNCHER" /> <!-- ❸ -->
      </intent-filter>
    </activity>

    <activity android:name=".PrefsActivity" android:label="@string/titlePrefs" />
    <activity android:name=".StatusActivity"
            android:label="@string/titleStatus" /> <!-- ❹ -->

    <service android:name=".UpdaterService" />

  </application>
  <uses-sdk android:minSdkVersion="8" />
```

```
    <uses-permission android:name="android.permission.INTERNET" />
</manifest>
```

❶ `<intent_filter>` registers this particular activity with the system to respond to certain intents.

❷ Tells the system that this is the main activity to start when users start your application.

❸ The category `LAUNCHER` tells the Home application to add this application into the list displayed in the launcher drawer.

❹ `StatusActivity` no longer needs any intent filters.

Initial App Setup

Now when the user runs our application, the Timeline screen will show up first. But unless the user knows she should set up the preferences and start the service, there will be no data and very little hand-holding telling her what to do.

One solution is to check whether preferences exist, and if they do not, redirect the user to the Preference activity with a message telling her what to do next:

```
...
@Override
protected void onCreate(Bundle savedInstanceState) {
  ...
  // Check whether preferences have been set
  if (yamba.getPrefs().getString("username", null) == null) { // ❶
    startActivity(new Intent(this, PrefsActivity.class)); // ❷
    Toast.makeText(this, R.string.msgSetupPrefs, Toast.LENGTH_LONG).show(); // ❸
  }
  ...
}
...
```

❶ We check whether a particular preference has been set. In this case, I've chosen to check `username` because it's likely to be set if any preferences at all are set. Since the preferences do not exist the first time the user runs the application, this means the value of `username` (or any other preference item we choose) will be `null`.

❷ We start the `PrefsActivity`. Note that `startActivity()` will dispatch an intent to the system, but the rest of `onCreate()` will execute as well. This is good because we're likely going to come back to the Timeline activity once we're done setting up preferences.

❸ We display a little pop-up message, i.e., a `Toast`, telling the user what to do. This assumes that you have created the appropriate `msgSetupPrefs` in your *strings.xml* file.

Base Activity

Now that we have a Timeline activity, we need to give it an options menu, just as we did for our Status activity in "The Options Menu" on page 89. This is especially important because the Timeline activity is the entry point into our application, and without the menu, the user cannot easily get to any other activity or start and stop the service.

As one approach, we could copy and paste the code we already have from the Status activity, but that's rarely a good strategy. Instead, we'll do what we usually do: refactor the code. In this case, we can take out the common functionality from the Status activity and place it in another activity that will serve as the base. See Figure 10-2.

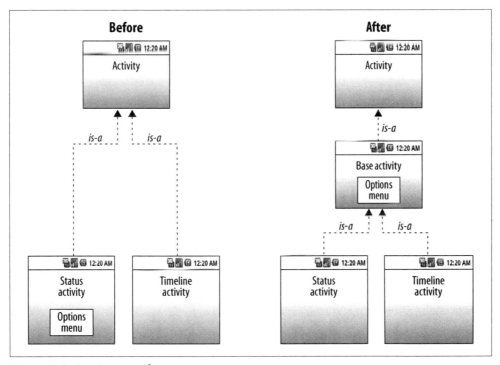

Figure 10-2. BaseActivity refactor

To do that, we'll create a new class called `BaseActivity` and move the common functionality into it. For us, the common functionality includes getting the reference to the `YambaApplication` object, as well as the `onCreateOptionsMenu()` and `onOptionsItem Selected()` methods that support the options menu.

Toggle Service

While we're at it, instead of having Start Service and Stop Service menu buttons, it would be nice to provide just one button that toggles between Start and Stop. To do that, we'll change our menu and add onMenuOpened() to the base activity to dynamically update the title and images for this toggle item.

First, we'll update the *menu.xml* file to include our new toggle menu item, as shown in Example 10-10. At the same time, we'll remove the Start Service and Stop Service items because our toggle feature makes them obsolete.

Example 10-10. res/menu/menu.xml[]

```xml
<?xml version="1.0" encoding="utf-8"?>
<menu xmlns:android="http://schemas.android.com/apk/res/android">

  <item android:id="@+id/itemStatus" android:title="@string/titleStatus"
    android:icon="@android:drawable/ic_menu_edit"></item>
  <item android:title="@string/titleTimeline" android:id="@+id/itemTimeline"
    android:icon="@android:drawable/ic_menu_sort_by_size"></item>
  <item android:id="@+id/itemPrefs" android:title="@string/titlePrefs"
    android:icon="@android:drawable/ic_menu_preferences"></item>
  <item android:icon="@android:drawable/ic_menu_delete"
    android:title="@string/titlePurge" android:id="@+id/itemPurge"></item>

  <!-- ❶ -->
  <item android:id="@+id/itemToggleService" android:title="@string/titleServiceStart"
    android:icon="@android:drawable/ic_media_play"></item>

</menu>
```

❶ This new `itemToggleService` now replaces both `itemServiceStart` and `itemService Stop`.

Next, we need to override onMenuOpened() in the base activity to change the menu item dynamically, shown in Example 10-11.

Example 10-11. BaseActivity.java

```java
package com.marakana.yamba5;

import android.app.Activity;
import android.content.Intent;
import android.os.Bundle;
import android.view.Menu;
import android.view.MenuItem;
import android.widget.Toast;

/**
 * The base activity with common features shared by TimelineActivity and
 * StatusActivity
 */
public class BaseActivity extends Activity { // ❶
  YambaApplication yamba; // ❷
```

```java
@Override
protected void onCreate(Bundle savedInstanceState) {
  super.onCreate(savedInstanceState);
  yamba = (YambaApplication) getApplication(); // ❸
}

// Called only once first time menu is clicked on
@Override
public boolean onCreateOptionsMenu(Menu menu) { // ❹
  getMenuInflater().inflate(R.menu.menu, menu);
  return true;
}

// Called every time user clicks on a menu item
@Override
public boolean onOptionsItemSelected(MenuItem item) { // ❺

  switch (item.getItemId()) {
  case R.id.itemPrefs:
    startActivity(new Intent(this, PrefsActivity.class)
        .addFlags(Intent.FLAG_ACTIVITY_REORDER_TO_FRONT));
    break;
  case R.id.itemToggleService:
    if (yamba.isServiceRunning()) {
      stopService(new Intent(this, UpdaterService.class));
    } else {
      startService(new Intent(this, UpdaterService.class));
    }
    break;
  case R.id.itemPurge:
    ((YambaApplication) getApplication()).getStatusData().delete();
    Toast.makeText(this, R.string.msgAllDataPurged, Toast.LENGTH_LONG).show();
    break;
  case R.id.itemTimeline:
    startActivity(new Intent(this, TimelineActivity.class).addFlags(
        Intent.FLAG_ACTIVITY_SINGLE_TOP).addFlags(
        Intent.FLAG_ACTIVITY_REORDER_TO_FRONT));
    break;
  case R.id.itemStatus:
    startActivity(new Intent(this, StatusActivity.class)
        .addFlags(Intent.FLAG_ACTIVITY_REORDER_TO_FRONT));
    break;
  }
  return true;
}

// Called every time menu is opened
@Override
public boolean onMenuOpened(int featureId, Menu menu) { // ❻
  MenuItem toggleItem = menu.findItem(R.id.itemToggleService); // ❼
  if (yamba.isServiceRunning()) { // ❽
    toggleItem.setTitle(R.string.titleServiceStop);
    toggleItem.setIcon(android.R.drawable.ic_media_pause);
  } else { // ❾
```

```
            toggleItem.setTitle(R.string.titleServiceStart);
            toggleItem.setIcon(android.R.drawable.ic_media_play);
        }
        return true;
    }

}
```

❶ BaseActivity is an Activity.

❷ We declare the shared YambaApplication to make it accessible to all the other subclasses.

❸ In onCreate(), we get the reference to yamba.

❹ onCreateOptionsMenu() is moved here from StatusActivity.

❺ onOptionsItemSelected() is also moved over from StatusActivity. Notice, however, that it now checks for itemToggleService instead of start and stop service items. Based on the state of the service, which we know from the flag in yamba, we request either to start or to stop the updater service.

❻ onMenuOpened() is the new method called by the system when the options menu is opened. This is a good callback for us to implement the toggle functionality. We're given the menu object that represents the options menu.

❼ Within the menu object, we find our new toggle item so that we can update it based on the current state of the updater service.

❽ We check whether the service is already running, and if it is, we set the appropriate title and icon for the toggle item. Notice that here we're setting up the title and icon programmatically using the Java APIs instead of the XML, which we used initially to set up the menu in *menu.xml*.

❾ If the service is stopped, we set the icon and title so that user can click on it and start the service. This way our single toggle button communicates the service's current state.

Now that we have a BaseActivity class, let's update our Timeline activity to use it. Example 10-12 shows what the completed Timeline activity looks like.

Example 10-12. TimelineActivity.java, final version

```
package com.marakana.yamba5;

import android.content.Intent;
import android.database.Cursor;
import android.os.Bundle;
import android.text.format.DateUtils;
import android.view.View;
import android.widget.ListView;
import android.widget.SimpleCursorAdapter;
import android.widget.TextView;
import android.widget.Toast;
```

```
import android.widget.SimpleCursorAdapter.ViewBinder;

public class TimelineActivity extends BaseActivity { // ❶
  Cursor cursor;
  ListView listTimeline;
  SimpleCursorAdapter adapter;
  static final String[] FROM = { DbHelper.C_CREATED_AT, DbHelper.C_USER,
      DbHelper.C_TEXT };
  static final int[] TO = { R.id.textCreatedAt, R.id.textUser, R.id.textText };

  @Override
  protected void onCreate(Bundle savedInstanceState) {
    super.onCreate(savedInstanceState);
    setContentView(R.layout.timeline);

    // Check if preferences have been set
    if (yamba.getPrefs().getString("username", null) == null) { // ❷
      startActivity(new Intent(this, PrefsActivity.class));
      Toast.makeText(this, R.string.msgSetupPrefs, Toast.LENGTH_LONG).show();
    }

    // Find your views
    listTimeline = (ListView) findViewById(R.id.listTimeline);
  }

  @Override
  protected void onResume() {
    super.onResume();

    // Setup List
    this.setupList(); // ❸
  }

  @Override
  public void onDestroy() {
    super.onDestroy();

    // Close the database
    yamba.getStatusData().close(); // ❹
  }

  // Responsible for fetching data and setting up the list and the adapter
  private void setupList() { // ❺
    // Get the data
    cursor = yamba.getStatusData().getStatusUpdates();
    startManagingCursor(cursor);

    // Setup Adapter
    adapter = new SimpleCursorAdapter(this, R.layout.row, cursor, FROM, TO);
    adapter.setViewBinder(VIEW_BINDER); // ❻
    listTimeline.setAdapter(adapter);
  }

  // View binder constant to inject business logic for timestamp to relative
  // time conversion
```

```
static final ViewBinder VIEW_BINDER = new ViewBinder() { // ❼

    public boolean setViewValue(View view, Cursor cursor, int columnIndex) {
      if (view.getId() != R.id.textCreatedAt)
        return false;

      // Update the created at text to relative time
      long timestamp = cursor.getLong(columnIndex);
      CharSequence relTime = DateUtils.getRelativeTimeSpanString(view
          .getContext(), timestamp);
      ((TextView) view).setText(relTime);

      return true;
    }

  };
}
```

❶ For starters, we now subclass our `BaseActivity` instead of just the system's `Activity`. This way we inherit the `yamba` object as well as all the support for the options menu.

❷ This is where we check whether preferences are already set. If not, we'll redirect the user to the Preference activity first.

❸ On resuming this activity, we set up the list. This is a private method, shown later in the code.

❹ When this activity is closed, we want to make sure we close the database to release this resource. The database is opened by the call to `getStatusUpdates()` in the `yamba` application.

❺ `setupList()` is the convenience method that gets the data, sets up the adapter, and connects it all to the list view.

❻ This is where we attach the view binder to the list, as discussed earlier in "View-Binder: A Better Alternative to TimelineAdapter" on page 149.

❼ `ViewBinder` is defined here.

At this point, we've done a lot of the refactoring work on our Timeline activity. We can also simplify the Status activity by cutting out the code related to the options menu. This also helps separate functional concerns among `BaseActivity`, `StatusDate`, and `TimelineActivity`.

Figure 10-3 shows what the final Timeline activity screen looks like.

Figure 10-3. TimelineActivity

Summary

At this point, Yamba can post a new status as well as list the statuses of our friends. Our application is complete and usable.

Figure 10-4 illustrates what we have done so far as part of the design outlined earlier in Figure 5-4.

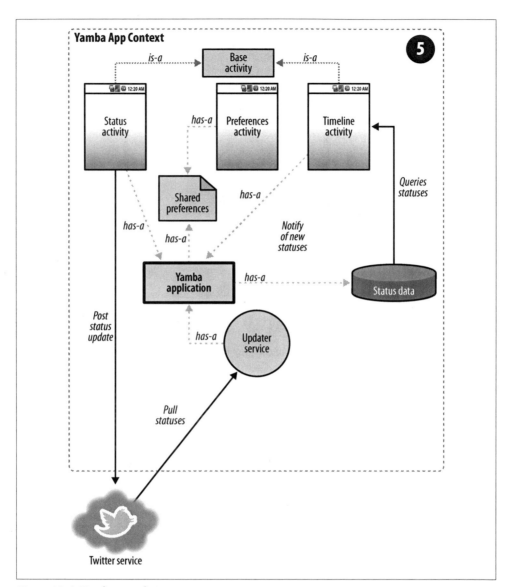

Figure 10-4. Yamba completion

Broadcast Receivers

In this chapter, you will learn about broadcast receivers and when to use them. We'll create a couple of different receivers that illustrate different usage scenarios. First, you'll create a broadcast receiver that will start up your update service at boot time, so that users always have their friends' latest timelines the first time they check for them (assuming their preferences are set). Next, you will create a receiver that will update the timeline when it changes while the user is viewing it. This will illustrate the programmatic registration of receivers and introduce you to broadcasting intents. We'll implement a receiver that is trigged by changes in network availability. And finally, we'll learn how to surround our app with some security by defining permissions.

By the end of this chapter, your app has most of the functionality that a user would need. The app can send status updates, get friends' timelines, update itself, and start automatically. It works even when the user is not connected to the network (although of course it cannot send or receive new messages).

About Broadcast Receivers

Broadcast receivers are Android's implementation of the Publish/Subscribe messaging pattern (*http://en.wikipedia.org/wiki/Publish/subscribe*), or more precisely, the Observer pattern (*http://en.wikipedia.org/wiki/Observer_pattern*). Applications (known as *publishers*) can generate broadcasts to simply send events without knowing who, if anyone, will get them. Receivers (known as *subscribers*) that want the information subscribe to specific messages via filters. If the message matches a filter, the subscriber is activated (if it's not already running) and notified of the message.

As you may recall from Chapter 4, a `BroadcastReceiver` is a piece of code to which an app subscribes in order to get notified when an action happens. That action is in the form of an *intent broadcast*. When the right intent is fired, the receiver wakes up and executes. The "wakeup" happens in the form of an `onReceive()` callback method.

BootReceiver

In our Yamba application, the `UpdaterService` is responsible for periodically updating the data from the online service. Currently, the user needs to start the service manually, which she does by starting the application and then clicking on the Start Service menu option.

It would be much cleaner and simpler if somehow the system automatically started `UpdaterService` when the device powered up. To do this, we create `BootReceiver`, a broadcast receiver that the system will launch when the boot is complete, which in turn will launch our `TimelineActivity` activity. Example 11-1 sets up our broadcast receiver.

Example 11-1. BootReceiver.java

```
package com.marakana.yamba6;

import android.content.BroadcastReceiver;
import android.content.Context;
import android.content.Intent;
import android.util.Log;

public class BootReceiver extends BroadcastReceiver { // ❶

  @Override
  public void onReceive(Context context, Intent intent) { // ❷
    context.startService(new Intent(context, UpdaterService.class)); // ❸
    Log.d("BootReceiver", "onReceived");
  }

}
```

❶ We create `BootReceiver` by subclassing `BroadcastReceiver`, the base class for all receivers.

❷ The only method that we need to implement is `onReceive()`. This method gets called when an intent matches this receiver.

❸ We launch an intent to start our Updater service. The system passed us a `Context` object when it invoked our `onReceive()` method, and we are expected to pass it on to the Updater service. The service doesn't happen to use the `Context` object for anything, but we'll see an important use for it later.

At this point, we have our boot receiver. But in order for it to get called—in other words, in order for the activity to start at boot—we must register it with the system.

Registering the BootReceiver with the AndroidManifest File

To register `BootReceiver`, we add it to the manifest file, shown in Example 11-2. We also add an *intent filter* to this file. This intent filter specifies which broadcasts trigger the receiver to become activated.

Example 11-2. AndroidManifest.xml: <application> section

```
...
<receiver android:name=".BootReceiver">
  <intent-filter>
    <action android:name="android.intent.action.BOOT_COMPLETED" />
  </intent-filter>
</receiver>
...
```

In order to get notifications for this particular intent filter, we must also specify that we're using a specific permission it requires, in this case `android.permission` `.RECEIVE_BOOT_COMPLETED` (see Example 11-3).

Example 11-3. AndroidManifest.xml: <manifest> section

```
...
<uses-permission android:name="android.permission.RECEIVE_BOOT_COMPLETED" />
...
```

 If we don't specify the permission we require, we simply won't be no-tified when this event occurs, and we won't have the chance to run our startup code. We won't even know we aren't getting notified, so this is potentially a hard bug to find.

Testing the Boot Receiver

At this point, you can reboot your device. Once it comes back up, your `UpdaterService` should be up and running. You can verify this either by looking at the LogCat for our output or by using System Settings and checking that the service is running.

To verify via System Settings, at the Home screen, click on the Menu button and choose Settings→Applications→Running Services. You should see `UpdaterService` listed there. At this point, you know the `BootReceiver` did indeed get the broadcast and has started the `UpdaterService`.

The TimelineReceiver

Currently, if you view your Timeline activity while a new status update comes in, you won't know about it. That's because the `UpdaterService` doesn't have a way to notify `TimelineActivity` to refresh itself.

To address this, we create another broadcast receiver, this time as an inner class of `TimelineActivity`, as shown in Example 11-4.

Example 11-4. TimelineActivity.java with TimelineReceiver inner class

```
...
class TimelineReceiver extends BroadcastReceiver { // ❶
  @Override
  public void onReceive(Context context, Intent intent) { // ❷
    cursor.requery(); // ❸
    adapter.notifyDataSetChanged(); // ❹
    Log.d("TimelineReceiver", "onReceived");
  }
}
...
```

❶ As before, to create a broadcast receiver, we subclass the `BroadcastReceiver` class.

❷ The only method we need to override is `onReceive()`. This is where we put the work we want done when this receiver is triggered.

❸ The work we want done is simply to tell the `cursor` object to refresh itself. We do this by invoking `requery()`, which executes the same query that was executed initially to obtain this cursor object.

❹ Notifies the adapter that the underlying data has changed.

At this point, our receiver is ready but not registered. Unlike `BootReceiver`, where we registered our receiver with the system statically via the manifest file, we'll register `TimelineReceiver` programmatically, as shown in Example 11-5. This is because `TimelineReceiver` makes sense only within `TimelineActivity` because purpose is refreshing the list when the user is looking at the Timeline activity.

Example 11-5. TimelineActivity.java with TimelineReceiver

```
...
@Override
protected void onResume() {
  super.onResume();

  // Get the data from the database
  cursor = db.query(DbHelper.TABLE, null, null, null, null, null,
      DbHelper.C_CREATED_AT + " DESC");
  startManagingCursor(cursor);

  // Create the adapter
  adapter = new TimelineAdapter(this, cursor);
  listTimeline.setAdapter(adapter);

  // Register the receiver
  registerReceiver(receiver, filter);   // ❶
}

@Override
protected void onPause() {
  super.onPause();
```

```
// UNregister the receiver
unregisterReceiver(receiver);  // ❷
}
...
```

❶ We register the receiver in onResume() so that it's registered whenever the
TimelineActivity is running. Recall that all paths to the running state go through
the onResume() method, as described in "Running state" on page 29.

❷ Similarly, we unregister the receiver on the way to the stopped state (recall "Stopped
state" on page 30). onPause() is a good place to do that.

What's missing now is the explanation of filter. To specify what triggers the receiver,
we need an instance of IntentFilter, which simply indicates which intent actions we
want to be notified about. In this case, we make up an action string through which we
filter intents, as shown in Example 11-6.

Example 11-6. TimelineActivity.java with update onCreate()

```
...
filter = new IntentFilter("com.marakana.yamba.NEW_STATUS"); // ❶
...
```

❶ Create a new instance of IntentFilter to filter for the com.marakana.yamba.NEW_STA
TUS intent action. Since this is a text constant, we'll define it as such and refer to it
as a constant later on. A good place to define it is the UpdaterService, because that's
the code that generates the events we're waiting for.

Broadcasting Intents

Finally, to trigger the filter, we need to broadcast an intent that matches the action the
intent filter is listening for. In the case of BootReceiver, earlier, we didn't have to do
this, because the system was already broadcasting the appropriate intent. However, for
TimelineReceiver, the broadcast is ours to make because the intent is specific to our
application.

If you recall from Chapter 8, our UpdaterService had an inner class called Updater (see
Example 11-7). This inner class was the separate thread that connected to the online
service and pulled down the data. Because this is where we know whether there are any
new statuses, this is a good choice for sending notifications as well.

Example 11-7. UpdaterService.java with the Updater inner class

```
...
private class Updater extends Thread {
  Intent intent;

  public Updater() {
    super("UpdaterService-Updater");
  }
```

```
@Override
public void run() {
  UpdaterService updaterService = UpdaterService.this;
  while (updaterService.runFlag) {
    Log.d(TAG, "Running background thread");
    try {
      YambaApplication yamba =
          (YambaApplication) updaterService.getApplication(); // ❶
      int newUpdates = yamba.fetchStatusUpdates();   // ❷
      if (newUpdates > 0) { // ❸
        Log.d(TAG, "We have a new status");
        intent = new Intent(NEW_STATUS_INTENT); // ❹
        intent.putExtra(NEW_STATUS_EXTRA_COUNT, newUpdates); // ❺
        updaterService.sendBroadcast(intent); // ❻
      }
      Thread.sleep(60000); // ❼
    } catch (InterruptedException e) {
      updaterService.runFlag = false; // ❽
    }
  }
}
}
...
```

❶ We get the application object to access our common application methods.

❷ If you recall, our application provides fetchStatusUpdates() to get all the latest status updates and populate the database. This method returns the number of new statuses.

❸ We check whether there are any new statuses.

❹ This is the intent we are about to broadcast. NEW_STATUS_INTENT is a constant that represents an arbitrary action. In our case, we define it as com.mara kana.yamba.NEW_STATUS, but it could be any string without spaces. However, using something that resembles your package name is a good practice.

❺ There's a way to add data to an intent. In our case, it would be useful to communicate to others as part of this broadcast how many new statuses there are. In this line, we use Intent's putExtra() method to add the number of new statuses under a key named NEW_STATUS_EXTRA_COUNT, which is just our arbitrary constant.

❻ At this point, we know there's at least one new status. sendBroadcast() is part of Context, which is a superclass of Service and therefore also a superclass of our UpdaterService. Since we're inside the Updater inner class, we have to refer to the parent's updaterService instance in order to call sendBroadcast(). This method simply takes the intent we just created.

❼ We tell this thread to sleep for a minute so that it doesn't overload the device's CPU while checking regularly for updates.

❽ In case this thread is interrupted for some reason, we update this service's runFlag so we know it's not currently running.

`UpdaterService` might send broadcasts even when the `Timeline` `Receiver` is not registered. That is perfectly fine. Those broadcasts will simply be ignored.

At this point, a new status received by `UpdaterService` causes an intent to be broadcast over to the `TimelineActivity`, where the message is received by the `TimelineReceiver`, which in turn refreshes the `ListView` of statuses.

The Network Receiver

With the current design, our service will start automatically at boot time and attempt to connect to the cloud and retrieve the latest updates approximately every minute. One problem with the current design is that the service will try to connect even when there's no Internet connection available. This adds unnecessary attempts to wake up the radio and connect to the server, all of which taxes the battery. Imagine how many wasteful attempts would be made while your phone is in flight mode on a cross-country flight. This highlights some of the inherit constraints when programming for mobile devices: we're limited by the battery life and network connectivity.

A better approach is to listen to network availability broadcasts and use that information to intelligently turn off the service when the Internet is unavailable and turn it back on when data connection comes back up. The system does send an intent whenever connection availability changes. Another system service allows us to find out what changed and act accordingly.

In this case, we're creating another receiver, `NetworkReceiver`, shown in Example 11-8. Just as before, we need to create a Java class that subclasses `BroadcastReceiver`, and then register it via the Android manifest file.

Example 11-8. NetworkReceiver.java

```
package com.marakana.yamba6;

import android.content.BroadcastReceiver;
import android.content.Context;
import android.content.Intent;
import android.net.ConnectivityManager;
import android.util.Log;

public class NetworkReceiver extends BroadcastReceiver { // ❶
  public static final String TAG = "NetworkReceiver";

  @Override
  public void onReceive(Context context, Intent intent) {

    boolean isNetworkDown = intent.getBooleanExtra(
        ConnectivityManager.EXTRA_NO_CONNECTIVITY, false);  // ❷
```

```
    if (isNetworkDown) {
      Log.d(TAG, "onReceive: NOT connected, stopping UpdaterService");
      context.stopService(new Intent(context, UpdaterService.class)); // ❸
    } else {
      Log.d(TAG, "onReceive: connected, starting UpdaterService");
      context.startService(new Intent(context, UpdaterService.class)); // ❹
    }
  }
}
```

❶ As we said before, when you create a new broadcast receiver, you typically start by subclassing Android's own `BroadcastReceiver` class.

❷ When the system broadcasts the particular intent action that this receiver subscribes, the intent will have an extra piece of information indicating whether the network is up or down. In this case, the variable is a Boolean value keyed to the `Connectivity Manager.EXTRA_NO_CONNECTIVITY` constant. In the previous section, we associated a value to a string of our own invention; here we're on the other end of the message, extracting a value from a Boolean. A value of `true` indicates that the network is down.

❸ If the network is down, we simply send an intent to our `UpdaterService`. We now have a use for the `Context` object that the system passed to this method. We call its `stopService()` method, passing the `Intent`.

❹ If the flag is `false`, we know that the network has changed and is now available. So we start our `UpdaterService`, the inverse of our previous stop action.

 Inside an activity or a service, we simply used the methods `start Activity()`, `startService()`, `stopService()`, and so on. This is because activities and services are subclasses of `Context`, and thus they inherited these methods. So, there's an is-a relationship (*http://en.wikipedia.org/ wiki/Is-a*) between them and `Context`. Broadcast receivers, on the other hand have a `Context` object passed into them, and thus have a has-a (*http://en.wikipedia.org/wiki/Has-a*) relationship with the object.

Now that we have created this new receiver, we need to register it with the manifest file, shown in Example 11-9.

Example 11-9. AndroidManifest.xml: <application> section

```
...
<receiver android:name=".NetworkReceiver">
  <intent-filter>
    <action android:name="android.net.conn.CONNECTIVITY_CHANGE" />
  </intent-filter>
</receiver>
...
```

We also need to update our application's permissions (Example 11-10) because the action filter for a network change is protected and requires us to ask the user to grant us this particular permission.

Example 11-10. AndroidManifest.xml: <manifest> section

```
...
<uses-permission android:name="android.permission.INTERNET" /> <!-- ❶ -->
<uses-permission android:name="android.permission.RECEIVE_BOOT_COMPLETED" /> <!-- ❷ -->
<uses-permission android:name="android.permission.ACCESS_NETWORK_STATE" /> <!-- ❸ -->
...
```

❶ Used by our `Twitter` object to connect to the Internet to get and post status updates. We saw this permission already in Chapter 6. Not having this permission will cause our app to crash when it attempts to access the network (unless we catch and handle that network exception).

❷ Required in order to receive broadcasts that the system has booted. As mentioned earlier, if we don't have this permission, we will silently be ignored at boot time and our boot code won't run.

❸ Needed in order to receive network state updates. Just as with the boot receiver, if we don't have this permission, we will be silently passed by when the network state changes.

Adding Custom Permissions to Send and Receive Broadcasts

As discussed in "Updating the Manifest File for Internet Permission" on page 60, an application must be granted permissions to access certain restricted features of the system, such as connecting to the Internet, sending SMS messages, making phone calls, reading the user's contacts, taking photos, and so on. The user has to grant all or none of the permissions to the application at installation time, and it is the job of the application developer to list all the permissions the app needs by adding the <uses-permission> element to the manifest file. So far, we've added permissions to Yamba in order to access the Internet, kick off our boot-time service, and learn about network changes.

But now that we have our Updater service sending a broadcast action to our Timeline receiver, we might want to restrict permission to send and receive that broadcast to our own app. Otherwise, another app, knowing what our action looks like, could send it and cause actions in our application that we didn't intend.

To fill up this security hole, we define our own permission and ask the user to grant it to the Yamba application. Next, we'll enforce both sending and receiving the permissions.

Declaring Permissions in the Manifest File

The first step is to declare our permissions, explaining what they are, how they are to be used, and setting their protection level, shown in Example 11-11.

Example 11-11. Adding permissions to manifest file

```
<manifest>

  ...
  <!-- ❶ -->
  <permission android:name="com.marakana.yamba.SEND_TIMELINE_NOTIFICATIONS"
  <!-- ❷ -->
    android:label="@string/send_timeline_notifications_permission_label"
  <!-- ❸ -->
    android:description="@string/send_timeline_notifications_permission_description"
  <!-- ❹ -->
    android:permissionGroup="android.permission-group.PERSONAL_INFO"
  <!-- ❺ -->
    android:protectionLevel="normal" />

  <!-- ❻ -->
  <permission android:name="com.marakana.yamba.RECEIVE_TIMELINE_NOTIFICATIONS"
    android:label="@string/receive_timeline_notifications_permission_label"
    android:description="@string/receive_timeline_notifications_permission_description"
    android:permissionGroup="android.permission-group.PERSONAL_INFO"
    android:protectionLevel="normal" />

  <!-- ❼ -->
  <uses-permission android:name="com.marakana.yamba.SEND_TIMELINE_NOTIFICATIONS" />
  <uses-permission android:name="com.marakana.yamba.RECEIVE_TIMELINE_NOTIFICATIONS" />

</manifest>
```

❶ This is the name of our permission, which we refer to later both when we request the permission and when we enforce it. In our app, we'll be using the permission to securely send timeline notifications.

❷ Label that will be displayed to the user when she is prompted to grant this permission to our app at installation time. It should be relatively short. Note that we have defined this label in our *strings.xml* resource file.

❸ A description should be provided to offer information about why this permission is needed and how it's going to be used.

❹ The permission group is optional, but it helps the system group your permission with other common permissions in one of the system-defined permission groups *http://d.android.com/reference/android/Manifest.permission_group.html*. You could also define your own group, but that is rarely done.

❺ The permission level, a required value, specifies the severity or risk posed by granting the permission. A "normal" level is the lowest and most basic of the four standard permission levels (*http://developer.android.com/reference/android/R.styleable.html #AndroidManifestPermission_protectionLevel*).

❻ We do the same to define the other permission, which allows us to receive the timeline notifications we are generating.

❼ Once our permissions are defined, we need to ask the user to grant them to the application. We do that via the `<uses-permission>` element, just as we did for the other system permissions we specified earlier.

At this point, we have defined our two custom permissions and have requested them for our application. Next, we need to make sure the sender and receiver both play by the rules.

Updating the Services to Enforce Permissions

Our Updater service broadcasts the intent to the rest of the system once there's a new status update. Because we do not want everyone to receive this intent, in Example 11-12 we ensure that the receiver won't be allowed to receive it unless the receiver defines the right permission.

Example 11-12. Updater in UpdaterService

```
...
private class Updater extends Thread {
  static final String RECEIVE_TIMELINE_NOTIFICATIONS =
      "com.marakana.yamba.RECEIVE_TIMELINE_NOTIFICATIONS"; // ❶
  Intent intent;

  public Updater() {
    super("UpdaterService Updater");
  }

  @Override
  public void run() {
    UpdaterService updaterService = UpdaterService.this;
    while (updaterService.runFlag) {
      Log.d(TAG, "Running background thread");
      try {
        YambaApplication yamba = (YambaApplication) updaterService
            .getApplication();
        int newUpdates = yamba.fetchStatusUpdates();
        if (newUpdates > 0) {
          Log.d(TAG, "We have a new status");
          intent = new Intent(NEW_STATUS_INTENT);
          intent.putExtra(NEW_STATUS_EXTRA_COUNT, newUpdates);
          updaterService.sendBroadcast(intent, RECEIVE_TIMELINE_NOTIFICATIONS); // ❷
        }
        Thread.sleep(DELAY);
      } catch (InterruptedException e) {
        updaterService.runFlag = false;
      }
```

```
      }
    }
  } // Updater
  ...
```

❶ This is the name of the permission that the receiver must have. It needs to be the same as the permission name in the manifest file that we specified previously.

❷ To enforce the permission on the receiver, we simply add it to the sendBroad cast() call as the optional second parameter. If the receiver doesn't have this particular permission granted to it by the user, the receiver won't be notified and will never know that our message just got dropped.

To complete the security in the sending direction, we don't have to do anything to TimelineReceiver. It will be able to receive the permission because the user granted it. But there is a corresponding responsibility on the TimelineReceiver side. It should check that the sender had permission to send the message it is receiving.

Updating TimelineReceiver to Enforce Permissions

Now we will check on the receiver side that the broadcaster is allowed to talk to us. When we register our receiver, we add the broadcast permission that the sender should have, as shown in Example 11-13.

Example 11-13. TimelineReceiver in TimelineActivity.java

```
...
public class TimelineActivity extends BaseActivity {
  static final String SEND_TIMELINE_NOTIFICATIONS =
      "com.marakana.yamba.SEND_TIMELINE_NOTIFICATIONS"; // ❶
  ...
  @Override
  protected void onResume() {
    super.onResume();
    ...
    // Register the receiver
    super.registerReceiver(receiver, filter,
        SEND_TIMELINE_NOTIFICATIONS, null); // ❷
  }
  ...
}
```

❶ We define the permission name as a constant. This needs to be the same name as the one we declared for this permission in the manifest file.

❷ In the onResume() method where we register our TimelineReceiver, we now add a parameter specifying this permission is a requirement for anyone who wants to send us this type of broadcast.

We now have a pair of custom permissions, and we are enforcing them in both the sender and the receiver of the broadcast. This illustrates some of the capabilities of Android to fine-tune the permission system.

Summary

Yamba is now complete and ready for prime time. Our application can now send status updates to our online service, get the latest statuses from our friends, start automatically at boot time, and refresh the display when a new status is received.

Figure 11-1 illustrates what we have done so far as part of the design outlined earlier in Figure 5-4.

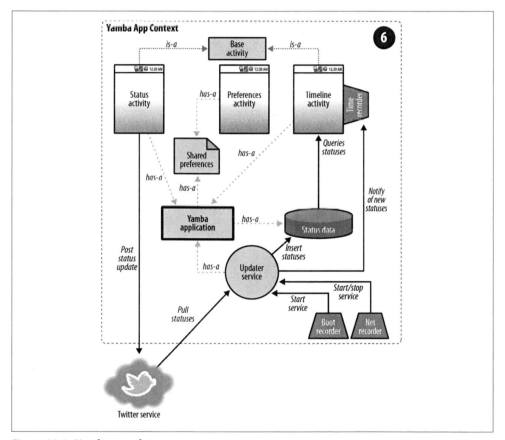

Figure 11-1. Yamba completion

Content Providers

Content providers are Android building blocks that can expose data across the boundaries between application sandboxes. As you recall, each application in Android runs in its own process with its own permissions. This means that an application cannot see another app's data. But sometimes you want to share data across applications. This is where content providers become very useful.

Take your contacts, for example. You might have a large database of contacts on your device, which you can view via the Contacts app as well as via the Dialer app. Some devices, such as HTC Android models, might even have multiple versions of the Contacts and Dialer apps. It would not make a lot of sense to have similar data live in multiple databases.

Content providers let you centralize content in one place and have many different applications access it as needed. In the case of the contacts on your phone, there is actually a ContactProvider application that contains a content provider, and other applications access the data via this interface. The interface itself is fairly simple: it has the same `insert()`, `update()`, `delete()`, and `query()` methods we saw in Chapter 9.

Android uses content providers quite a bit internally. In addition to contacts, your settings represent another example, as do all your bookmarks. All the media in the system is also registered with MediaStore, a content provider that dispenses images, music, and videos in your device.

Creating a Content Provider

To create a content provider:

1. Create a new Java class that subclasses the system's `ContentProvider` class.
2. Declare your `CONTENT_URI`.
3. Implement all the unimplemented methods, such as `insert()`, `update()`, `delete()`, `query()`, `getID()`, and `getType()`.
4. Declare your content provider in the *AndroidManifest.xml* file.

We are going to start by creating a brand-new Java class in the same package as all other classes. Its name will be `StatusProvider`. This class, like any of Android's main building blocks, will subclass an Android framework class, in this case `ContentProvider`.

In Eclipse, select your package, click on File→New→Java Class, and enter "StatusProvider". Then, update the class to subclass `ContentProvider`, and organize the imports (Ctrl-Shift-O) to import the appropriate Java packages. The result should look like this:

```
package com.marakana.yamba7;

import android.content.ContentProvider;

public class StatusProvider extends ContentProvider {

}
```

Of course, this code is now broken because we need to provide implementations for many of its methods. The easiest way to do that is to click on the class name and choose "Add unimplemented methods" from the list of quick fixes. Eclipse will then create stubs, or templates, of the missing methods.

Defining the URI

Objects within a single app share an address space, so they can refer to each other simply by variable names. But objects in different apps don't recognize the different address spaces, so they need some other mechanism to find each other. Android uses a Uniform Resource Identifier (*http://en.wikipedia.org/wiki/Uniform_Resource_Identifier*), a string that identifies a specific resource, to locate a content provider. A URI has three or four parts, shown in Example 12-1.

Example 12-1. Parts of a URI

```
content://com.marakana.yamba.statusprovider/status/47
   A              B                          C    D
```

- Part A, `content://`, is always set to this value. This is written in stone.
- Part B, `com.marakana.yamba.provider`, is the so-called *authority*. It is typically the name of the class, all in lowercase. This authority must match the authority that we specify for this provider when we later declare it in the manifest file.
- Part C, `status`, indicates the type of data that this particular provider provides. It could contain any number of *segments* separated with a slash, including none at all.
- Part D, `47`, is an optional ID for the specific item that we are referencing. If not set, the URI will represent the entire set. Number 47 is an arbitrary number picked for this example.

Sometimes you need to refer to the content provider in its entirety, and sometimes to only one of the items of data it contains. If you refer to it in its entirety, you leave off

Part D; otherwise, you include that part to identify one item within the content provider. Actually, since we have only one table, we do not need Part C of the URI.

One way to define the constants for our example is like this:

```
public static final Uri CONTENT_URI = Uri
    .parse("content://com.marakana.yamba7.statusprovider");
public static final String SINGLE_RECORD_MIME_TYPE =
    "vnd.android.cursor.item/vnd.marakana.yamba.status";
public static final String MULTIPLE_RECORDS_MIME_TYPE =
    "vnd.android.cursor.dir/vnd.marakana.yamba.mstatus";
```

In "Getting the Data Type" on page 180, we'll explore the reason for two MIME types. We are also going to define the status data object in a class-global variable so that we can refer to it:

```
StatusData statusData;
```

We'll be using the status data object all over our app because all our database connectivity is centralized in that class. So now the StatusProvider class has a reference to an object of class StatusData.

Inserting Data

To insert a record into a database via the content provider interface, we need to override the insert() method. The caller provides the URI of this content provider (without an ID) and the values to be inserted. A successful call to insert the new record returns the ID for that record. We end by returning a new URI concatenating the provider's URI with the ID we just got back:

```
@Override
public Uri insert(Uri uri, ContentValues values) {
  SQLiteDatabase db = statusData.dbHelper.getWritableDatabase(); // ❶
  try {
    long id = db.insertOrThrow(StatusData.TABLE, null, values); // ❷
    if (id == -1) {
      throw new RuntimeException(String.format(
          "%s: Failed to insert [%s] to [%s] for unknown reasons.", TAG,
          values, uri)); // ❸
    } else {
      return ContentUris.withAppendedId(uri, id); // ❹
    }
  } finally {
    db.close(); // ❺
  }
}
```

❶ We need to open the database for writing.

❷ We attempt to insert the values into the database and, upon a successful insert, receive the ID of the new record from the database.

❸ If anything fails during the insert, the database will return -1. We can than throw a runtime exception because this is an error that should never have happened.

❹ If the insert was successful, we use the `ContentUris.withAppendedId()` helper method to craft a new URI containing the ID of the new record appended to the standard provider's URI.

❺ We need to close the database no matter what, so a `finally` block is a good place to do that.

Updating Data

To update the data via the Content Provider API, we need:

The URI of the provider
> This may or may not contain an ID. If it does, the ID indicates the specific record that needs to be updated, and we can ignore the selection. If the ID is not specified, it means that we are updating many records and need the selection to indicate which are to be changed.

The values to be updated
> The format of this parameter is a set of name/value pairs that represent column names and new values.

Any selection and arguments that go with it
> These together make up a `WHERE` clause in SQL, selecting the records that will change. The selection and its arguments are omitted when there is an ID, because the ID is enough to select the record that is being updated.

The code that handles both types of update—by ID and by selection—can be as follows:

```
@Override
public int update(Uri uri, ContentValues values, String selection,
    String[] selectionArgs) {
  long id = this.getId(uri); // ❶
  SQLiteDatabase db = statusData.dbHelper.getWritableDatabase(); // ❷
  try {
    if (id < 0) {
      return db.update(StatusData.TABLE, values, selection, selectionArgs); // ❸
    } else {
      return db.update(StatusData.TABLE, values,
                  StatusData.C_ID + "=" + id, null); // ❹
    }
  } finally {
    db.close(); // ❺
  }
}
```

❶ We use the local helper method `getId()` to extract the ID from the URI. If no ID is present, this method returns -1. `getId()` will be defined later in this chapter.

❷ We need to open the database for writing the updates.

❸ If there's no ID, that means we're simply updating all the database records that match the `selection` and `selectionArgs` constraints.

❹ If an ID is present, we are using that ID as the only part of the WHERE clause to limit the single record that we're updating.

❺ Don't forget to close the database.

Deleting Data

Deleting data is similar to updating data. The URI may or may not contain the ID of the particular record to delete:

```
@Override
public int delete(Uri uri, String selection, String[] selectionArgs) {
  long id = this.getId(uri); // ❶
  SQLiteDatabase db = statusData.dbHelper.getWritableDatabase(); // ❷
  try {
    if (id < 0) {
      return db.delete(StatusData.TABLE, selection, selectionArgs); // ❸
    } else {
      return db.delete(StatusData.TABLE, StatusData.C_ID + "=" + id, null); // ❹
    }

  } finally {
    db.close(); // ❺
  }
}
```

❶ The getId() helper method extracts the ID from the URI that we get. If no ID is present, this method returns -1.

❷ We need to open the database for writing the updates.

❸ If there's no ID, we simply delete all the database records that match the selection and selectionArgs constraints.

❹ If an ID is present, we use that ID as the only part of the WHERE clause to limit the operation to the single record the user wants to delete.

❺ Don't forget to close the database.

Querying Data

To query the data via a content provider, we override the query() method. This method has a long list of parameters, but usually we just forward most of them to the database call with the same name:

```
@Override
public Cursor query(Uri uri, String[] projection, String selection,
    String[] selectionArgs, String sortOrder) {
  long id = this.getId(uri); // ❶
  SQLiteDatabase db = statusData.dbHelper.getReadableDatabase(); // ❷
```

```
      if (id < 0) {
        return db.query(StatusData.TABLE, projection, selection, selectionArgs, null,
            null, sortOrder); // ❸
      } else {
        return db.query(StatusData.TABLE, projection,
            StatusData.C_ID + "=" + id, null, null, null, null); // ❹
      }
    }
```

❶ The getId() helper method extracts the ID from the URI that we get.

❷ We need to open the database, in this case just for reading.

❸ If there's no ID, we simply forward what we got for the content provider to the equivalent database call. Note that the database call has two additional parameters that correspond to the SQL GROUPING and HAVING components. Because content providers do not support this feature, we simply pass in null.

❹ If an ID is present, we use that ID as the WHERE clause to limit what record to return.

 We do not close the database here, because closing the database will destroy the cursor and we still need it on the receiving end to go over the data returned by the query. One way to handle the cursor is to have the receiver manage it. Activities have a simple startManagingCursor() method for this purpose.

Getting the Data Type

A content provider must return the MIME type (*http://en.wikipedia.org/wiki/MIME*) of the data it is returning. The MIME type indicates either a single item or all the records for the given URI. Earlier in this chapter we defined the single-record MIME type as vnd.android.cursor.item/vnd.marakana.yamba.status and the directory of all statuses as vnd.android.cursor.dir/vnd.marakana.yamba.status. To let others retrieve the MIME type, we must define the call getType().

The first part of the MIME type is either vnd.android.cursor.item or vnd.android .cursor.dir, depending on whether the type represents a specific item or all items for the given URI. The second part, vnd.marakana.yamba.status or vnd.marakana .yamba.mstatus for our app, is a combination of the constant vnd followed by your company or app name and the actual content type.

As you may recall, the URI can end with a number. If it does, that number is the ID of the specific record. If it doesn't, the URI refers to the entire collection.

The following source shows the implementation of getType() as well as the getId() helper method that we've already used several times:

```
    @Override
    public String getType(Uri uri) {
      return this.getId(uri) < 0 ? MULTIPLE_RECORDS_MIME_TYPE
```

```
        : SINGLE_RECORD_MIME_TYPE;   // ❶
    }

    private long getId(Uri uri) {
      String lastPathSegment = uri.getLastPathSegment();  // ❷
      if (lastPathSegment != null) {
        try {
          return Long.parseLong(lastPathSegment);  // ❸
        } catch (NumberFormatException e) { // ❹
          // at least we tried
        }
      }
      return -1;   // ❺
    }
```

❶ getType() uses the helper method getId() to determine whether the URI has an ID part. If it does not—as indicated by a negative return value—we return vnd.android.cursor.dir/vnd.marakana.yamba.status for the MIME type. Otherwise, we're referring to a single record and the MIME type is vnd.android.cursor.item/vnd.marakana.yamba.status. Of course, we previously defined these values as class constants.

❷ To extract the ID in our implementation of getId(), we take the last part of the URI.

❸ If that last part is not null, we try to parse it as a long and return it.

❹ It could be that the last part is not a number at all, in which case the parse will fail.

❺ We return -1 to indicate that the given URI doesn't contain a valid ID.

Updating the Android Manifest File

As with any major building block, we want to define our content provider in the Android manifest XML file. Notice that in this case the android:authorities property specifies the URI authority permitted to access this content provider. Typically, this authority would be your content provider class—which we use here—or your package:

```
<application>
  ...
  <provider android:name=".StatusProvider"
    android:authorities="com.marakana.yamba7.statusprovider" />
  ...
</application>
```

At this point our content provider is complete, and we are ready to use it in other building blocks of Yamba. But since our application already centralizes all data access in a StatusData object that is readily accessible via YambaApplication, we don't really have a good use for this content provider within the same application. Besides, content providers mostly make sense when we want to expose the data to another application.

Using Content Providers Through Widgets

As mentioned before, content providers make the most sense when you want to expose the data to other applications. It is a good practice to always think of your application as part of a larger Android ecosystem and, as such, a potential provider of useful data to other applications.

To demonstrate how content providers can be useful, we'll create a Home screen widget. We're not using the term *widget* here as a synonym for Android's View class, but as a useful embedded service offered by the Home screen.

Android typically ships with a few Home screen widgets. You can access them by going to your Home screen, long-pressing on it to pull up an Add to Home Screen dialog, and choosing Widgets. Widgets that come with Android include Alarm Clock, Picture Frame, Power Controls, Music, and Search. Our goal is to create our own Yamba widget that the user will be able to add to the Home screen.

The Yamba widget will be simple, displaying just the latest status update. To create it, we'll make a new YambaWidget class that subclasses AppWidgetProviderInfo. We'll also have to register the widget with the manifest file.

Implementing the YambaWidget class

YambaWidget is the main class for our widget. It is a subclass of AppWidgetProvider, a special system class that makes widgets. This class itself is a subclass of Broadcast Receiver, so our Yamba widget is a broadcast receiver automatically. Basically, whenever our widget is updated, deleted, enabled, or disabled, we'll get a broadcast intent with that information. So this class inherits the onUpdate(), onDeleted(), onEnabled(), onDisabled(), and onReceive() callbacks. We can override any of these, but typically we care mostly about the updates and general broadcasts we receive.

Now that we understand the overall design of the widget framework, Example 12-2 shows how we implement it.

Example 12-2. YambaWidget.java

```
package com.marakana.yamba7;

import android.app.PendingIntent;
import android.appwidget.AppWidgetManager;
import android.appwidget.AppWidgetProvider;
import android.content.ComponentName;
import android.content.Context;
import android.content.Intent;
import android.database.Cursor;
import android.text.format.DateUtils;
import android.util.Log;
import android.widget.RemoteViews;

public class YambaWidget extends AppWidgetProvider { // ❶
```

```java
private static final String TAG = YambaWidget.class.getSimpleName();

@Override
public void onUpdate(Context context, AppWidgetManager appWidgetManager,
    int[] appWidgetIds) { // ❷
  Cursor c = context.getContentResolver().query(StatusProvider.CONTENT_URI,
    null, null, null, null); // ❸
  try {
    if (c.moveToFirst()) { // ❹
      CharSequence user = c.getString(c.getColumnIndex(StatusData.C_USER)); // ❺
      CharSequence createdAt = DateUtils.getRelativeTimeSpanString(context, c
          .getLong(c.getColumnIndex(StatusData.C_CREATED_AT)));
      CharSequence message = c.getString(c.getColumnIndex(StatusData.C_TEXT));

      // Loop through all instances of this widget
      for (int appWidgetId : appWidgetIds) { // ❻
        Log.d(TAG, "Updating widget " + appWidgetId);
        RemoteViews views = new RemoteViews(context.getPackageName(),
            R.layout.yamba_widget); // ❼
        views.setTextViewText(R.id.textUser, user); // ❽
        views.setTextViewText(R.id.textCreatedAt, createdAt);
        views.setTextViewText(R.id.textText, message);
        views.setOnClickPendingIntent(R.id.yamba_icon, PendingIntent
            .getActivity(context, 0, new Intent(context,
                TimelineActivity.class), 0));
        appWidgetManager.updateAppWidget(appWidgetId, views); // ❾
      }
    } else {
      Log.d(TAG, "No data to update");
    }
  } finally {
    c.close(); // ❿
  }
  Log.d(TAG, "onUpdated");
}

@Override
public void onReceive(Context context, Intent intent) { // ⓫
  super.onReceive(context, intent);
  if (intent.getAction().equals(UpdaterService.NEW_STATUS_INTENT)) { // ⓬
    Log.d(TAG, "onReceived detected new status update");
    AppWidgetManager appWidgetManager = AppWidgetManager.getInstance(context); // ⓭
    this.onUpdate(context, appWidgetManager, appWidgetManager
        .getAppWidgetIds(new ComponentName(context, YambaWidget.class))); // ⓮
  }
}
}
```

❶ As mentioned before, our widget is a subclass of `AppWidgetProvider`, which itself is a `BroadcastReceiver`.

❷ This method is called whenever our widget is to be updated, so it's where we'll implement the main functionality of the widget. When we register the widget with the system in the manifest file later, we'll specify the update frequency we'd like. In our case, this method will be called about every 30 minutes.

❸ We finally get to use our content provider. The whole purpose of this widget in this chapter is to illustrate how to use the StatusProvider that we created earlier. As you saw earlier when we implemented the content provider, its API is quite similar to the SQLite database API. The main difference is that instead of passing a table name to a database object, we're passing a content URI to the ContentResolver. We still get back the very same Cursor object as we did with databases in Chapter 9.

❹ In this particular example, we care only about the very latest status update from the online service. So we position the cursor to the first element. If one exists, it's our latest status update.

❺ In the next few of lines of code, we extract data from the cursor object and store it in local variables.

❻ Since the user could have multiple Yamba widgets installed, we need to loop through them and update them all. We don't particularly care about the specific appWidgetId because we're doing identical work to update every instance of the Yamba widget. The appWidgetId becomes an opaque handle we use to access each widget in turn.

❼ The actual view representing our widget is in another process. To be precise, our widget is running inside the Home application, which acts as its host and is the process we are updating. Hence the RemoteViews constructor. The RemoteViews framework is a special shared memory system designed specifically for widgets.

❽ Once we have the reference to our widget views' Java memory space in another process, we can update those views. In this case, we're setting the status data in the row that represents our widget.

❾ Once we update the remote views, the AppWidgetManager call to updateAppWidget() actually posts a message telling the system to update our widget. This will happen asynchronously, but shortly after onUpdate() completes.

❿ Regardless of whether the StatusProvider found a new status, we release the data that we might have gotten from the content provider. This is just a good practice.

⓫ The call to onReceive() is not necessary in a typical widget. But since a widget is a broadcast receiver, and since our Updater service does send a broadcast when we get a new status update, this method is a good opportunity to invoke onUpdate() and get the latest status data updated on the widget.

⓬ We check whether the intent was for the new status broadcast.

⓭ If it was, we get the instance of AppWidgetManager for this context.

⓮ We then invoke onUpdate().

At this point, we have coded the Yamba widget, and as a receiver, it will be notified periodically or when there are new updates, and it will loop through all instances of this widget on the Home screen and update them.

Next, we need to set up the layout for our widget.

Creating the XML Layout

The layout for the widget is fairly straightforward. Note that we're reusing our existing *row.xml* file that displays status data properly in the Timeline activity. In Example 12-3, we just include it along with a little title and an icon to make it look good on the Home screen.

Example 12-3. res/layout/yamba_widget.xml

```
<?xml version="1.0" encoding="utf-8"?>
  <!-- ❶ -->
<LinearLayout xmlns:android="http://schemas.android.com/apk/res/android"
  android:layout_height="wrap_content" android:layout_width="fill_parent"
  android:background="@color/edit_text_background"
  android:layout_margin="5dp" android:padding="5dp">
  <!-- ❷ -->
  <ImageView android:layout_width="wrap_content" android:src="@drawable/icon"
    android:layout_height="fill_parent" android:id="@+id/yamba_icon"
    android:clickable="true" />
  <!-- ❸ -->
  <include layout="@layout/row" />
</LinearLayout>
```

❶ We're using LinearLayout to hold our widget together. It runs horizontally, with the icon on the left and the status data on the right.

❷ This is our standard Yamba icon.

❸ Notice the use of the `<include>` element. This is how we include our existing *row.xml* into this layout so we don't have to duplicate the code.

This layout is simple enough, but it does the job for our particular needs. Next, we need to define some basic information about this widget and its behavior.

Creating the AppWidgetProviderInfo File

The XML file shown in Example 12-4 is responsible for describing the widget. It typically specifies which layout this widget uses, how frequently it should be updated by the system, and its size.

Example 12-4. res/xml/yamba_widget_info.xml

```
<?xml version="1.0" encoding="utf-8"?>
<appwidget-provider xmlns:android="http://schemas.android.com/apk/res/android"
  android:initialLayout="@layout/yamba_widget" android:minWidth="294dp"
```

```
android:minHeight="72dp" android:label="@string/msgLastTimelineUpdate"
android:updatePeriodMillis="1800000" />
```

In this case we specify that we'd like to have our widget updated every 30 minutes or
so (1,800,000 milliseconds). Here, we also specify the layout to use, the title of this
widget, and its size.

Updating the Manifest File

Finally, we need to update the manifest file and register the widget:

```
...
<application .../>
  ...
  <receiver android:name=".YambaWidget"
            android:label="@string/msgLastTimelineUpdate">
    <intent-filter>
      <action android:name="android.appwidget.action.APPWIDGET_UPDATE" />
    </intent-filter>
    <intent-filter>
      <action android:name="com.marakana.yamba.NEW_STATUS" />
    </intent-filter>
    <meta-data android:name="android.appwidget.provider"
      android:resource="@xml/yamba_widget_info" />
  </receiver>
  ...
</application>
...
```

Notice that the widget is a receiver, as we mentioned before. So, just like other broadcast
receivers, we declare it within a <receiver> tag inside an <application> element. It is
important to register this receiver to receive ACTION_APPWIDGET_UPDATE updates. We do
that via the <intent-filter>. The <meta-data> specifies the meta information for this
widget in the yamba_widget_info XML file described in the previous section.

That's it. We now have the widget and are ready to test it.

Testing the Widget

To test this widget, install your latest application on the device. Next, go to the Home
screen, long-press it, and click on the Widgets choice. You should be able to navigate
to the Yamba widget at this point. After adding it to the Home screen, the widget should
display the latest status update.

If your Updater service is running, the latest updates should show up on the Home
screen. This means your widget is running properly.

Summary

At this point, the Yamba app is complete. Congratulations! You are ready to fine-tune it, customize it, and publish it to the market.

Figure 12-1 illustrates what we have done so far as part of the design outlined earlier in Figure 5-4.

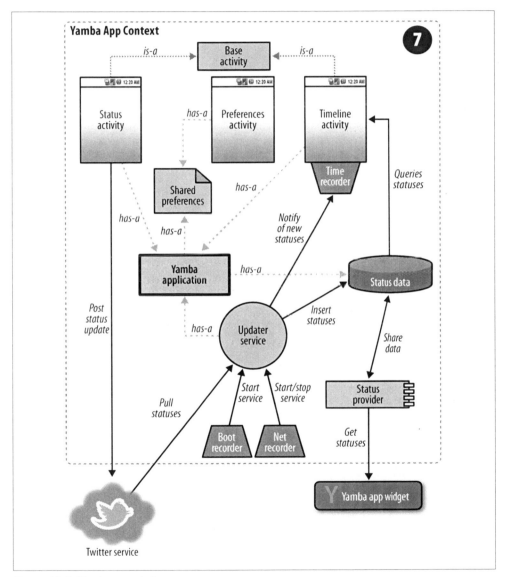

Figure 12-1. Yamba completion

System Services

Like many modern operating systems, Android comes with a number of system services that are always on, always running, and readily available for developers to tap into. These system services include things like the Location service, Sensor service, WiFi service, Alarm service, Telephony service, Bluetooth service, and so on. System services are started at boot time and are guaranteed to be running by the time your application launches.

In this chapter, we'll see how we can use some of the system services to further expand the Yamba application. First, we'll take a look at the Sensor service in a small example to demonstrate some of the concepts that are common to most of the system services. Then, we'll add support for location information to our status updates via the Location service.

Additionally, we're going to refactor the Yamba application to take advantage of Intent Service support. This will demonstrate how to use the Alarm service and will make our Updater slightly simpler and more efficient.

Compass Demo

To start with system services, we are going to look at a simple, self-contained example of a compass application. This application uses the Sensor service to get updates from the orientation sensor and use its information to rotate a Rose, our custom UI component. The Sensor service is very typical of system services and a relatively easy one to understand.

To build this example, we'll create an activity that will get the Sensor service and register for updates from a particular sensor. Next, we'll build the Rose that will rotate on the screen based on the sensor readings.

Common Steps in Using System Services

To get any system service, issue the `getSystemService()` call. This returns a `Manager` object representing that system service, which you then use to access the service. Most system services work on some sort of publish/subscribe mechanism. In other words, you generally register your app for notifications from that service and provide your own callback methods that the service will invoke when an event happens. To do this in Java, create a listener that implements an interface so that the service can call the callback methods.

Keep in mind that requesting notifications from a system service can be costly in terms of battery usage. For example, getting a GPS signal or processing sensor updates takes a lot of energy from the device. To preserve the battery, we typically want to be doing the work of processing updates only when the user is looking at the activity itself. In terms of the activity life cycle (see "Activity Life Cycle" on page 28), this means we want to get the notifications only while in the running state (see "Running state" on page 29).

To ensure that you request service updates only while in the running state, register for updates in `onResume()` and unregister in `onPause()`. This is because all roads into the running state go via `onResume()` and all roads out of it go via `onPause()`. In certain other situations, you may want to cast the net wider and register the activity between `onStart()` and `onStop()`, or even between `onCreate()` and `onDestroy()`. In our case, we don't want to register in `onCreate()`, because it would waste a lot of battery and processing time by making us listen and process sensor updates even when our activity is not in the foreground. You can now see how understanding the activity life cycle plays an important role in optimizing the usage of system services for battery consumption.

Getting Updates from the Compass

To code our Compass demo application, we get `SensorManager`, the class that represents the Sensor system service. We make our main activity implement `SensorEvent Listener` so that we can register it (i.e., `this`) to get updates for a specific sensor. We register and unregister the listener in `onResume()` and `onPause()`, respectively. To implement the sensor listeners, our activity provides `onAccuracyChanged()` and `onSensorCh anged()`. The former is a requirement, but we'll leave it empty because the accuracy of the orientation sensor is not expected to change. The latter call is what's really of interest to us.

When the orientation sensor changes, the Sensor service calls back our sensor listener via `onSensorChanged()` and reports the new sensor data. The data always comes back as an array of `float` values that represent degrees and therefore range from 0 to 359. In the case of the orientation sensor, the elements represent the following dimensions, illustrated in Figure 13-1:

Index [0], the azimuth
> The amount of rotation around the Z axis from the vertical position around the back and then around the bottom toward the front

Index [1], the pitch
> The amount of rotation around the X axis from the front to the left and then around the back toward the right

Index [2], the roll
> The amount of rotation around the Y axis from the vertical position to the left and then the around the bottom toward the right

For the Compass demo, we are interested only in the first element, i.e., the azimuth. The data returned by each sensor has a different meaning, and you should look up the particulars in the documentation at *http://d.android.com/reference/android/hardware/ SensorManager.html*.

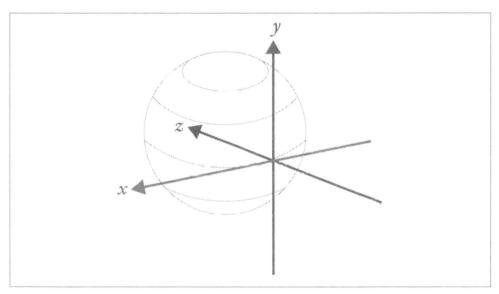

Figure 13-1. Axis

Compass Main Activity

Example 13-1, the main Compass activity, sets the Rose as its only widget on the screen. It also registers with `SensorManager` to listen to sensor events and updates the Rose orientation accordingly.

Example 13-1. Compass.java

```java
package com.marakana;

import android.app.Activity;
import android.content.res.Configuration;
import android.hardware.Sensor;
import android.hardware.SensorEvent;
import android.hardware.SensorEventListener;
import android.hardware.SensorManager;
import android.os.Bundle;
import android.util.Log;
import android.view.Window;
import android.view.WindowManager;

// implement SensorListener
public class Compass extends Activity implements SensorEventListener { // ❶
  SensorManager sensorManager; // ❷
  Sensor sensor;
  Rose rose;

  /** Called when the activity is first created. */
  @Override
  public void onCreate(Bundle savedInstanceState) { // ❸
    super.onCreate(savedInstanceState);

    // Set full screen view ❹
    getWindow().setFlags(WindowManager.LayoutParams.FLAG_FULLSCREEN,
        WindowManager.LayoutParams.FLAG_FULLSCREEN);
    requestWindowFeature(Window.FEATURE_NO_TITLE);

    // Create new instance of custom Rose and set it on the screen
    rose = new Rose(this); // ❺
    setContentView(rose); // ❻

    // Get sensor and sensor manager
    sensorManager = (SensorManager) getSystemService(SENSOR_SERVICE); // ❼
    sensor = sensorManager.getDefaultSensor(Sensor.TYPE_ORIENTATION); // ❽

    Log.d("Compass", "onCreated");
  }

  // Register to listen to sensors
  @Override
  public void onResume() {
    super.onResume();
    sensorManager.registerListener(this, sensor,
        SensorManager.SENSOR_DELAY_NORMAL); // ❾
  }

  // Unregister the sensor listener
  @Override
  public void onPause() {
    super.onPause();
    sensorManager.unregisterListener(this); // ❿
  }
```

```
// Ignore accuracy changes
public void onAccuracyChanged(Sensor sensor, int accuracy) { // ⓫
}

// Listen to sensor and provide output
public void onSensorChanged(SensorEvent event) { // ⓬
  int orientation = (int) event.values[0]; // ⓭
  Log.d("Compass", "Got sensor event: " + event.values[0]);
  rose.setDirection(orientation); // ⓮
}

@Override
public void onConfigurationChanged(Configuration newConfig) {
  super.onConfigurationChanged(newConfig);
}
}
```

❶ Since Compass listens to sensor events, it needs to implement the SensorEvent Listener interface.

❷ We define the local variable for the sensor, the sensor manager, and the Rose.

❸ Because accessing the sensor is a one-time activity, we do it when our app is created.

❹ The window manager flags set the activity into full-screen mode.

❺ We create a new instance of the Rose widget, our custom compass rose.

❻ In this case, the activity content is the single Rose widget. This is unlike the usual reference to an XML layout resource.

❼ We get the sensor manager from the system service.

❽ From the sensor manager, we can obtain the actual sensor object that we are interested in.

❾ We register to listen to sensor updates in the activity's onResume() method, as described earlier.

❿ We unregister from sensor updates in onPause(), the counterpart to onResume().

⓫ onAccuracyChanged() is implemented because it is required by the SensorEvent Listener interface, but is left empty for the reasons explained earlier.

⓬ onSensorChanged() is called whenever the sensor changes, indicating a rotation of the device in some direction. The particular information about the change is stored in SensorEvent.

⓭ We are interested in the first element of the array of new values.

⓮ Once we have the new orientation, we update our Rose widget to rotate accordingly.

The way a device reports sensor data can be very erratic, coming at uneven intervals. There are ways to suggest to the system how frequently we'd like the sensor updates, but these are just suggestions and not a guarantee. Also, sensors are not supported by the emulator, so to really test your application, you'll need a physical device with support for the orientation sensor. Most Android phones have that support.

Custom Rose Widget

Shown in Example 13-2, Rose is our custom UI widget showing a compass rose that can be rotated like a real compass. Every UI widget in Android needs to be a subclass of View. But because this is an image, we'll choose a higher starting point, in this case the ImageView class, which is a View. By subclassing ImageView, our Rose inherits some useful methods to load an image and draw it on the screen.

With any custom UI widget, one of the most important methods is onDraw(), which draws the widget onto a Canvas that is provided to the method. In the case of our Rose, we rotate this canvas around its middle point for the same number of degrees as reported by the orientation sensor. Next, we draw the image onto this rotated sensor as it would normally be drawn by the super class. The result is a rotated compass rose representing the direction in which we are pointing.

Example 13-2. Rose.java

```
package com.marakana;

import android.content.Context;
import android.graphics.Canvas;
import android.widget.ImageView;

public class Rose extends ImageView { // ❶
  int direction = 0;

  public Rose(Context context) {
    super(context);

    this.setImageResource(R.drawable.compassrose); // ❷
  }

  // Called when component is to be drawn
  @Override
  public void onDraw(Canvas canvas) { // ❸
    int height = this.getHeight(); // ❹
    int width = this.getWidth();

    canvas.rotate(direction, width / 2, height / 2); // ❺
    super.onDraw(canvas); // ❻
  }

  // Called by Compass to update the orientation
  public void setDirection(int direction) { // ❼
```

```
      this.direction = direction;
      this.invalidate(); // request to be redrawn ❽
  }

}
```

❶ Our widget has to be a subclass of View, but since our widget is an image, we get more functionality by starting from ImageView.

❷ ImageView already knows how to set an image as its content. We just specify to super which image resource to use. Note that the file *compassrose.jpg* is in our */res/drawable* folder.

❸ onDraw() is the method that the layout manager calls to have each widget draw itself. The layout manager passes the Canvas to this method. This method is where you typically do any custom drawing to the canvas.

❹ Once we have the canvas, we can figure out its size.

❺ We simply rotate the entire canvas for some amount (in degrees) around its midpoint.

❻ We tell super to draw the image on this rotated canvas. At this point we have our rose drawn at the proper angle.

❼ setDirection() is called by the Compass activity to update the direction of the rose based on the values that the sensor manager reported.

❽ Calling invalidate() on a view marks it for redrawing, which happens later via a call to onDraw().

At this point, your compass application is working. The compass rose should be pointing north, more or less, when the device is held upright as usual. Keep in mind that you should run this application on a physical device because the emulator doesn't support it.

Location Service

Now that you have seen how the sensor manager works, we can look at the Location API, another system service provided by Android. Just like sensors, the Location API is supported via the Location manager. And just like sensors, we get the Location manager via a getSystemService() call.

Once we have access to the Location service, we need to register a Location listener with it so the service can call back when there's a change in location. Again, we'll do this by implementing a Location listener interface.

If you recall from "Common Steps in Using System Services" on page 190, processing GPS and other location updates can be very taxing for the battery. To minimize the battery consumption, we want to listen to location updates only while in the running state. To do that, we'll register for the updates in onResume() and unregister in onPause(), taking advantage of the activity life cycle.

Where Am I? Demo

This example illustrates how to use location-based services in Android. First, we use LocationManager to figure out our current location based on the resources in the environment available to the device, such as GPS or a wireless network. Second, we use Geocoder to convert this location to an address.

The layout

The layout for this example is trivial, as you can see in Example 13-3. Our resource file provides a TextView widget for the title and another TextView widget for the output. Since the output could be longer than the screen size, we wrap the output in a Scroll View widget.

Example 13-3. res/layout/main.xml

```xml
<?xml version="1.0" encoding="utf-8"?>
<LinearLayout xmlns:android="http://schemas.android.com/apk/res/android"
  android:layout_height="fill_parent" android:layout_width="fill_parent"
  android:background="#fff" android:orientation="vertical">
  <!-- ❶ -->
  <TextView android:layout_width="wrap_content"
    android:layout_height="wrap_content" android:layout_gravity="center"
    android:textColor="#333" android:textSize="30dp" android:text="@string/title"/>
  <!-- ❷ -->
  <ScrollView android:layout_height="fill_parent"
    android:layout_width="fill_parent">
    <!-- ❸ -->
    <TextView android:textColor="#333" android:layout_gravity="center"
      android:layout_height="fill_parent" android:layout_width="fill_parent"
      android:gravity="center" android:textSize="25dp" android:text="Waiting..."
      android:id="@+id/textOut"></TextView>
  </ScrollView>
</LinearLayout>
```

❶ The title for our application.

❷ A ScrollView to enable scrolling if the output grows beyond the size of the screen.

❸ A TextView to represent the output. It will be programmatically set from the Where-AmI activity.

The activity for our Location listener

The code in Example 13-4 is our main activity, which sets up the screen, connects to LocationManager, and uses the Geocoder to figure out our address. The Location Manager uses location providers, such as GPS or Network, to figure out our current location. The location is expressed as latitude and longitude values. The Geocoder searches an online database for known addresses in the vicinity of the location provided. It may come up with multiple results, some more specific than others.

Example 13-4. WhereAmI.java

```java
package com.marakana;

import java.io.IOException;
import java.util.List;

import android.app.Activity;
import android.location.Address;
import android.location.Geocoder;
import android.location.Location;
import android.location.LocationListener;
import android.location.LocationManager;
import android.os.Bundle;
import android.util.Log;
import android.widget.TextView;

public class WhereAmI extends Activity implements LocationListener { // ❶
  LocationManager locationManager; // ❷
  Geocoder geocoder; // ❸
  TextView textOut; // ❹

  @Override
  public void onCreate(Bundle savedInstanceState) {
    super.onCreate(savedInstanceState);
    setContentView(R.layout.main);

    textOut = (TextView) findViewById(R.id.textOut);

    locationManager = (LocationManager) getSystemService(LOCATION_SERVICE); // ❺
    geocoder = new Geocoder(this); // ❻

    // Initialize with the last known location
    Location lastLocation = locationManager
        .getLastKnownLocation(LocationManager.GPS_PROVIDER); // ❼
    if (lastLocation != null)
      onLocationChanged(lastLocation);
  }

  @Override
  protected void onResume() { // ❽
    super.onRestart();
    locationManager.requestLocationUpdates(LocationManager.GPS_PROVIDER, 1000,
        10, this);
  }

  @Override
  protected void onPause() { // ❾
    super.onPause();
    locationManager.removeUpdates(this);
  }
```

```
// Called when location has changed
public void onLocationChanged(Location location) { // ❿
  String text = String.format(
      "Lat:\t %f\nLong:\t %f\nAlt:\t %f\nBearing:\t %f", location
          .getLatitude(), location.getLongitude(), location.getAltitude(),
      location.getBearing()); // ⓫
  textOut.setText(text);

  // Perform geocoding for this location
  try {
    List<Address> addresses = geocoder.getFromLocation(
        location.getLatitude(), location.getLongitude(), 10); // ⓬
    for (Address address : addresses) {
      textOut.append("\n" + address.getAddressLine(0)); // ⓭
    }
  } catch (IOException e) {
    Log.e("WhereAmI", "Couldn't get Geocoder data", e);
  }
}

// Methods required by LocationListener ⓮
public void onProviderDisabled(String provider) {
}

public void onProviderEnabled(String provider) {
}

public void onStatusChanged(String provider, int status, Bundle extras) {
}

}
```

❶ Notice that WhereAmI implements LocationListener. This is the interface that Location Manager uses to notify us of changes to the location.

❷ Local reference to LocationManager.

❸ Local reference to Geocoder.

❹ textOut is the text view to which we print our output so the user can see it.

❺ To get the local reference to LocationManager, we ask the context to get the location manager system service. For more about context, see "Application Context" on page 34.

❻ We create a new instance of Geocoder and pass the current context to it.

❼ The location manager memorizes its last known location. This is useful because it might take a while until we get the location lock via either a network or a GPS provider.

❽ As usual, we register in onResume(), since that is the method that is called en route to the running state. We use the location manager's requestLocationUpdates() method to register for updates.

❾ We unregister in onPause(), which will be called just before the activity goes into the stopped state.

❿ onLocationChanged() is the callback method called by the location manager when it detects that the location has changed.

⓫ We get the Location object, which contains a lot of useful information about the current location. We create a human-readable string with this info.

⓬ Once we have the location, we can try to "geocode" the location, a process of converting latitude and longitude to a known address.

⓭ If we do find known addresses for this location, we print them out.

⓮ Some other callback methods are required to implement the LocationListener interface. We don't use them for this example.

The manifest file

As shown in Example 13-5, the manifest file for this app is fairly standard. Notice that in order to register as a location listener, we have to hold the appropriate permissions. Keep in mind that although we have GPS and Network as the two most commonly used location providers, Android is built with extensibility in mind. In the future, we might have other types of providers as well. For that reason, Android breaks down the location permissions into abstract *fine location* and *coarse location* permissions.

Example 13-5. AndroidManifest.xml

```
<?xml version="1.0" encoding="utf-8"?>
<manifest xmlns:android="http://schemas.android.com/apk/res/android"
  package="com.marakana" android:versionCode="1" android:versionName="1.0">
  <application android:icon="@drawable/icon" android:label="@string/app_name">
    <activity android:name=".WhereAmI" android:label="@string/app_name">
      <intent-filter>
        <action android:name="android.intent.action.MAIN" />
        <category android:name="android.intent.category.LAUNCHER" />
      </intent-filter>
    </activity>
  </application>
  <uses-sdk android:minSdkVersion="4" />
  <!-- ❶ -->
  <uses-permission android:name="android.permission.ACCESS_FINE_LOCATION" />
  <uses-permission android:name="android.permission.ACCESS_COARSE_LOCATION" />

</manifest>
```

❶ Declares that this app uses location providers. The location permissions could be android.permission.ACCESS_FINE_LOCATION for a GPS provider or android.permission.ACCESS_COARSE_LOCATION for a wireless network provider.

At this point, your WhereAmI application is complete. It illustrates how to use LocationManager to get the actual location via a specific location provider and how to convert that location into a known address via Geocoder. An example of the result is shown in Figure 13-2.

Figure 13-2. WhereAmI

Updating Yamba to Use the Location Service

The WhereAmI application was a small standalone test to make sure we can get location information. Now we'll incorporate location information into our larger Yamba app.

Updating Our Preferences

First, the user might not want to broadcast her location to the world, so we should ask. A good place to ask would be the Preferences. This time around, we'll use a List Preference property. This is somewhat different from the EditTextPreferences we've seen before in Chapter 7, in that it requires a list of items. In fact, it requires two lists: one to display and one to use for actual values.

So we'll add a couple of strings to our *strings.xml* file and create two new string resources: one to represent names of our location providers in a form friendly to human readers and the other to represent their values. To do that, we'll add the following to our *strings.xml* file:

```xml
<?xml version="1.0" encoding="utf-8"?>
<resources>
  ...
  <string-array name="providers">
    <item>None, please</item>
    <item>GPS via satellites!</item>
    <item>Mobile Network will do</item>
  </string-array>
```

```
    <string-array name="providerValues">
      <item>NONE</item>
      <item>gps</item>
      <item>network</item>
    </string-array>
  </resources>
```

Notice that both string arrays have the same number of elements. They basically represent name-value pairs and match each other.

Now that we have the names and values for our location providers, we can update *prefs.xml* with that information, as shown in Example 13-6.

Example 13-6. Updated res/xml/prefs.xml

```
<?xml version="1.0" encoding="utf-8"?>
<PreferenceScreen xmlns:android="http://schemas.android.com/apk/res/android">
  <EditTextPreference android:title="@string/titleUsername"
    android:summary="@string/summaryUsername" android:key="username"></EditTextPreference>
  <EditTextPreference android:title="@string/titlePassword"
    android:password="true" android:summary="@string/summaryPassword"
    android:key="password"></EditTextPreference>
  <EditTextPreference android:title="@string/titleApiRoot"
    android:summary="@string/summaryApiRoot" android:key="apiRoot"></EditTextPreference>
  <ListPreference android:title="@string/titleProvider"
    android:summary="@string/summaryProvider" android:key="provider"
    android:entryValues="@array/providerValues" android:entries="@array/providers" />
    <!-- ❶ -->
  <ListPreference android:entryValues="@array/intervalValues"
    android:summary="@string/summaryUpdaterInterval"
    android:title="@string/titleUpdaterInterval"
    android:entries="@array/interval" android:key="interval"></ListPreference>
</PreferenceScreen>
```

❶ The new ListPreference displaying the names and values of various location providers that we support: GPS, network, and none at all.

Updating the Yamba Application

Now that we have the location provider preferences, we have to expose those preferences via YambaApplication to rest of the app, namely StatusActivity.

To do that, add a getter method to *YambaApplication.java* (see Example 13-7).

Example 13-7. YambaApplication.java

```
public class YambaApplication extends Application implements
    OnSharedPreferenceChangeListener {
  ...
  public static final String LOCATION_PROVIDER_NONE = "NONE";
  ...
  public String getProvider() {
    return prefs.getString("provider", LOCATION_PROVIDER_NONE);
```

```
    }
}
```

Now that we have support for providers in the preferences and in the Yamba app object, we're ready to update the Status activity.

Updating the Status Activity

The Status activity is the main place where we use the location information. Just as in the WhereAmI demo, we're going to get the Location manager by calling getSys temService() and register for location updates. We're also going to implement the LocationListener interface, which means adding a number of new callback methods to this activity. When the location does change, we'll update the location object, and next time around when we update our status online, we'll have the proper location information. Example 13-8 shows the updated code.

Example 13-8. StatusActivity.java

```java
package com.marakana.yamba8;

import winterwell.jtwitter.Twitter;
import android.graphics.Color;
import android.location.Location;
import android.location.LocationListener;
import android.location.LocationManager;
import android.os.AsyncTask;
import android.os.Bundle;
import android.text.Editable;
import android.text.TextWatcher;
import android.util.Log;
import android.view.View;
import android.view.View.OnClickListener;
import android.widget.Button;
import android.widget.EditText;
import android.widget.TextView;
import android.widget.Toast;

public class StatusActivity extends BaseActivity implements OnClickListener,
    TextWatcher, LocationListener { // ❶
  private static final String TAG = "StatusActivity";
  private static final long LOCATION_MIN_TIME = 3600000; // One hour
  private static final float LOCATION_MIN_DISTANCE = 1000; // One kilometer
  EditText editText;
  Button updateButton;
  TextView textCount;
  LocationManager locationManager; // ❷
  Location location;
  String provider;

  /** Called when the activity is first created. */
  @Override
  public void onCreate(Bundle savedInstanceState) {
```

```java
    super.onCreate(savedInstanceState);
    setContentView(R.layout.status);

    // Find views
    editText = (EditText) findViewById(R.id.editText);
    updateButton = (Button) findViewById(R.id.buttonUpdate);
    updateButton.setOnClickListener(this);

    textCount = (TextView) findViewById(R.id.textCount);
    textCount.setText(Integer.toString(140));
    textCount.setTextColor(Color.GREEN);
    editText.addTextChangedListener(this);
}

@Override
protected void onResume() {
    super.onResume();

    // Setup location information
    provider = yamba.getProvider(); // ❸
    if (!YambaApplication.LOCATION_PROVIDER_NONE.equals(provider)) { // ❹
        locationManager = (LocationManager) getSystemService(LOCATION_SERVICE); // ❺
    }
    if (locationManager != null) {
        location = locationManager.getLastKnownLocation(provider); // ❻
        locationManager.requestLocationUpdates(provider, LOCATION_MIN_TIME,
            LOCATION_MIN_DISTANCE, this); // ❼
    }

}

@Override
protected void onPause() {
    super.onPause();

    if (locationManager != null) {
        locationManager.removeUpdates(this);  // ❽
    }
}

// Called when button is clicked
public void onClick(View v) {
    String status = editText.getText().toString();
    new PostToTwitter().execute(status);
    Log.d(TAG, "onClicked");
}

// Asynchronously posts to twitter
class PostToTwitter extends AsyncTask<String, Integer, String> {
    // Called to initiate the background activity
    @Override
    protected String doInBackground(String... statuses) {
        try {
            // Check if we have the location
            if (location != null) { // ❾
```

```
        double latlong[] = {location.getLatitude(), location.getLongitude()};
        yamba.getTwitter().setMyLocation(latlong);
      }
      Twitter.Status status = yamba.getTwitter().updateStatus(statuses[0]);
      return status.text;
    } catch (RuntimeException e) {
      Log.e(TAG, "Failed to connect to twitter service", e);
      return "Failed to post";
    }
  }

  // Called once the background activity has completed
  @Override
  protected void onPostExecute(String result) {
    Toast.makeText(StatusActivity.this, result, Toast.LENGTH_LONG).show();
  }
}

// TextWatcher methods
public void afterTextChanged(Editable statusText) {
  int count = 140 - statusText.length();
  textCount.setText(Integer.toString(count));
  textCount.setTextColor(Color.GREEN);
  if (count < 10)
    textCount.setTextColor(Color.YELLOW);
  if (count < 0)
    textCount.setTextColor(Color.RED);
}

public void beforeTextChanged(CharSequence s, int start, int count, int after) {
}

public void onTextChanged(CharSequence s, int start, int before, int count) {
}

// LocationListener methods
public void onLocationChanged(Location location) { // ❿
  this.location = location;
}

public void onProviderDisabled(String provider) { // ⓫
  if (this.provider.equals(provider))
    locationManager.removeUpdates(this);
}

public void onProviderEnabled(String provider) { // ⓬
  if (this.provider.equals(provider))
    locationManager.requestLocationUpdates(this.provider, LOCATION_MIN_TIME,
        LOCATION_MIN_DISTANCE, this);
}

public void onStatusChanged(String provider, int status, Bundle extras) { // ⓭
}

}
```

❶ `StatusActivity` now implements `LocationListener`, the interface for callbacks from the location manager.

❷ Here we define local variables for `LocationManager`, `Location`, and our provider.

❸ We get the provider from the Yamba application object, as we explained earlier. And ultimately, the user chooses the provider in the preferences.

❹ We check whether the user wants us to provide her location information at all.

❺ If we pass that test, we get the location information via `getSystemService()`. This call is relatively inexpensive, even if it happens every time the method runs, because we're just getting a reference to an already running system service.

❻ Get the cached location if the location manager has it.

❼ Register with the location manager to receive location updates. Here, we get to specify how often we'd like to receive notifications and for what kind of change in location. In our example, we care only about the general vicinity at a city level, so we set these values to 1,000 meters (one kilometer) and 3,600,000 milliseconds (one hour). Note that this is just a hint to the system.

❽ When this activity is no longer visible, we unregister from the location manager and no longer receive any updates to help save battery power.

❾ Once the user is about to update her status, we check whether we have a location. If we do, we pack it into the required `double` array and pass it on to `setMyLocation()` in Yamba's `Twitter` object.

❿ Now we implement the methods that the location manager calls. `onLocationChanged()` is called whenever there's a change in location and provides us with the actual new `Location` object.

⓫ This method is called when the provider is no longer available. We can simply remove any updates so that we don't waste the battery.

⓬ When the provider we care about becomes available, we can request location updates again.

⓭ This method is called when there's a change with the provider in general. In this case, we ignore it.

At this point our Yamba application supports location updates. The user can set preferences to indicate what location provider to use, if any.

Next, we're going to see another system service, this time the Alarm service, which we'll use to trigger an Intent service.

Intent Service

Now that we understand how system services work, we can use another service concept to substantially simplify our Updater service. If you recall, our Updater service is an always-on, always-running service that periodically goes to the cloud and pulls down the latest timeline updates. Since by default a service runs in the same thread as the user interface (i.e., it runs on the UI thread), we had to create a separate thread called Updater within the Updater service that is responsible for the actual network connection. We then started this thread in the service's onCreate() and onStartCommand() methods. We ran it forever until onDestroy() got called. However, our Updater thread would sleep between the updates for some amount of time. All this worked well in Chapter 8, but there's a simpler way to accomplish this task, shown in Example 13-9.

An IntentService is a subclass of Service and is also activated by a startService() intent. Unlike a regular service, it runs on its own *worker* thread, so it doesn't block our precious UI thread. Also, once it's done, it's done. This means it runs only once, but we will use an Alarm later to run it periodically. Any call to the intent's startSer vice() will recreate it.

Unlike a regular service, we don't override onCreate(), onStartCommand(), onDestroy(), and onBind(), but rather a new onHandleIntent() method. This method is where we want to put our code that goes online and handles the network updates. Also, unlike a regular service, an IntentService has a default constructor that must be provided.

In short, instead of creating a separate thread and delaying network updates as in a regular service, we can simplify our code by using an IntentService to run status updates on its worker thread. Now we just need something to periodically wake up our IntentService so it knows it needs to handle the updating job. For that, we'll use the Alarm manager, another system service.

The key to Intent services is the onHandleIntent() method, a block of code that will run on a separate thread.

Example 13-9. UpdaterService.java based on IntentService

```
package com.marakana.yamba8;

import android.app.IntentService;
import android.content.Intent;
import android.util.Log;

public class UpdaterService1 extends IntentService { // ❶
  private static final String TAG = "UpdaterService";

  public static final String NEW_STATUS_INTENT = "com.marakana.yamba.NEW_STATUS";
  public static final String NEW_STATUS_EXTRA_COUNT = "NEW_STATUS_EXTRA_COUNT";
  public static final String RECEIVE_TIMELINE_NOTIFICATIONS
    = "com.marakana.yamba.RECEIVE_TIMELINE_NOTIFICATIONS";
```

```
public UpdaterService1() { // ❷
  super(TAG);

  Log.d(TAG, "UpdaterService constructed");
}

@Override
protected void onHandleIntent(Intent inIntent) { // ❸
  Intent intent;
  Log.d(TAG, "onHandleIntent'ing");
  YambaApplication yamba = (YambaApplication) getApplication();
  int newUpdates = yamba.fetchStatusUpdates();
  if (newUpdates > 0) { // ❹
    Log.d(TAG, "We have a new status");
    intent = new Intent(NEW_STATUS_INTENT);
    intent.putExtra(NEW_STATUS_EXTRA_COUNT, newUpdates);
    sendBroadcast(intent, RECEIVE_TIMELINE_NOTIFICATIONS);
  }
}
}
```

❶ We now subclass IntentService instead of its parent, Service.

❷ A default constructor is needed. This is a good place to give your service a name, which can be useful in TraceView, for example, to help identify various threads.

❸ This is the key method. The work inside of it takes place on a separate worker thread and doesn't interfere with the main UI thread.

❹ The rest of the code in this section broadcasts the change, as described in "Broadcasting Intents" on page 165.

At this point, our service is updated. An easy way to test it would be to change the Start/Stop Service menu item to a Refresh button. To do that, update your *menu.xml* file to include the new item shown in Example 13-10, and change its handling in our BaseActivity class.

Example 13-10. res/xml/menu.xml

```
<?xml version="1.0" encoding="utf-8"?>
<menu xmlns:android="http://schemas.android.com/apk/res/android">
  ...
  <item android:title="@string/titleRefresh" android:id="@+id/itemRefresh"
    android:icon="@android:drawable/ic_menu_rotate"></item>
</menu>
```

I've replaced itemToggle with itemRefresh so that the names make more sense. We must also add the appropriate string to the *strings.xml* file.

Now we need to update our *BaseActivity.java* file to handle this new Refresh button (see Example 13-11). To do that, we change the appropriate case statement in onOptionsItemSelected(). Additionally, we can now remove onMenuOpened() altogether because we no longer need to change the state of that toggle button—it doesn't exist any more.

Example 13-11. BaseActivity.java with support for the Refresh button

```java
public class BaseActivity extends Activity {
  ...
  @Override
  public boolean onOptionsItemSelected(MenuItem item) {

    switch (item.getItemId()) {
    ...
    case R.id.itemRefresh:
      startService(new Intent(this, UpdaterService.class)); // ❶
      break;
    ...
    }
    return true;
  }
  ...
}
```

❶ We simply fire off an intent to start our Updater service.

So our options menu now has a Refresh button that will start a service and have it update the status data in the background. We can use this button to test whether this new feature works well.

Another way to add the same functionality would have been to use an `AsyncTask`. In fact, `AsyncTask` would probably be slightly more appropriate in this case from a design point of view, to keep all the functionality at the UI level, but we've already discussed it in "Threading in Android" on page 65. Here we wanted to demonstrate quickly how an `IntentService` is started, and as you can see, it works just like any other service.

Next, we want to have our Updater service triggered periodically. To do that, we'll use the Alarm manager.

Alarms

The previous incarnation of our Updater service had a regular service that was always running in a loop, pulling network updates, then sleeping for some amount of time, and then looping again. With `IntentService`, we turned the process around. Our Updater service now runs only once when fired up by the `startService()` intent. Now we need a way to have something fire these intents every so often.

Android comes with yet another system service just for that. The Alarm service, represented by the `AlarmManager` class, lets you schedule certain things to happen at certain times. The time can be recurring, which makes it easy to start our service every so often. And the event that happens is an intent, or more precisely, a `PendingIntent`.

Pending intents

A `PendingIntent` is a combination of an intent and an action to be executed on it. Typically this is used for future intents that you are passing to someone else. Create a pending intent via one of the static methods in the `PendingIntent` class. Since there are only a handful of ways to send an intent, there are only a handful of static methods to create pending intents along with their actions. If you recall, you typically use an intent to start an activity via `startActivity()`, start a service via `startService()`, or send a broadcast via `sendBroadcast()`. So, to create a pending intent that will execute `startService()` with our intent in the future, we call the `getService()` static method.

Adding an Interval to Preferences

Now that we know how to leave an intent for someone to execute later and how to tell an Alarm service to repeat that periodically, we need to choose where to implement this feature. One good place is our existing `BootReceiver`, but before we do that, we'll add another option to our preferences, shown in Example 13-12.

Example 13-12. strings.xml with arrays for interval options

```xml
<?xml version="1.0" encoding="utf-8"?>
<resources>
  ...

  <!-- ❶ -->
  <string-array name="interval">
    <item>Never</item>
    <item>Fifteen minutes</item>
    <item>Half hour</item>
    <item>An hour</item>
    <item>Half day</item>
    <item>Day</item>
  </string-array>

  <!-- ❷ -->
  <string-array name="intervalValues">
    <item>0</item>
    <item>900000</item>
    <item>1800000</item>
    <item>3600000</item>
    <item>43200000</item>
    <item>86400000</item>
  </string-array>
</resources>
```

❶ These will be the names of options that show up in the list.

❷ These will be their corresponding values.

Now that we have these arrays, we can update *prefs.xml* as shown in Example 13-13 to add to our list of intervals.

Example 13-13. prefs.xml with support for interval preference setting

```xml
<?xml version="1.0" encoding="utf-8"?>
<PreferenceScreen xmlns:android="http://schemas.android.com/apk/res/android">
  ...
  <!-- ❶ -->
  <ListPreference android:entryValues="@array/intervalValues"
    android:summary="@string/summaryUpdaterInterval"
    android:title="@string/titleUpdaterInterval"
    android:entries="@array/interval" android:key="interval" />
</PreferenceScreen>
```

❶ This is the list preference. It shows a list of entities, as represented by `android:enti ties`. The value associated with it comes from `android:entityValues`.

Now we are ready to update `BootReceiver` and add the Alarm service alarms.

Updating BootReceiver

If you recall from "BootReceiver" on page 162, a `BootReceiver` wakes up every time the device is booted up. So far, our `BootReceiver` just starts our Updater service. That was fine when the Updater service was always on and running, but now it would cause only a one-time execution of the Updater.

We can use the Alarm service instead to periodically fire intents that start our Updater service, as shown in Example 13-14. To do that, we'll get the reference to the Alarm manager, create a pending intent to be started each time, and set up the interval at which to start the updates. Because our pending intent is meant to start a service, we'll use the `PendingIntent.getService()` call, as described in "Pending intents" on page 209.

Example 13-14. BootReceiver.java updated with Alarm service calls to periodically start the Updater service

```java
package com.marakana.yamba8;

import android.app.AlarmManager;
import android.app.PendingIntent;
import android.content.BroadcastReceiver;
import android.content.Context;
import android.content.Intent;
import android.util.Log;

public class BootReceiver extends BroadcastReceiver {

  @Override
  public void onReceive(Context context, Intent callingIntent) {

    // Check if we should do anything at boot at all
    long interval = ((YambaApplication) context.getApplicationContext())
      .getInterval(); // ❶
    if (interval == YambaApplication.INTERVAL_NEVER)  // ❷
```

```
        return;

    // Create the pending intent
    Intent intent = new Intent(context, UpdaterService.class);  // ❸
    PendingIntent pendingIntent = PendingIntent.getService(context, -1, intent,
        PendingIntent.FLAG_UPDATE_CURRENT); // ❹

    // Setup alarm service to wake up and start service periodically
    AlarmManager alarmManager = (AlarmManager) context
        .getSystemService(Context.ALARM_SERVICE); // ❺
    alarmManager.setInexactRepeating(AlarmManager.ELAPSED_REALTIME, System
        .currentTimeMillis(), interval, pendingIntent); // ❻

    Log.d("BootReceiver", "onReceived");
  }

}
```

 The previous code assumes that the phone is awake and will not work when the device is asleep. When your device is asleep, a different approach is needed (not discussed in this book).

❶ Our Yamba application has a simple getter method to return the value of the interval preference.

❷ We check the user's preference to set the frequency of checks for network updates. A value of INTERVAL_NEVER (zero) means not to check for updates at all.

❸ This is the intent that will run to start our Updater service.

❹ Here we wrap that intent with the action to start a service and get a new pending intent. The value -1 is for a request code that is currently not being used. The flag in the final argument indicates whether this intent already exists. We need just to update it and not recreate it.

❺ We get the reference to AlarmManager via the usual getSystemService() call.

❻ setInexactRepeating() specifies that we'd like this pending intent to be sent repeatedly, but we're not concerned with being exactly on time. The ELAPSED_REALTIME flag will keep the alarm from waking up the phone just to run the updates. The other parameters are the current time as the start time for this alarm, our desired interval, and the actual pending intent to execute when the alarm runs.

You can now install this application on a device (and thus install the updated BootReceiver), and then reboot the device. Once the device starts, the LogCat should indicate that the BootReceiver ran and started the Updater service by posting a pending intent to the Alarm service.

Sending Notifications

Here's an opportunity to introduce yet another system service—this time the Notification service. We worked hard to have our Updater service run in the background and get the latest status updates, but what's the point of all this work if the user is not made aware that there's something new to look at? A standard Android UI approach to this would be to post a notification to the notification bar up at the top of the screen. To do that, we use the Notification system service.

We're going to make the Updater service responsible for posting the notifications, since it is the part of the app that knows of new statuses in the first place. To do that, we'll get the reference to the system Notification service, create a new **Notification** object, and update it with the latest information. The notification itself will contain a pending intent so that when the user clicks on it, it takes the user to Timeline activity to view the latest status updates. Example 13-15 shows the new code.

Example 13-15. UpdaterService.java with Notifications

```
package com.marakana.yamba8;

import android.app.IntentService;
import android.app.Notification;
import android.app.NotificationManager;
import android.app.PendingIntent;
import android.content.Intent;
import android.util.Log;

public class UpdaterService extends IntentService {
  private static final String TAG = "UpdaterService";

  public static final String NEW_STATUS_INTENT = "com.marakana.yamba.NEW_STATUS";
  public static final String NEW_STATUS_EXTRA_COUNT = "NEW_STATUS_EXTRA_COUNT";
  public static final String RECEIVE_TIMELINE_NOTIFICATIONS = "com.marakana.yamba.
    RECEIVE_TIMELINE_NOTIFICATIONS";

  private NotificationManager notificationManager; // ❶
  private Notification notification; // ❷

  public UpdaterService() {
    super(TAG);

    Log.d(TAG, "UpdaterService constructed");
  }

  @Override
  protected void onHandleIntent(Intent inIntent) {
    Intent intent;
    this.notificationManager = (NotificationManager) getSystemService(NOTIFICATION_
        SERVICE); // ❸
    this.notification = new Notification(android.R.drawable.stat_notify_chat,
        "", 0); // ❹
```

```
    Log.d(TAG, "onHandleIntent'ing");
    YambaApplication yamba = (YambaApplication) getApplication();
    int newUpdates = yamba.fetchStatusUpdates();
    if (newUpdates > 0) {
      Log.d(TAG, "We have a new status");
      intent = new Intent(NEW_STATUS_INTENT);
      intent.putExtra(NEW_STATUS_EXTRA_COUNT, newUpdates);
      sendBroadcast(intent, RECEIVE_TIMELINE_NOTIFICATIONS);
      sendTimelineNotification(newUpdates); // ❺
    }
  }

  /**
   * Creates a notification in the notification bar telling user there are new
   * messages
   *
   * @param timelineUpdateCount
   *           Number of new statuses
   */
  private void sendTimelineNotification(int timelineUpdateCount) {
    Log.d(TAG, "sendTimelineNotification'ing");
    PendingIntent pendingIntent = PendingIntent.getActivity(this, -1,
        new Intent(this, TimelineActivity.class),
        PendingIntent.FLAG_UPDATE_CURRENT); // ❻
    this.notification.when = System.currentTimeMillis(); // ❼
    this.notification.flags |= Notification.FLAG_AUTO_CANCEL; // ❽
    CharSequence notificationTitle = this
        .getText(R.string.msgNotificationTitle); // ❾
    CharSequence notificationSummary = this.getString(
        R.string.msgNotificationMessage, timelineUpdateCount);
    this.notification.setLatestEventInfo(this, notificationTitle,
        notificationSummary, pendingIntent); // ❿
    this.notificationManager.notify(0, this.notification);
    Log.d(TAG, "sendTimelineNotificationed");
  }
}
```

❶ This is just our local reference to the NotificationManager class, which is our access to the Notification system service.

❷ We create a class-global Notification object and update it each time there's a new notification for our listeners.

❸ We obtain the reference to the Notification service by using the usual getSystem Service() call.

❹ We create the notification object that we'll reuse later. For now, we just specify the standard icon to use with our notification, and leave the text and timestamp to be updated later when we are about to post this notification.

❺ We call our private sendTimelineNotification() method once we know there are new statuses for the user.

❻ This pending intent will be kicked off when the user checks the notification in the notification bar and clicks on the actual item. In this case, we want to take the user to the Timeline activity, so we create an intent for that.

❼ We're now updating the data for the most recent notification. This is the timestamp that indicates when it happened.

❽ This flag tells the Notification manager to cancel this notification as soon as the user clicks on it. The notification will be removed from the notification bar at that point.

❾ Here we get the notification's title and summary from our *strings.xml* file. Notice that the summary has parameters, so we can use `String.format()` to update the actual number of new statuses.

❿ Finally, we tell the Notification manager to post this notification. In this case, we do not need the ID, so we specify zero. An ID can be used to refer to a notification later, usually in order to cancel it.

At this point our application is yet again complete. We now have a way to notify the user of any new status updates so he can stay on top of what is going on in the world.

Summary

At this point you have seen a few system services—Sensor, Location, Alarm, and Notification—and Android provides a few more services in addition to these. You might have noticed that most of them have a lot of similarities, and hopefully you have started extrapolating certain patterns. We have also used this chapter to somewhat simplify our Updater service and introduce Intent services and pending intents.

The Android Interface Definition Language

Each application in Android runs in its own process. For security reasons, an application cannot directly access the data of another application. However, a couple of mechanisms allow communication between applications. One such mechanism that you've seen throughout this book is Intents. Intents are asynchronous, meaning that you can post a message for someone to receive at some future point in time and just continue with your application.

Every once in a while we need a more direct, synchronous access to another process. There are many ways to implement this across process boundaries, and collectively they are called Interprocess Communication (*http://en.wikipedia.org/wiki/Inter-process _communication*), or IPC for short.

To allow cross-application communication, Android provides its own version of an IPC protocol. One of the biggest challenges in IPC is passing data around, such as when passing parameters to method calls on the remote systems. IPC protocols tend to get complicated because they have to convert data from its in-memory format to a format that's convenient for sending to another process. This is called *marshaling*, and the unpacking at the receiver is called *unmarshaling*.

To help with this, Android provides the Android Interface Definition Language, or AIDL. This lightweight implementation of IPC uses a syntax that is very familiar to Java developers, and there is a tool that automatically creates the hidden code required to connect a client and a remote service.

To illustrate how to use AIDL to create an interprocess communication, we'll create two applications: a remote service called LogService and a client called LogClient that will bind to that remote service.

Implementing the Remote Service

Our remote service, `LogService`, will simply allow remote clients to log a message to it.

We are going to start by creating the *interface* for the remote service. This interface represents the API, or set of capabilities that the service provides. We write this interface in the AIDL language and save it in the same directory as our Java code with an *.aidl* extension.

The AIDL syntax is very similar to a regular Java interface. You simply define the method signature. The datatypes supported by AIDL are somewhat different from regular Java interfaces. However, all Java primitive datatypes are supported, and so are the `String`, `List`, `Map`, and `CharSequence` classes.

If you have a custom complex data type, such as a class, you need to make it `Parcelable` so that the Android runtime can marshal and unmarshal it. In this example, we'll create a `Message` as a custom type.

Writing the AIDL

We start by defining the interface for our service. As you can see in Example 14-1, the interface very much resembles a typical Java interface. For readers who might have worked with CORBA in the past, AIDL has its roots in CORBA's IDL.

Example 14-1. ILogService.aidl

```
package com.marakana.logservice; // ❶

import com.marakana.logservice.Message; // ❷

interface ILogService { //❸
  void log_d(String tag, String message); // ❹
  void log(in Message msg); // ❺
}
```

❶ Just as in Java, our AIDL code specifies what package it's part of.

❷ However, unlike Java, we have to explicitly import other AIDL definitions, even if they are in the same package.

❸ We specify the name of our interface. Interface names conventionally start with *I* for interface.

❹ This method is simple because it doesn't return anything and takes only primitives as inputs. Note that the `String` class is not a Java primitive, but AIDL considers it to be one.

❺ This method takes our custom `Message` parcel as its input. We'll define `Message` next.

Next, we'll look at the implementation of the `Message` AIDL, shown in Example 14-2.

Example 14-2. Message.aidl

```
package com.marakana.logservice; // ❶

/* ❷ */
parcelable Message;
```

❶ Specifies the package it's in.

❷ Declares that `Message` is a parcelable object. We will define this object later in Java.

At this point, we are done with the AIDL. As you save your files, Eclipse automatically builds the code to which the client will connect, called the *stub* because it looks like a complete method to the client but actually just passes on the client request to your remote service. The new Java file is located in the *gen* folder under */gen/com/marakana/logservice/LogService.java*. Because this file is derived from your AIDL, you should never modify it. The *aidl* tool that comes with the Android SDK will regenerate it whenever you make changes to your AIDL files.

Now that we have the AIDL and the generated Java stub, we are ready to implement the service.

Implementing the Service

Just like any Android service, we implement `LogService` in a Java class that subclasses the system `Service` class. But unlike our earlier Service implementations, where we ignored `onBind()` but implemented `onCreate()`, `onStartCommand()`, and `onDestroy()`, here we're going to do the opposite. A method in a remote service starts when the client makes its request, which is called *binding* to the service, and therefore the client request triggers the service's `onBind()` method.

To implement our remote service, we'll return an `IBinder` object from the `onBind()` method in our service class. `IBinder` represents the implementation of the remote service. To implement `IBinder`, we subclass the `ILogService.Stub` class from the auto-generated Java code, and provide the implementation for our AIDL-defined methods, in this case various `log()` methods. Example 14-3 shows the code.

Example 14-3. LogService.java

```
package com.marakana.logservice;

import android.app.Service;
import android.content.Intent;
import android.os.IBinder;
import android.os.RemoteException;
import android.util.Log;

public class LogService extends Service { // ❶

  @Override
  public IBinder onBind(Intent intent) { // ❷
```

```
    final String version = intent.getExtras().getString("version");

    return new ILogService.Stub() { // ❸

        public void log_d(String tag, String message) throws RemoteException { // ❹
            Log.d(tag, message + " version: " + version);
        }

        public void log(Message msg) throws RemoteException { // ❺
            Log.d(msg.getTag(), msg.getText());
        }
    };
  }

}
```

❶ LogService is an Android class derived from Service. We've seen many services, but this time around, it's a bound service, as opposed to UpdaterService, which was unbound.

❷ Since this is a bound service, we must implement onBind() and have it return a correct instance of IBinder class. The client passes us an Intent, from which we extract some string data. During the client implementation, we'll see how it sets this, and thus how we can pass small amounts of data into the remote service as part of the binding process.

❸ This instance of IBinder is represented by ILogService.Stub(), a helper method that is generated for us in the Java stub file created by the *aidl* tool when we saved our AIDL interface. This code is part of */gen/com/marakana/logservice/LogService.java*.

❹ log_d() is the simple method that takes two strings and logs them. Our implementation simply invokes the system's Log.d().

❺ We also provide a log() method that gets our Message parcel as its input parameter. Out of this object we extract the tag and the message. Again, for this trivial implementation, we just invoke Android's logging mechanism.

Now that we have implemented the service in Java, we have to provide the Java implementation of the Message parcel as well.

Implementing a Parcel

Since Message is a Java object that we're passing across processes, we need a way to encode and decode this object—marshal and unmarshal it—so that it can be passed. In Android, the object that can do that is called a Parcel and implements the Parcelable interface.

To be a parcel, this object must know how to write itself to a stream and how to recreate itself. Example 14-4 shows the code.

Example 14-4. Message.java

```java
package com.marakana.logservice;

import android.os.Parcel;
import android.os.Parcelable;

public class Message implements Parcelable { // ❶
  private String tag;
  private String text;

  public Message(Parcel in) { // ❷
    tag = in.readString();
    text = in.readString();
  }

  public void writeToParcel(Parcel out, int flags) { // ❸
    out.writeString(tag);
    out.writeString(text);
  }

  public int describeContents() { // ❹
    return 0;
  }

  public static final Parcelable.Creator<Message> CREATOR
      = new Parcelable.Creator<Message>() { // ❺

    public Message createFromParcel(Parcel source) {
      return new Message(source);
    }

    public Message[] newArray(int size) {
      return new Message[size];
    }

  };

  // Setters and Getters ❻
  public String getTag() {
    return tag;
  }

  public void setTag(String tag) {
    this.tag = tag;
  }

  public String getText() {
    return text;
  }

  public void setText(String text) {
    this.text = text;
  }

}
```

❶ As we said before, `Message` implements the `Parcelable` interface.

❷ To be parcelable, this object must provide a constructor that takes in a `Parcel` and recreates the object. Here we read the data from the parcel into our local variables. The order in which we read in data is important: it must correspond to the order in which the data was written out.

❸ `writeToParcel()` is the counterpart to the constructor. This method is responsible for taking the current state of this object and writing it out into a parcel. Again, the order in which variables are written out must match the order in which they are read in by the constructor that gets this parcel as its input.

❹ We're not using this method, because we have no special objects within our parcel.

❺ A parcelable object must provide a `Creator`. This `Creator` is responsible for creating the object from a parcel. It simply calls our other methods.

❻ These are just various setter and getter methods for our private data.

At this point, we have implemented the required Java code. We now need to register our service with the manifest file.

Registering with the Manifest File

As always, whenever we provide one of the new main building blocks for an application, we must register it with the system. The most common way to do that is to define it in the manifest file.

Just as we registered `UpdaterService` earlier, we provide a `<service>` element specifying our service. The difference this time around is that this service is going to be invoked remotely, so we should specify what action this service responds to. To do that, we specify the action and the intent filter as part of this service registration:

```
<?xml version="1.0" encoding="utf-8"?>
<manifest xmlns:android="http://schemas.android.com/apk/res/android"
  package="com.marakana.logservice" android:versionCode="1"
  android:versionName="1.0">
  <application android:icon="@drawable/icon" android:label="@string/app_name">

  <!-- ❶ -->
    <service android:name=".LogService">
      <!-- ❷ -->
      <intent-filter>
        <action android:name="com.marakana.logservice.ILogService" />
      </intent-filter>
    </service>

  </application>
  <uses-sdk android:minSdkVersion="4" />
</manifest>
```

❶ This is where we define our service. It is a `<service>` element within the application block.

❷ The difference between this service and our `UpdaterService` is that this service is going to be remote to the client. Therefore, calling it by an explicit class name wouldn't work well, because the client might not have access to the same set of classes. So instead, we provide the intent filter and action to which this service is registered to respond.

At this point, our service is complete. We can now move on to the client implementation.

Implementing the Remote Client

Now that we have the remote service, we are going to create a client that connects to that service to test that it all works well. Note that in this example we purposely separated the client and the server into two separate projects with different Java packages altogether, in order to demonstrate how they are separate apps.

So we're going to create a new Android project in Eclipse for this client, just as we've done before for various other applications. However, this time around we are also going to make this project depend on the `LogService` project. This is important because `LogClient` has to find the AIDL files we created as part of `LogService` in order to know what that remote interface looks like. To do this in Eclipse:

1. After you have created your `LogClient` project, right-click on your project in Package Explorer and choose Properties.

2. In the "Properties for LogClient" dialog box, choose Java Build Path, and then click on the Projects tab.

3. In this tab, click on "Add...", and point to your `LogService` project.

This procedure will add `LogService` as a dependent project for `LogClient`.

Binding to the Remote Service

Our client is going to be an activity so that we can see it working graphically. In this activity, we're going to bind to the remote service, and from that point on, use it as if it were just like any other local class. Behind the scenes, the Android binder will marshal and unmarshal the calls to the service.

The binding process is asynchronous, meaning we request it and it happens at some later point in time. To handle that, we need a callback mechanism to handle remote service connections and disconnections.

Once we have the service connected, we can make calls to it as if it were any other local object. However, if we want to pass any complex data types, such as a custom Java object, we have to create a parcel for it first. In our case, we have `Message` as a custom type, and we have already made it parcelable. Example 14-5 shows the code.

Example 14-5. LogActivity.java

```java
package com.marakana.logclient;

import android.app.Activity;
import android.content.ComponentName;
import android.content.Context;
import android.content.Intent;
import android.content.ServiceConnection;
import android.os.Bundle;
import android.os.IBinder;
import android.os.Parcel;
import android.os.RemoteException;
import android.util.Log;
import android.view.View;
import android.view.View.OnClickListener;
import android.widget.Button;

import com.marakana.logservice.ILogService;
import com.marakana.logservice.Message;

public class LogActivity extends Activity implements OnClickListener {
  private static final String TAG = "LogActivity";
  ILogService logService;
  LogConnection conn;

  @Override
  public void onCreate(Bundle savedInstanceState) {
    super.onCreate(savedInstanceState);
    setContentView(R.layout.main);

    // Request bind to the service
    conn = new LogConnection(); // ❶
    Intent intent = new Intent("com.marakana.logservice.ILogService"); // ❷
    intent.putExtra("version", "1.0"); // ❸
    bindService(intent, conn, Context.BIND_AUTO_CREATE); // ❹

    // Attach listener to button
    ((Button) findViewById(R.id.buttonClick)).setOnClickListener(this);
  }

  class LogConnection implements ServiceConnection { // ❺

    public void onServiceConnected(ComponentName name, IBinder service) { // ❻
      logService = ILogService.Stub.asInterface(service); // ❼
      Log.i(TAG, "connected");
    }

    public void onServiceDisconnected(ComponentName name) { // ❽
      logService = null;
      Log.i(TAG, "disconnected");
    }
```

```
    }

    public void onClick(View button) {
      try {
        logService.log_d("LogClient", "Hello from onClick()"); // ❾
        Message msg = new Message(Parcel.obtain()); // ❿
        msg.setTag("LogClient");
        msg.setText("Hello from inClick() version 1.1");
        logService.log(msg); // ⓫
      } catch (RemoteException e) { // ⓬
        Log.e(TAG, "onClick failed", e);
      }

    }

    @Override
    protected void onDestroy() {
      super.onDestroy();
      Log.d(TAG, "onDestroyed");

      unbindService(conn); // ⓭

      logService = null;
    }
  }
```

❶ LogConnection is our class that both connects to and handles disconnections from the remote service. The class is explained later.

❷ This is the action intent that we're using to connect to the remote service. It must match the action that LogService specified in the manifest file as part of its intent filter.

❸ Here is where we add the data to the intent, to be extracted by the remote method.

❹ The bindService() method asks the Android runtime to bind this activity to the remote service specified by the intent action. In addition to the intent, we pass on the Service Connection class to handle the actual connection. The BIND_AUTO_CREATE flag indicates that if the service we're trying to connect to doesn't already exist, it should be created.

❺ LogConnection is the class that will be called back upon successful connection to the remote service and whenever the service disconnects. This class needs to subclass ServiceConnection and implement onServiceConnected() and onServiceDisconnected().

❻ onServiceConnected() is called once the bind succeeds. At this point, the IBinder instance represents our remote service.

❼ We now need to cast the bound service into our LogService instance. To do that, we use a helper method named ILogService.Stub.asInterface(), provided by that

Java stub that was created automatically by the *aidl* tool when we saved our AIDL files.

❽ onServiceDisconnected() is called once the remote service is no longer available. It is an opportunity to handle any necessary cleanup. In this case, we just set log Service to null to help with the garbage collection.

❾ Assuming that we have successfully bound to the remote service, we can now make calls to it as if it were a local call. logService.log_d() simply passes two strings to the log_d() method that we saw defined in LogService.

❿ As mentioned earlier, if we want to pass a Message to the remote method, we have to create a parcel for it first. This is possible because Message is a parcelable object. We then set its properties using appropriate setters.

⓫ Once we have the parcel, we simply call logService.log() and pass it to LogSer vice, where it gets logged.

⓬ Whenever we make a remote call, it could fail for a variety of reasons outside of our control. Because of that, it is a good practice to handle a possible RemoteException.

⓭ When this activity is about to be destroyed, we ask to unbind the service and free those resources.

At this point our client is complete. There's a simple UI with a single button that triggers an onClick() call. Once the user clicks the button, our client should invoke the remote call in the service.

Testing That It All Works

Try to run the client from within Eclipse. Since Eclipse knows that LogClient is dependent on LogService, it should install both packages onto your device. Once the client starts, it should bind to the service. Try clicking on the button and check that LogService is indeed logging. Your adb logcat call should give you something like this:

```
...
I/LogActivity(  613): connected
...
D/LogClient(  554): Hello from onClick() version: 1.0
D/LogClient(  554): Hello from inClick() version 1.1
...
```

The first line is from the LogConnection in the client, indicating that we've successfully bound to the service. The other two lines are from the remote service, one for Log Service.log_d() and the other one for LogService.log(), where we passed in the Message parcel.

If you run `adb shell ps` to see the running processes on your device, you'll notice two separate line items for the client and the server:

```
app_43    554   33    130684 12748 ffffffff afd0eb08 S com.marakana.logservice
app_42    613   33    132576 16552 ffffffff afd0eb08 S com.marakana.logclient
```

This indicates that indeed the client and server are two separate applications.

Summary

Android provides an interprocess communication mechanism based on its binder, a high-performance, shared-memory system. To create a remote service, we define it using the Android Interface Definition Language (AIDL), in a way similar to Java interfaces. We then implement the remote interface and connect to it via the `IBinder` object. This allows us to connect our client to a remote service in a different process altogether.

The Native Development Kit (NDK)

The Native Development Kit, or NDK, is an add-on to SDK that helps you integrate native code—code that uses platform-specific features, generally exposed through C or C++ language APIs—within your Android application. The NDK allows your Android application to call some native code and even include some native libraries.

In the Gingerbread release of Android, NDK takes support for native code even further with the introduction of the `NativeActivity` class (*http://developer.android.com/refer ence/android/app/NativeActivity.html*). You can now write your entire activity in C or C++. However, `NativeActivity` is not the subject of this chapter. Here, we'll look at integrating native C code within your Java Android application.

What Is and Isn't the NDK For?

The main motivation for developing parts of your app in native code is performance. As you can see, the NDK supports math and graphics libraries well, as well as some supporting system libraries. So graphically and computationally intensive applications are the best candidates for NDK. One could argue that the recent boom in the popularity of mobile games is driving this development as well.

Note that any native code accessible from your app via the Java Native Interface (JNI) still runs inside your application's Dalvik VM. So it's subject to the same security sandboxing rules that an Android application lives by. Writing parts of your application in C or C++ just so you can do something that might not be possible in Java usually is not a good reason for NDK. Keep in mind that most of the low-level hardware features are already elegantly exposed via the Android framework in Java and are usually what you want to use anyhow.

Problems Solved by the NDK

The NDK addresses several of the major issues you'd have to deal with if you were doing native development directly.

The Toolchain

Java offers access to native code via the Java Native Interface (JNI). To make it work, you would typically have to compile everything on your host computer for the target architecture, which would require you to have the entire tool chain on your development machine. Setting up the proper cross-compiler and other tools is not easy.

NDK provides the complete toolchain you need to compile and build your native code so it can run on your target platform. The build system makes it very easy to set up your environment and integrate your native code into your project.

Packaging Your Libs

If you had a native library and wanted it to be available to your application, you'd have to make sure it is part of the library path where the system searches for libraries to load. This is typically `LD_LIBRARY_PATH` on Linux. On an Android device, only the */system/lib* directory is part of this path. This is a problem because the entire */system* partition is read-only and thus unavailable for installing libraries.

NDK solves this problem by providing for a mechanism to ship your native library as part of your Application Package (APK) file. Basically, when the user installs an APK that contains a native library, the system creates a directory named */data/data/your.package/lib/*. If you recall from "The Filesystem Explained" on page 95, this partition is private just to your application and thus is a safe place to keep your libraries for the user, while blocking other applications from loading and using your libraries. This packaging mechanism is a dramatic change to the rules for distributing applications on Android devices, and is a big deal because it brings the huge range of legacy and new native code into the game.

Documentation and Standardized Headers

The NDK comes with helpful documentation and a sample application explaining how to get things done in native code. It also standardizes on certain guaranteed C and C++ headers, such as:

- `libc` (C library) headers
- `libm` (math library) headers
- JNI interface headers
- `libz` (Zlib compression) headers
- `liblog` (Android logging) header
- OpenGL ES 1.1 and OpenGL ES 2.0 (3D graphics libraries) headers
- `libjnigraphics` (Pixel buffer access) header (for Android 2.2 and above)
- A minimal set of headers for C++ support

- OpenSL ES native audio libraries
- Android native application APIs

Given this set of standard headers, you might have extrapolated what NDK is well suited for. We'll examine that in the next section.

An NDK Example: Fibonacci

Because the NDK is well-suited for computationally intensive applications, I wanted to find an example where we can implement a relatively simple algorithm in both native code and Java to compare their relative speeds.

So I picked a Fibonacci algorithm (*http://en.wikipedia.org/wiki/Fibonacci_number*) as the example. It's a fairly simple algorithm that can be implemented easily in both C and Java. Additionally, we can implement it recursively as well as iteratively.

As a quick refresher, the Fibonacci series is defined as:

```
fib(0)=0
fib(1)=1
fib(n)=fib(n-1)+fib(n-2)
```

So the Fibonacci sequence looks like this: 0, 1, 1, 2, 3, 5, 8, 13, 21, 34, 55, 89, 144, and so on.

In this example, we are going to:

- Create the Java class representing the Fibonacci library.
- Create the native code header file.
- Implement the native code by writing C code.
- Compile everything and build a shared library.
- Use this native code inside an Android activity.

FibLib

FibLib is where we declare our algorithms for computing the Fibonacci sequence. We have a total of four versions of the Fibonacci algorithm:

- Java recursive version
- Java iterative version
- Native recursive version
- Native iterative version

We'll write the Java implementation in Example 15-1 and do the native ones in C later.

Example 15-1. FibLib.java

```java
package com.marakana;

public class FibLib {

  // Java implementation - recursive
  public static long fibJ(long n) {  // ❶
    if (n <= 0)
      return 0;
    if (n == 1)
      return 1;
    return fibJ(n - 1) + fibJ(n - 2);
  }

  // Java implementation - iterative
  public static long fibJI(long n) { // ❷
    long previous = -1;
    long result = 1;
    for (long i = 0; i <= n; i++) {
      long sum = result + previous;
      previous = result;
      result = sum;
    }
    return result;
  }

  // Native implementation
  static {
    System.loadLibrary("fib"); // ❸
  }

  // Native implementation - recursive
  public static native long fibN(int n); // ❹

  // Native implementation - iterative
  public static native long fibNI(int n);  // ❺
}
```

❶ This is the Java recursive version of the Fibonacci recursive algorithm.

❷ The iterative version of the same Java recursive algorithm. Everything that can be implemented recursively can be reduced to an iterative algorithm as well.

❸ The native version will be implemented in a shared library. Here, we tell the Java virtual machine to load that library so the function can be found when called.

❹ We declare the native Fibonacci method, but don't implement it. Notice the use of the native keyword here. It tells the Java VM that the implementation of this method is in a shared library. The library should be loaded prior to this method call.

❺ The previous declaration is for the recursive native implementation. This one is for the iterative version.

At this point, our FibLib is complete, but we still need to back the native methods with their C implementations. To do that, first we need to create the appropriate JNI header file.

The JNI Header File

The next step is to create the C header file based on our FibLib Java file. To do that, we use Java's standard *javah* tool. Note that you must have the Java Development Kit (JDK) installed in order to find this tool in the *JDK/bin* directory.

Now, to create the C header, go to your project's *bin* directory and execute:

```
[Fibonacci/bin]> javah -jni com.marakana.FibLib
```

javah -jni takes a Java class as the parameter. Not all the classes are in the Java classpath by default, so it is easiest to just change directory to your project's *bin* directory. Here, we assume that the current working directory is part of your Java classpath and thus that javah -jni com.marakana.FibLib at this location will work.

The result should be a new file named *com_marakana_FibLib.h*. This is the C header file that we need to implement next.

Before implementing our native files, let's organize our project a little bit. Although Eclipse did a lot to set up our Android application directories in a meaningful way thus far, it doesn't yet offer that level of support and automation for NDK development. We are going to do a couple of steps manually here.

For one, create a directory named *jni* inside your Eclipse Fibonacci project. This will be the place where you'll store all your native code and related files. You can create this directory from within Eclipse by selecting the Fibonacci project in Package Explorer, right-clicking on it, and choosing New→Folder.

Next, move this new header file into that folder:

```
[Fibonacci/bin]> mv com_marakana_FibLib.h ../jni/
```

You can look into this file:

```
/* DO NOT EDIT THIS FILE - it is machine generated */
#include <jni.h>
/* Header for class com_marakana_FibLib */

#ifndef _Included_com_marakana_FibLib
#define _Included_com_marakana_FibLib
#ifdef __cplusplus
extern "C" {
#endif
/*
 * Class:     com_marakana_FibLib
 * Method:    fibN
 * Signature: (I)J
 */
```

```
JNIEXPORT jlong JNICALL Java_com_marakana_FibLib_fibN
  (JNIEnv *, jclass, jint);

/*
 * Class:     com_marakana_FibLib
 * Method:    fibNI
 * Signature: (I)J
 */
JNIEXPORT jlong JNICALL Java_com_marakana_FibLib_fibNI
  (JNIEnv *, jclass, jint);

#ifdef __cplusplus
}
#endif
#endif
```

As you can see, this file is automatically generated and is not to be modified by the programmer directly. You may observe signatures for two of our native functions that we're yet to implement:

```
...
JNIEXPORT jlong JNICALL Java_com_marakana_FibLib_fibN
  (JNIEnv *, jclass, jlong);
...
JNIEXPORT jlong JNICALL Java_com_marakana_FibLib_fibNI
  (JNIEnv *, jclass, jlong);
...
```

These are standard JNI signatures. They are generated by a naming convention indicating that the function contains code defined in Java as part of the com.mara kana.FibLib class for the native methods fibN and fibNI. You can also see that both methods return jlong, a JNI-standardized integer value.

Their input parameters are also interesting: JNIEnv, jclass, and jlong. The first two are always part of a Java class, created to interface with native code. The JNIEnv points back to the virtual machine environment, and the next parameter points back to the class or object where this method is from; the parameter is jclass for a class method or jobject for an instance method. The third parameter, jlong, is just our input into the Fibonacci algorithm, or our n.

Now that we have this header file, it is time to provide its implementation in C.

C Implementation

We are going to create a C file that will implement our native algorithms. For simplicity's sake, we'll call it *fib.c*. Like the header file we looked at earlier, this file will reside in the *jni* folder. To create it, right-click on the *jni* folder and choose New→File. Save it as *fib.c*.

When you open the C file, it might open up in another editor outside of Eclipse. That's because the Java version of Eclipse typically doesn't have support for C development. You could extend your Eclipse with C development tools by opening Eclipse and going to Help→Install New Software. Alternatively, you can just open the file with the standard Eclipse text editor by selecting the file and choosing Open With→Text Editor.

Next, we provide the implementation of the Fibonacci algorithm in C in this *fib.c* file, as shown in Example 15-2. The C versions of our algorithms are almost identical to the Java versions.

Example 15-2. jni/fib.c

```
#include "com_marakana_FibLib.h" /* ❶ */

/* Recursive Fibonacci Algorithm ❷ */
long fibN(long n) {
  if(n<=0) return 0;
  if(n==1) return 1;
  return fibN(n-1) + fibN(n-2);
}

/* Iterative Fibonacci Algorithm ❸ */
long fibNI(long n) {
  long previous = -1;
  long result = 1;
  long i=0;
  int sum=0;
  for (i = 0; i <= n; i++) {
    sum = result + previous;
    previous = result;
    result = sum;
  }
  return result;
}

/* Signature of the JNI method as generated in header file ❹ */
JNIEXPORT jlong JNICALL Java_com_marakana_FibLib_fibN
  (JNIEnv *env, jclass obj, jlong  n) {
  return fibN(n);
}
/* Signature of the JNI method as generated in header file ❺ */
JNIEXPORT jlong JNICALL Java_com_marakana_FibLib_fibNI
  (JNIEnv *env, jclass obj, jlong  n) {
  return fibNI(n);
}
```

❶ We import *com_marakana_FibLib.h*, the header file that was produced when we called `javah -jni com.marakana.FibLib`.

❷ The actual recursive Fibonacci algorithm. This is fairly similar to the Java version.

❸ An iterative version of Fibonacci. Again, very similar to the Java version.

❹ JNI provides this function to us. Copy and paste the prototype from *com_marakana_FibLib.h*, add variable names, and call the appropriate C function to produce the result.

❺ Same for the iterative signature of the method.

Now that we have implemented C versions of Fibonacci, we want to build the shared library. To do that, we need an appropriate makefile.

The Makefile

To build the native library, the *Android.mk* makefile must describe our files. The file is shown in Example 15-3.

Example 15-3. jni/Android.mk

```
LOCAL_PATH := $(call my-dir)

include $(CLEAR_VARS)

LOCAL_MODULE    := fib
LOCAL_SRC_FILES := fib.c

include $(BUILD_SHARED_LIBRARY)
```

The makefile is a part of the standard Android *make* system. All we are adding here is our specific input (*fib.c*) and our specific output (the `fib` module). The name of the module we specify is important and will determine the name of the library based on the operating system convention. For example, on ARM-based systems, the output will be a *libfib.so* file.

Once we have this makefile, we're ready to initiate the build.

Building the Shared Library

Assuming you have the NDK installed properly, you can now build the native shared library by running `ndk-build` in your project directory. Here, `ndk-build` is a tool in the directory where your NDK is installed. We assume you put this directory into your environment PATH.

At this point, you should have a subdirectory named *lib* containing your shared library. When you deploy the Fibonacci application in the next section, this library is packaged as part of the APK.

 The shared library is compiled to run on the emulator by default, so it's based on ARM architecture.

Finally, we need an application to put this library to good use.

The Fibonacci Activity

The Fibonacci Activity asks the user to input a number. Then, it runs the four algorithms to compute the Fibonacci value of that number. It also times the computation and prints the results to the screen. This activity basically uses the FibLib class that in turn uses *libfib.so* for its native part. Example 15-4 shows the code.

Example 15-4. FibActivity.java

```java
package com.marakana;

import android.app.Activity;
import android.os.Bundle;
import android.view.View;
import android.view.View.OnClickListener;
import android.widget.Button;
import android.widget.EditText;
import android.widget.TextView;

public class Fibonacci extends Activity implements OnClickListener {
  TextView textResult;
  Button buttonGo;
  EditText editInput;

  @Override
  public void onCreate(Bundle savedInstanceState) {
    super.onCreate(savedInstanceState);
    setContentView(R.layout.main);

    // Find UI views
    editInput = (EditText) findViewById(R.id.editInput);
    textResult = (TextView) findViewById(R.id.textResult);
    buttonGo = (Button) findViewById(R.id.buttonGo);
    buttonGo.setOnClickListener(this);
  }

  public void onClick(View view) {

    int input = Integer.parseInt(editInput.getText().toString()); // ❶

    long start, stop;
    long result;
    String out = "";

    // Dalvik - Recursive
    start = System.currentTimeMillis(); // ❷
    result = FibLib.fibJ(input);  // ❸
    stop = System.currentTimeMillis();  // ❹
    out += String.format("Dalvik recur  sive: %d (%d msec)", result,
                    stop - start);

    // Dalvik - Iterative
```

```
            start = System.currentTimeMillis();
            result = FibLib.fibJI(input); // ❺
            stop = System.currentTimeMillis();
            out += String.format("\nDalvik iterative: %d (%d msec)", result,
                                  stop - start);

            // Native - Recursive
            start = System.currentTimeMillis();
            result = FibLib.fibN(input); // ❻
            stop = System.currentTimeMillis();
            out += String.format("\nNative recursive: %d (%d msec)", result,
                                  stop - start);

            // Native - Iterative
            start = System.currentTimeMillis();
            result = FibLib.fibNI(input); // ❼
            stop = System.currentTimeMillis();
            out += String.format("\nNative iterative: %d (%d msec)", result,
                                  stop - start);

            textResult.setText(out); // ❽
    }
}
```

❶ We convert the string we get from the user into a number.

❷ Before we start the calculation, we take the current timestamp.

❸ We perform the actual Fibonacci calculation by invoking the appropriate static method in FibLib. In this case, it's the Java recursive implementation.

❹ We take another timestamp and subtract the previous one. The delta is the length of the computation, in milliseconds.

❺ We do the same for the iterative Java implementation of Fibonacci.

❻ Here we use the native recursive algorithm.

❼ And finally, we use the native iterative algorithm.

❽ We format the output and print out the results on the screen.

Testing That It All Works

At this point, we can fire up the Fibonacci application and run some tests on it. Keep in mind that larger values for n take quite a bit longer to process, especially using the recursive algorithms. One suggestion would be to keep n in the 25–30 range. Also keep in mind that we are doing all this processing on Activity's main UI thread, and blocking that thread for a long period of time will lead to the Application Not Responding (ANR) error we showed in Figure 6-9. As an exercise, you might want to move the actual calculation into an AsyncTask, as described in "AsyncTask" on page 67, to prevent blocking the main thread.

As you run some tests, you might notice that the native version of the algorithm runs about one order of magnitude (*http://en.wikipedia.org/wiki/Order_of_magnitude*) faster than the Java implementation (see Figure 15-1).

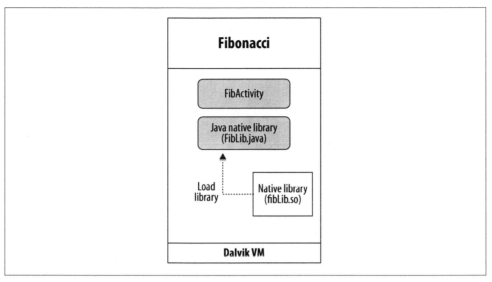

Figure 15-1. Fibonacci of 33

These results alone should provide enough motivation to consider moving some of your computationally intensive code into native code. NDK makes the job of integrating native code into your app much simpler.

Summary

Starting with the Gingerbread version of Android, NDK also supports Native activities, a way to create an entire activity in C and still have it adhere to the activity life cycle rules, as discussed in "Activity Life Cycle" on page 28. This makes game development in Android even easier.

Index

We'd like to hear your suggestions for improving our indexes. Send email to *index@oreilly.com*.

About the Author

Marko Gargenta is the founder and chief Android expert at Marakana, a training company in San Francisco. Marko has developed Android Bootcamp and Android Internals courses, and has trained over 1,000 developers on four continents. His clients include Qualcomm, Sony-Ericsson, Motorola, Sharp, Cisco, the US Department of Defense, and many more. Marko frequently speaks on Android at technical conferences and events, and is the founder of the San Francisco Android Users Group.

Colophon

The animal on the cover of *Learning Android* is a Little Owl.

The Little Owl is part of the taxonomic family Strigdae, which is informally known as "typical owl" or "true owl" (the other taxonomic family includes barn owls). True to its name, the Little Owl is small, measuring between 23 and 27.5 centimeters in length. It is native to the warmer areas of east Asia (particularly Korea), Europe, and North Africa and has been introduced and naturalized in Great Britain and the South Island of New Zealand.

The Little Owl is characterized by long legs and a round head with yellow eyes and white eyebrows; the eyebrows are said to give the owl a serious expression. The most widespread species, *Athene noctua*, is white and speckled brown on top and white-and-brown streaked on bottom. A species commonly found in the Middle East, *A. n. lilith*, or the Syrian Little Owl, is a pale grayish-brown.

The sedentary Little Owl typically makes its home in open country, such as parkland and farmland. It preys on amphibians, earthworms, insects, and even smaller mammals and birds; despite its diminutive stature, the Little Owl is able to attack many game birds. Unlike many of its true owl family members, the Little Owl is diurnal, or active during the day, during which it often perches openly. Depending on the habitat, the Little Owl builds nests in cliffs, rocks, holes in trees, river banks, and buildings. Little Owls that live in areas with human activity tend to get used to people and may perch in full view when humans are present.

The cover image is from Cassell's *Natural History*. The cover font is Adobe ITC Garamond. The text font is Linotype Birka; the heading font is Adobe Myriad Condensed; and the code font is LucasFont's TheSansMonoCondensed.

Buy this book and get access to the online edition for 45 days—for free!

Learning Android
By Marko Gargenta
March 2011, $34.99
ISBN 9781449390501

With Safari Books Online, you can:

Access the contents of thousands of technology and business books

- Quickly search over 7000 books and certification guides
- Download whole books or chapters in PDF format, at no extra cost, to print or read on the go
- Copy and paste code
- Save up to 35% on O'Reilly print books
- **New!** Access mobile-friendly books directly from cell phones and mobile devices

Stay up-to-date on emerging topics before the books are published

- Get on-demand access to evolving manuscripts.
- Interact directly with authors of upcoming books

Explore thousands of hours of video on technology and design topics

- Learn from expert video tutorials
- Watch and replay recorded conference sessions

To try out Safari and the online edition of this book FREE for 45 days, go to **www.oreilly.com/go/safarienabled** and enter the coupon code QPDQFDB. To see the complete Safari Library, visit safari.oreilly.com.

Spreading the knowledge of innovators   safari.oreilly.com

©2011 O'Reilly Media, Inc. O'Reilly logo is a registered trademark of O'Reilly Media, Inc. 00000

Breinigsville, PA USA
16 March 2011
257501BV00001BA/2/P

9 781449 390501